Intermediate-Level:

SOCIAL STUDIES

BIG 8 REVIEW

Authors
Paul Stich & Sue Ann Kime & Howard VanAckooy

Editor
Wayne Garnsey

Artwork & Graphics
Eugene B. Fairbanks & Wayne Garnsey

N&N Publishing Company, Inc.
18 Montgomery Street   Middletown, New York 10940-5116

For Ordering & Information
1-800-NN 4 TEXT
internet: www.nn4text.com   email: nn4text@warwick.net

DEDICATION & THANKS

This book is dedicated to all of our students, past and present, and to all students who use our book as a resource to improve their knowledge. It is our students who have inspired us to do better as teachers.

This book is also dedicated to all of our colleagues who strive to help their students with knowledge and understanding so they can become better decision-makers.

————————————

Special thanks to

Eric Fiore,
Fran Harrison, and
Maureen VanAckooy

for their editorial assistance in the preparation of this manuscript.

© Copyright 2001

N&N Publishing Company, Inc.

internet: www.nn4text.com   phone: 1-800-NN 4 TEXT   email: nn4text@warwick.net

SAN # - 216-4221   600   ISBN # - 0935487-72-7

1 2 3 4 5 6 7 8 9 0 BookMart Press 2007 2006 2005 2004 2003 2002 2001

TABLE OF CONTENTS

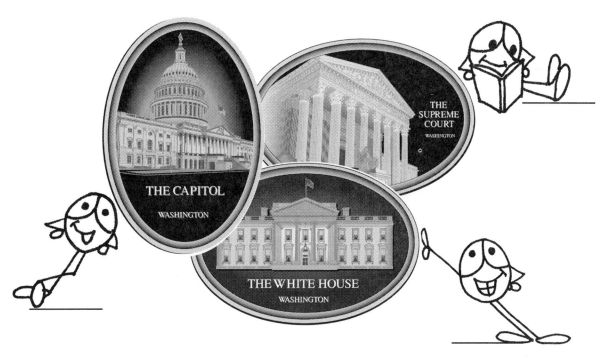

INTRO-DUC-TION

INTRODUCTION

EXAM BLUEPRINT

Part I: 45 Multiple Choice (50%)

Part II: 3-4 Constructed Response (20%)

Part III: 1 Document-Based Question (30%)
- 10% scaffolding questions
- 20% essay question

GETTING READY FOR THE EXAM

This book is designed to help you prepare for the intermediate examination in Social Studies. It can be used in many ways – among them, as a gradual term-long training or intensive end-term drill. Your teacher will explain how it is to be used and issue the appropriate assignments.

The comprehensive examination helps determine whether you have the foundation to do high school work. It evaluates your thinking and writing skills. The comprehensive examination also tests your grasp of a range of events that helped the United States develop into an industrial nation and a world power.

Keep in mind that the state has very broad goals for the examination. The test can only touch on the key ideas and events. There was a very large amount of material originally taught, but you have only a short time to review. Therefore, any review for the examination has to be on a broad, general level. Getting bogged down in detail is counter-productive. It is only possible to touch on the key ideas and events. This book helps you focus on the main ideas and the kinds of questions you can expect on the examination.

At the end of each unit in this book, there are practice questions on that unit's material. The purpose of these drills is to show you the kind of questions that will be on the examination. With practice, you will get an idea of the different styles of questions and how to answer them effectively without overdoing it.

As you go through the book, there are built-in *hints* and directions as to where to turn for help when you are doing certain *types of questions*. At the back of the book (see pages 184-188), there is a special **self-help chart** with advice on how to handle certain types of questions. It is a valuable tool for review. It is wise to put a bookmark in the chart pages. Always look over the chart before you begin answering questions and refer to it often as you work.

Remember to check the **Index/Glossary**. It is an important tool giving you more information and showing you where in the book the term is used.

Pacific Coast, Northern California ©PhotoDisc

A GEOGRAPHIC OVERVIEW

In your studies over the past few semesters, you have covered many ideas and events. Before you begin looking at the highlights, you should look at the stage on which the action takes place. To visualize *where* all these events occurred. In the next few pages, you can take a brief look at the geography of the United States. Visualizing the physical setting of the country is good preparation for any journey through United States history.

Geographic features have a significant impact on people. Climate, water, land forms, and mineral deposits influence where people live and how they interact with others. Distances and technology alter such relationships, too. For example, once railroads began crossing the undeveloped Western U.S., settlement and commerce increased in a very short time.

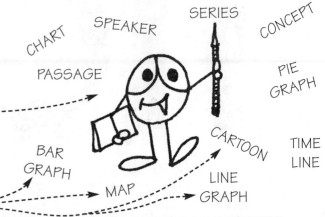

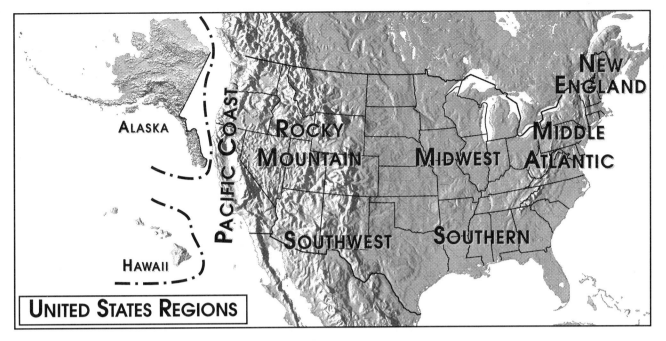

UNITED STATES REGIONS

Climate plays an important role in human development. Knowing general climatic conditions can often help explain why events occurred in the region throughout history.

An area's livelihood may spring from geographic factors. For example, early European colonists came to New England to be farmers. The poor soils, heavy forests, and rugged coasts made them turn to fishing. It became a chief industry for New England.

U.S. GEOGRAPHIC FACTORS

The United States is almost as large as the entire European continent. Only three countries (Russia, Canada, China) have a larger land mass. The 48 states that adjoin each other (excluding Alaska

Rocky Mountains, ©PhotoDisc

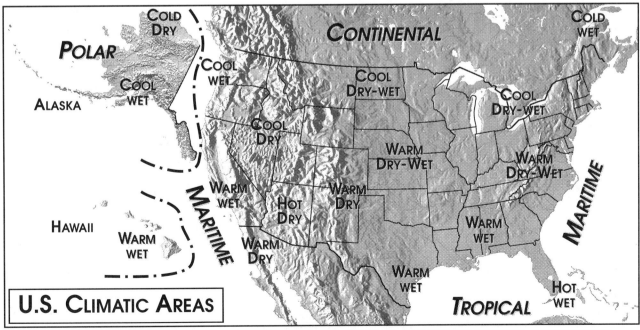

U.S. CLIMATIC AREAS

VEGETATION

Human settlement has swept away much of the naturally growing vegetation of the United States, especially in the areas east of the Rockies.

General Area	Original Vegetation
Atlantic Coast to the edge of the Great Plains	evergreen forests in the northern and mountain regions
the rest of the East (southern)	deciduous forests (broad leaf)
Great Plains	prairie grasses
Rockies and westward	great variations – majestic forests in the mountains; grasses and small plants in the basins and desert regions

Great Plains, ©PhotoDisc

Wisconsin Farm Land, ©PhotoDisc

and Hawaii) extend nearly 3,000 miles in a west to east direction and over 1,200 miles north-south. The entire 4,000 mile northern border of the United States is with Canada, while Mexico comprises the 1,900 mile southern border. This southern boundary extends from the Gulf of Mexico to the Pacific Ocean. The United States is often divided into 8 regions: New England, Middle Atlantic, Midwest, Southern, Southwest, Rocky Mountain, Pacific Coast, Alaska and Hawaii.

The United States has a total of 50 states. Of the 48 states that adjoin each other (excluding Alaska and Hawaii), all are in the temperate or middle latitudes – north of the Tropic of Cancer (23° 30' N.) and

Mississippi River, ©PhotoDisc

AGRICULTURAL AREAS

The United States produces enormous surpluses of food. It produces nearly 40% of the world's corn and between 10% - 20% of the world's cotton and wheat.

General Area	Main Crops
New England to the Upper Midwest	Dairy farming is common; smaller farms grow a variety of corn, grain, and vegetables in a short growing season.
Midwest and the Plains	Corn, soybeans, wheat, and oats are grown in large quantities, and pastures are filled with cattle.
South	A longer growing season permits cultivation of cotton, tobacco, and rice.
Florida and Texas	Citrus fruits are grown.
California	Irrigation and a mild climate give farmers the ability to grow fresh vegetables and produce a large citrus crop.

GEOGRAPHIC FACTORS THAT INFLUENCE THE UNITED STATES

The topography (physical features of Earth's surface) greatly influenced the settlement and development of the nation. Some features served as barriers to transportation and communication (see map on pg. 10).

Topographic Factors	Features
Major Mountain Ranges	The **Appalachians** extend 1,500 miles from New England, south westward to Georgia and Alabama. These are older, eroded mountains that are relatively low when compared to other mountain ranges around the world. They form a nearly continuous chain; however, they were a formidable barrier in earlier centuries. The **Rocky Mountains** extend in an irregular pattern from Canada through to Northern New Mexico. Many of the mountains rise above the timber line and are snow covered for much of the year. The **Sierra Nevada, Cascades**, and the Pacific Coast mountains run in a general north-south arrangement, along the **Pacific Coast Plain** from the Canadian border to southern California.
Intermountain Region	Area between the Rockies and the Sierra Nevada and Cascades is relatively dry since moist Pacific air is stopped from advancing eastward by the mountains. Some parts of the southern region are arid deserts.
Major River Systems	The **Mississippi River** is served as the most vital water highway. Its main tributaries – the **Ohio River** in the east and the **Missouri River** in the west – drain the country from Appalachians to the Rockies. The delta at the mouth of the Mississippi provides for a fertile agricultural region in Louisiana. The **Delaware, Potomac, Hudson**, and **Connecticut Rivers** are some of the eastern rivers that flow toward the Atlantic Ocean. The **St. Lawrence River** (with the St. Lawrence Seaway and other locks and canals) provides a route from the Atlantic through to the Great Lakes connecting cities such as Chicago, Cleveland, Detroit, and Buffalo to the ocean. The **Columbia** and **Colorado Rivers** have dams that divert water to the desert areas as they flow west of the Rockies.
The Great Plains	Large area between the Rocky Mountains and the Appalachian Mountains is called the **Interior Plains**. In the eastern part are the Central Lowlands, a fertile area with adequate rainfall. The area west of the Mississippi to the foothills of the Rockies is the **Great Plains**. This drier grassland has been transformed for pasture land and farming.
Coastal Areas	The **Atlantic** and **Gulf Coastal Plains** extend in a broad sweep from New York to Texas. The gentle slope to the sea, together with the eastern rivers, give the region excellent ports for shipping and farming. On the **Pacific Coast**, some mountain ranges drop sharply toward the sea, providing little or no coastal plain. The battering storms make the northern part of the coastline a harsh place to live. The southern half of the California coast is usually impacted much less by storms.
Atlantic/Pacific Oceans	The **Atlantic** and **Pacific Oceans** created a boundary thousands of miles wide from the political, economic, and social problems of Europe and Asia. (Until the 20th century, it took weeks or even months to cross these oceans.)

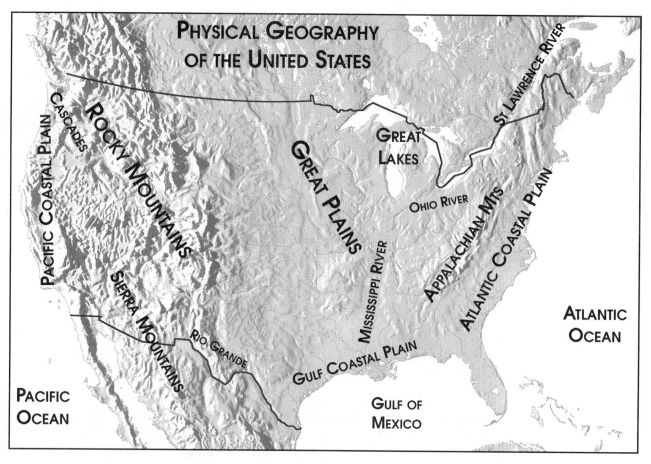

PHYSICAL GEOGRAPHY OF THE UNITED STATES

PACIFIC COASTAL PLAIN

CASCADES

ROCKY MOUNTAINS

SIERRA MOUNTAINS

RIO GRANDE

GREAT PLAINS

GREAT LAKES

OHIO RIVER

MISSISSIPPI RIVER

ST. LAWRENCE RIVER

APPALACHIAN MTS.

ATLANTIC COASTAL PLAIN

ATLANTIC OCEAN

GULF COASTAL PLAIN

PACIFIC OCEAN

GULF OF MEXICO

south of the Arctic Circle (66° 33' N.). Because of Continental (dry) and Maritime (wet) and Polar (cold) and Tropical (warm) air influences, the climate varies greatly. The West Coast is generally wet, the eastern side of the Rocky Mountains dry, and the Midwest plains vary from stormy to dry spells. Along the Mississippi River and east to the Appalachian Mountains, it is seasonable with year round moisture. Along the Atlantic coast the climate ranges from cool and moist in New England to warm and humid in Florida. (See the climate map on page 7.)

This great variety of climate has determined agricultural zones since the earliest times. Colonial Americans stayed near the moderating influence of the Atlantic. In the 19th century, settlers battled blizzards and droughts as they moved west. Recently, climate has been one of the factors in the movement of people to the southern and southwestern states, popularly called the "Sunbelt."

NATURAL RESOURCES

The United States became a leading industrial nation because of its substantial natural resources. While gold and silver rushes in California, Nevada, and Alaska drew thousands to claim their fortune, most came away disappointed. More important in the long run have been other natural resources, such as petroleum, natural gas, iron ore, and coal.

Petroleum and natural gas are found mostly in Texas, Louisiana, California, and Alaska. The Mesabi region around Lake Superior provided iron ore for steel during the industrial expansion. In the Appalachian Mountains, coal has been mined for over 150 years. Arkansas provides most of the domestic production of bauxite to make aluminum. Copper comes from Arizona and Utah. The wide variety and vast supply of natural resources helped the United States grow into a major industrial nation and world power.

Portland Head Light, Maine ©PhotoDisc

38000 to 10000	MIGRATIONS FROM ASIA
100	ANASAZI BASKET MAKERS
50	MAYAN CIVILIZATION
BC/AD	
700	ANASAZI PUEBLO BUILDERS
800	CAHOKIA ARTIFACTS
1350	INCA CIVILIZATION
1400	AZTEC CIVILIZATION
1700	IROQUOIS LEAGUE

UNIT 1

THE GLOBAL HERITAGE OF THE AMERICAN PEOPLE PRIOR TO 1500

THE GLOBAL HERITAGE OF THE AMERICAN PEOPLE PRIOR TO 1500

If you would study America, think first that this is more than just a place to live. Think of it as a state of being that has done much and has meaning for all the ages. You are in a land that holds the keys to the future. You are in a place to be a gatekeeper of the new millennium. If you would be a part of all of this, you must know its people, from where they have come and why.

Citizens of the United States have now entered the third century of their national life. In the first century, came independence and the setting forth of marvelous rules. In the second, came the building into a power never before seen in the world. In the third, comes the most enduring monument to all who came to America in the past – the building of a just and open society.

HISTORY AND THE SOCIAL SCIENCES: FRAMEWORK FOR A SYSTEMATIC STUDY OF PEOPLE

THE WORK OF HISTORIANS

Historians study past human events to build accurate records of the past.

- Historians interpret past events from written records, oral traditions, and physical evidence (artifacts). For example, they might gather information from parish records or tax registers; symbols found in art, religion, customs, or folklore.

- Historians examine primary and secondary sources (primary sources include accounts from letters, chronicles, diaries, documents, and newspapers written at the time of an event; secondary sources are investigations, books, and accounts written after the event takes place).

- Historians test sources of the past to find truth (cross-checking with other accurate sources and other proven events to see if the new discoveries are trustworthy and reliable).

- Historians make assumptions, hypotheses, and inferences. **Assumptions** are guesses based on preliminary evidence ("This evidence seems to indicate …"). **Hypotheses** are firm positions or beliefs based on evidence that is being tested. **Inferences** are judgments based on an accumulation and cross-checking of proven facts).

OTHER SOCIAL SCIENCES

Prologue: Early historians focused on official accounts of major political events, treaties, wars, crusades, and colonization. Modern historians look beyond politics and major events. They now include geography, the economy, society, and culture to view life in a broader way.

Social Science	What They Study
Anthropology	Anthropologists study human social life and culture.
Economics	Economists study how three broad human activities (production, exchange, and consumption) affect individuals and societies in general.
Geography	Geographers study location of various elements in the environment and try to describe how they affect human life and societies.
Political Science (civics)	Political scientists study the structures and activities of government and try to describe how they affect human life and societies.
Psychology	Psychologists study why living humans act the way they do, how they grow up, how they learn and change, how they differ from one another, and even how they get into trouble or become disturbed.
Sociology	Sociologists study human social relations or group life and how they affect human life and societies.

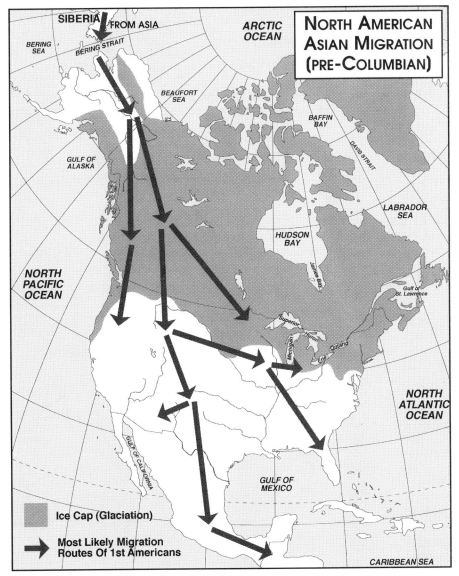

NORTH AMERICAN ASIAN MIGRATION (PRE-COLUMBIAN)

Ice Cap (Glaciation)

Most Likely Migration Routes Of 1st Americans

By 9,000 BC, as the glaciers melted and climate warmed, the early people gradually wiped out mammoths and other grass-eating animals, and turned to hunting deer and bison.

GEOGRAPHIC FACTORS AFFECTED THE SETTLEMENT PATTERNS AND LIVING CONDITIONS OF THE EARLIEST AMERICANS

Between 5,000 and 2,000 BC, herds of wild animals thinned. Some people in warmer climates began setting up semi-permanent agricultural settlements. Maize (corn) became a major crop that sustained the early farmers. New food-processing tools such as the mortar and pestle made new foods available.

MAJOR NATIVE AMERICAN INDIAN CIVILIZATIONS
CIVILIZATIONS IN NORTH AMERICA

MISSISSIPPIAN PEOPLE (MOUND BUILDERS)

Civilizations arose in the valleys along the Mississippi and Ohio Rivers because natural sources of water provided fish, transportation, game, and fertile soil. The Adena and Hopewell cultures built mound cities: Cahokia artifacts (MO) include pipes and ceremonial masks (c. 800 AD); burial mounds show the influence of Mesoamericans. Cooler climatic changes led to decline of these cultures.

THE PEOPLE OF THE GREAT PLAINS

From the Rocky Mountains to the Mississippi River, the Great Plains formed the home of 30 million bison (American buffalo) that migrated seasonally in huge herds. Three dozen or more tribes made use of the Great Plains in the early historic period (c. 1700-1850), including the Arapaho, Blackfoot, Cheyenne, Crow, Iowa, Mandan, Osage, Pawnee, Sioux, Kiowa, and Apache.

For thousands of years, the nomadic people of the Great Plains foraged a living in its river bottoms. They developed many ways of using the bison herds. After 1600, when horses were introduced by European settlers, the area became a melting pot of mounted hunter-warriors from neighboring areas. They spent the summers in bison hunting camps. The camps had dozens of portable tipis (teepees) covered

GEOGRAPHIC FACTORS
INFLUENCE CULTURE
THEORIES ATTEMPT TO EXPLAIN
HUMAN SETTLEMENT IN THE AMERICAS

Anthropologists have one theory that more than 12,000 years ago, Asian peoples migrated across a land bridge or in small boats between Northeastern Asia and North America. They slowly moved southward and eastward. These early people were fishers and nomadic hunter-gathers.

Newer evidence shows settlements in Pennsylvania and Virginia as early as 17,000 years ago. These findings indicate there may have been earlier settlers from across the Atlantic. Native American Indians believe that they were the original people in the Americas and that migration patterns went in both directions.

MESOAMERICAN EMPIRES
Organization and Contributions

OLMEC EMPIRE **1200 BC – 400 BC** Southern Mexico El Salvador	• formed the first truly complex Mesoamerican culture • established civic-ceremonial centers at San Lorenzo and La Venta, with temples and palaces • built towns with clay building platforms and stone pavements and drainage systems • traded in raw materials such as jade • created large stone jade sculptures of human heads • developed rudimentary hieroglyphic writing
MAYAN EMPIRE **50 BC – 1400 AD** Southern Mexico Yucatan Guatemala Central America	• invented writing system which mixed script with ideographs and phonetics • wrote historic records on pots, stone stele (upright inscribed slabs), and palace walls • cultivated corn as staple crop • produced a complex astronomical calendar • established religious rituals which included human sacrifice, mythology, and ancestral worship • created a monarchy that united small settlements into larger states • built flat-topped pyramids as temples and rulers' tombs • built palaces, shrines, large ball courts for ceremonial sport. and astronomical observatories • invented math system, including zero base
AZTEC EMPIRE **1300 AD – 1535 AD** Central Mexico	• founded island capital Tenochtitlan (modern Mexico City) • created a highly specialized, strictly hierarchal society • conquered and dominated neighbors for tribute (protection payments), not for territory • elected by nobility, ruler-emperor (tlatoani) had near god status and supreme authority • formed a powerful priestly hierarchy to administer government • produced a severe legal code of laws with judgments based on generally accepted ideas of reasonable behavior • developed a sophisticated agricultural economy, carefully adjusted to the land with crop rotation and extensive aqueduct and irrigation systems • adopted Nahuatl as a language of learning that accompanied a hieroglyphic writing system • created a 365-day solar calendar system divided into 19 months of 20 days each
INCA EMPIRE **1200 AD – 1535 AD** Andes Mountains (Peru, Ecuador, parts of Chile, Bolivia, and Argentina)	• established largest empire of the Americas – at its height in the 16th century, the Inca Empire controlled 12 million people, over 100 cultures with 20 different languages • formed a strong monarchy ruled from Cuzco by using strategic resettlement of loyal "colonists" among rebellious groups • believed emperors descended from the Sun god and worshiped them as divine beings • adapted an intricate 12,000 mile road system for traveling messengers and services for traveling bureaucratic officials • created agricultural terracing and irrigation systems • adapted various "vertical climates" of the Andes' elevations for a variety of crops • built elaborate fortress cities such as Machu Picchu • developed refined spoken language (Quechua) • instituted quipu (knot-cord) record keeping system • developed a religion centered on the worship of the Sun • mined gold for use by the elite for decorative and ritual purposes

NORTH AMERICAN CULTURES (c 1500)

Map labels: KWAKIUTL, BLACK FEET, EASTERN WOODLANDS, NEZ PERCE, NORTHWEST COAST, CROW, PLAINS, HURON, ALGONQUIN, SAC FOX, IROQUOIS, POTAWATOMI, CHEYENNE, SIOUX, GREAT BASIN, CHINOOK, UTE, MIAMI, DELAWARE, HOPI, WICHITA, POWHATAN, SERRANO, NAVAJO, ARAPAHO, TUSKARORA, SOUTHWEST, APACHE, CHEROKEE, COMANCHE, CHOCTAW, SOUTHEAST, CREEK, SEMINOLE, MEXICO, COAHUILTEC, TAINO, ARAWAK, AZTEC, MAYA, CARIBBEAN

16th century, the Seneca, Cayuga, Onondaga, Oneida, and Mohawk people joined in an alliance against their enemies, the Huron and Algonquin-speaking tribes. In the early 18th century, they were joined by the Tuscarora as the sixth member of the League.

The League had a Grand Council of male sachems (peace chiefs) who kept peace among the tribes and unified warfare against outsiders. The League was successful in dealing with the British and French colonists and conquered neighboring tribes. Some historians claim that the Iroquois League may have served as a model for the writers of the *Constitution of the United States*.

Algonquin-speaking people to the north and east of the Iroquois League allied themselves with the French to control the fur trade in Eastern North America. Over the years, the better unified Iroquois forced the Algonquins to move west to the Lake Huron region.

The Eastern Woodland People lived in dwellings that were often cabin-like, but large enough to accommodate extended families. The longhouses of the northern groups were solid walled to preserve heat; in the south they were more open for greater air circulation. Their villages were located near good fishing, hunting, and gathering areas. Some groups burned off forest sections for beans and maize crops, using the ash as fertilizer.

in bison hides and arranged in large circles. Their public ceremonies united groups in common purpose. They participated in raids on enemies. They became warrior societies where success in raids (usually carried out by fewer than a dozen men) and possession of many horses were important.

ANASAZI OR PUEBLO PEOPLE OF THE SOUTHWEST

As early as 700 AD, the Anasazi built the communal dwellings, or pueblos, on the high plateau of the Four Corners region, where Arizona, Colorado, New Mexico, and Utah join. At the time of its greatest extent, the Anasazi culture was spread over most of New Mexico, northern Arizona, southwestern Colorado, and much of Utah. They were semi-nomadic people that hunted deer and small game with light spears and darts. They lived in simple shelters in shallow caves or rock shelters. Some of them made more substantial houses of logs and mud. Later, they made cotton cloth, built above-ground houses of stone and adobe masonry, and developed decorated pottery with black and white designs.

IROQUOIS AND ALGONQUIN CIVILIZATIONS

Eastern Woodlands People occupied a large territory. It stretched from the Mississippi-Ohio Valley area eastward to the Atlantic Ocean. Some groups concentrated around the Great Lakes, others lived along the ocean coast. In the forests in between, Woodland People merged into several great language groupings or tribes. In New York's Mohawk Valley and Finger Lakes region, the **Iroquois League** (Haudenosaunee – People of the Longhouse) became a Confederation of Iroquoian-speakers. In the early

CIVILIZATIONS IN MESOAMERICA: CENTRAL AND SOUTH AMERICA

The Olmec
The Aztecs
The Mayas
The Incas

(See chart on Page 14.)

Unit 1

Multiple Choice

1 Discovery of an arrowhead, an ancient basket made of woven plant fibers, or ancient cave drawings would be of most interest to a (an)
1 economist
2 sociologist
3 archaeologist
4 political scientist

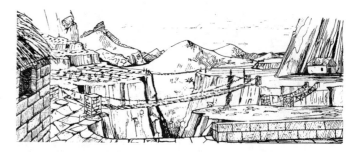

2 An example of a primary source for the colonial period in American History is
1 a letter written by President Woodrow Wilson
2 a pamphlet written by Sam Adams
3 President Franklin Roosevelt's "Four Freedoms" speech
4 an account of the Salem witch trials written by a 20th century historian

CONCEPT

3 A political scientist would be concerned with how a society
1 preserves its environment
2 produces goods and services
3 is influenced by religious beliefs
4 sets up its government

4 Which civilization used runners carrying messages on quipu (knotted ropes) to carry the emperor's commands and messages throughout the empire?
1 Aztec   3 Olmec
2 Incan   4 Mayan

5 The Inuit live in igloos, the Iroquois in wooden long houses, and the Anasazi in cliff dwellings. All three civilizations are using shelters which
1 are adaptations to their environment
2 will accommodate large numbers of people
3 are easily defended against enemies
4 will survive for centuries

SERIES

Directions: Base your answer to question 6 on the illustrations below and on your knowledge of social studies.

6 From the illustration, it is possible to conclude that the Incas (1200-1535)
1 were deficient in building skills
2 had an advanced civilization for its time
3 were primarily concerned about trade
4 lived on a large plain near the Pacific

7 Civilizations arose in the valleys along the Mississippi and Ohio Rivers because they provided
1 sources of food and transportation
2 stone for building monuments
3 access to rain forests
4 protection during ice ages

8 The goal of the League of the Iroquois was to
1 end wars among members and provide for defense against outsiders
2 promote trade within the League and stop trade with tribes to the west
3 divide fishing grounds and limit the hunting seasons
4 increase production of corn and end dependence on trade goods

Directions: Base your answer to question 9 on the Venn diagram below and on your knowledge of social studies.

CHART

9 Which best completes the Venn diagram?
1 understood concept of zero
2 had emperor with absolute power
3 refused to make human sacrifices
4 developed a calendar

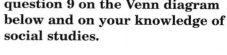

Mayans
• construction of huge stone pyramids
• invented system of hieroglyphics

Both
• structured social classes
• _____

Aztecs
• capital constructed on an island
• grew crops on floating gardens

10 Native American groups of the Great Plains were
   1 pyramid builders
   2 nomadic hunters
   3 unified in a confederacy
   4 cliff dwellers

CONSTRUCTED RESPONSE

Directions: Base your answers to questions 1 through 3 on the Mesoamerican Empire chart on page 14 and on your knowledge of social studies.

1 Which Mesoamerican empire had the largest empire? _____

2 What is one way that the Mayan and Incan approach to language and communication differed?

   _____

   _____

   _____

3 It is often said that the Mesoamerican empires had advanced civilizations. What are FOUR (4) of their achievements that would support this statement?

   _____

   _____

   _____

   _____

   _____

   _____

   _____

PRACTICE SKILLS FOR DBQ

Directions: The following task is based on the accompanying documents. The documents may have been edited for the purposes of this exercise. The task is designed to test your ability to work with historical documents. As you analyze the documents, take into account both the source of the document and the author's point of view where relevant.

Historical Context: The Iroquois people or People of the Longhouse lived in New York's Mohawk Valley and Finger Lakes region.

Part A - Short Answer
The two documents (on the next page) show how the Iroquois people used the environment to meet their basic needs. Examine each document carefully, then answer the question(s) which follow.

Document 1

1 What are TWO (2) ways the Iroquois obtained food?

_____

_____

_____

_____

_____

Document 2

2a Near what geographical fea-
ture did the Iroquois locate
their villages?

_____

_____

_____

2b Why did the Iroquois chose
the location identified
above?

_____

INDIAN SETTLEMENTS (c 1650)

_____

_____

Part B - Essay Response

Task: Write a one paragraph explanation of why the environment was important in meeting the basic
needs of the Iroquois. (State your thesis in the introduction.)

_____

_____

_____

ADDITIONAL SUGGESTED TASK

From your knowledge of social studies, make a list of ways the Iroquois used their environment not included in the documents above.

UNIT 2

EUROPEAN EXPLORATION AND COLONIZATION OF THE AMERICANS

He Whispers

EUROPEAN EXPLORATION AND COLONIZATION OF THE AMERICANS

Before the 15th century, most Europeans knew very little of the world beyond their farms and towns. However, a few Europeans had always wandered to far-off lands. **Marco Polo** of Italy is an example. Around 1260, his father and uncle took 17 year-old Marco to the court of Emperor Kublai Khan in China. They stayed in China for 17 years before returning to Venice. Polo's written account of his adventures became the primary source of knowledge of Asia.

In the 1400s, Europe was recovering from the **Black Death** (bubonic plague). It had killed nearly one-third of the people in some countries. This broke down some of the old feudal ties and altered the system of self-sufficient manors of feudal lords. Slowly, Europe revived. Towns and cities grew and sought trade beyond Europe. However, trade routes to Asia and its spices were difficult and dangerous. The Turkish Empire also blocked the old overland routes.

"GOD, GOLD, AND GLORY"
EUROPEAN COLONIAL EXPANSION (1487-1609)

Causes
- Growth of urban population and wealth generated markets
- Desire for spices and luxury goods (silks, jewels)
- Need for sea routes to Asia (Ottomans and Turks blocked overland routes)
- Development of better navigational techniques
- Development of better geographic knowledge and maps
- National monarchs needed wealth to consolidate power and compete with other nations
- Desire to spread Christian faith

Nations adopted mercantilist* economic philosophy escalating expansionism

---

(*accumulating gold bullion, establishing colonies and a merchant marine, and developing industry and mining to attain a favorable balance of trade)

Effects
- Europeans exploited the wealth of the Americas, Africa, India, Southeast Asia
- Colonial empires and political competition grew
- Slavery and the slave trade spread globally
- Forced labor systems emerged on colonial plantations in the Americas and Southeast Asia
- Mesoamerican civilizations destroyed (Aztec, Inca)
- European diseases killed many indigenous (native) people
- Cultural diffusion accelerated
- Capitalism expanded
- Large numbers of Europeans migrated to other regions (especially the Western Hemisphere)

Also in the early 1400s, breakthroughs in navigation – especially by the Portuguese under **Prince Henry the Navigator** – made seafaring exploration safer and more popular. Portuguese captains, such as Pedro de Sintra and Bartolomeu Dias, went southward, exploring the west coast of Africa for a break toward the east. In 1497, explorer Vasco da Gama rounded the Cape of Good Hope and sailed north eastward into the Indian Ocean and finally reached India.

Other explorers felt Asia could be reached by sailing west, across the Atlantic Ocean. In the 1490s, when Spain became a unified country, its rulers wanted wealth to make their country powerful. They wanted to compete commercially with Portugal. **Christopher Columbus**, an Italian mariner, convinced Spain's Queen Isabella to outfit an expedition to sail west to the Indies and China.

In 1492, Columbus' expedition reached the Caribbean. He believed he had reached the outer islands of Asia. It took several more voyages before others concluded he encountered not Asia, but another unknown land – the Americas. In this "New World," Spanish rulers of the 1500s saw a chance to gain power and wealth. What followed has become known as the **Columbian Exchange**. Plants and animals from Europe

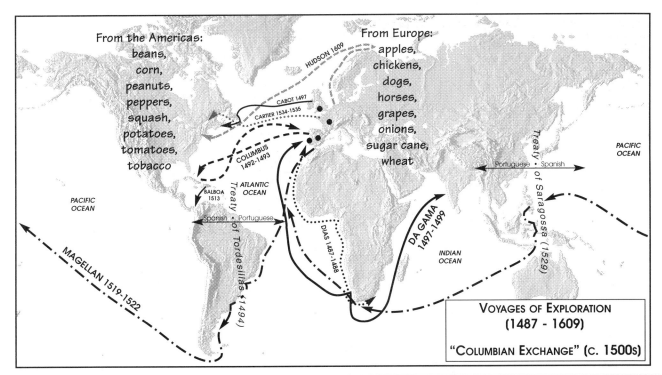

From the Americas:
beans,
corn,
peanuts,
peppers,
squash,
potatoes,
tomatoes,
tobacco

From Europe:
apples,
chickens,
dogs,
horses,
grapes,
onions,
sugar cane,
wheat

HUDSON 1609
CABOT 1497
CARTIER 1534-1535
COLUMBUS 1492-1493
BALBOA 1513
MAGELLAN 1519-1522
DIAS 1487-1488
DA GAMA 1497-1499
Treaty of Tordesillas (1494)
Treaty of Saragossa (1529)
Portuguese · Spanish
Spanish · Portuguese

PACIFIC OCEAN
ATLANTIC OCEAN
PACIFIC OCEAN
INDIAN OCEAN

VOYAGES OF EXPLORATION (1487 - 1609)

"COLUMBIAN EXCHANGE" (c. 1500s)

and the Americas traveled across the Atlantic, changing both civilizations. Also, bacteria and viral infections crossed the Atlantic. Native Americans' immune systems could not combat smallpox and cholera. The Columbian Exchange brought epidemics that laid waste to Native American civilization.

News of New World treasure ships returning to Spain and Portugal brought other countries into the Age of Exploration. England, France, and Holland sent expeditions across the Atlantic, too.

The early explorers paved the way for a second stage of development – commercial enterprise (see Early Voyages of Discovery chart on page 22). Business investors pooled some of their wealth to set up joint stock companies. These companies wanted to set up colonies, plantations, and trading stations in the New World. In 1587, an investor group headed by **Sir Walter Raleigh** tried to set up a colony on Roanoke Island (NC). When ships returned to bring supplies in

SPAIN BUILDS A NEW WORLD EMPIRE (1492-1600)

Explorers
- Christopher Columbus (Caribbean, Honduras, 1492-1502)
- Ponce de León (Puerto Rico, Florida, Venezuela, Colombia, c. 1513)
- Vasco Núñez de Balboa (Panama, Pacific Ocean, c. 1513)
- Francisco Fernández de Córdoba (Mexico, c. 1517)
- Fernand Magellan (South America, Philippines, 1519-1522)

Conquistadores
- Diego Velazquez de Cuellar, c. 1514 (Cuba & Caribbean)
- Hernando Cortés, c. 1521 (Mexico)
- Francisco Pizarro, c. 1534 (Peru)

Viceroys
- The Spanish monarchs set up a near feudal administration for the New World. They appointed Spanish nobles as **viceroys** (regional governors) with almost absolute power to oversee the royally chartered **encomiendas** (plantations) and mining operations granted to **peninsulares** (lesser nobles) usually administered by **criollos** (American-born children of peninsulares).

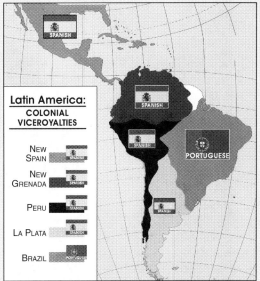

Latin America:
COLONIAL VICEROYALTIES

NEW SPAIN	SPANISH
NEW GRENADA	SPANISH
PERU	SPANISH
LA PLATA	SPANISH
BRAZIL	PORTUGUESE

SPANISH
PORTUGUESE

EARLY VOYAGES OF DISCOVERY

YEAR	EXPLORER (COUNTRY)	AREA
1487-1488	Dias (Portugal)	West coast of Africa, Cape of Good Hope
1492-1502	Columbus (Spain)	West Indies, Caribbean
1497-1499	da Gama (Portugal)	East coast of Africa, India
1497	Cabot (England)	Canada, No. America
1513	Balboa (Spain)	Central America, Pacific
1519-1522	Magellan (Spain)	Circumnavigates globe
1534-1535	Cartier (France)	Canada - St. Lawrence R.
1608	Champlain (France)	Eastern Canada, northern U.S.
1609	Hudson (Netherlands)	Arctic Ocean, North America

Commerce was a driving force for colonization, but religion played a role in settlement, too. As the 1500s went on, the **Protestant Reformation** gained strength in Europe. The religious rivalries spilled into the New World. Spain wanted to win converts for the Roman Catholic Faith. Spanish priests set up missions to the Amerindians. Some, like St. Augustine (FL) and San Diego (CA) grew into permanent settlements.

1590, the colonists could not be traced. Roanoke became known as the **Lost Colony**.

Almost two decades went by before the first permanent English settlement took place in 1607, at Jamestown, Virginia. Like Roanoke, **Jamestown** nearly failed. Colonists sought gold and mineral wealth. They were unprepared to struggle with the primitive, unfamiliar environment. Many died, and only with the help of a Native American chieftain, **Powhatan**, and his daughter **Pocahontas**, was the colony able to survive. The Native Americans shared food and taught the colonists agricultural skills. **Captain John Smith** took control of the colony and forced the settlers to organize for survival. When the Europeans learned to cultivate tobacco, they found economic success. They exported it to England, and the pipe smoking fad made the Virginia colony profitable to investors.

Protestant groups also wanted to spread their beliefs to the New World. They arranged to set up colonies and settlements away from oppression. The **Pilgrims** are an example. They disagreed with the doctrines and rites of the Anglican Church. Also called the Church of England, the **Anglican Church** was set up by **King Henry VIII** after disagreements with the Pope in 1534. The Pilgrims were persecuted in England, because they wished to separate from the Anglican Church. After a short exile in Holland, Pilgrim leaders arranged to set up an English colony in Virginia. Off course and short on supplies, they landed in **Plymouth**, Massachusetts in 1620. Before going ashore, the passengers signed the *Mayflower Compact*. This document was a pledge to cooperate, to form a local government, and to abide by the group's rules and laws. The *Compact* set a democratic **precedent** (example) for succeeding colonial governments in British colonies.

The mid-1600s saw New World colonies set up and strengthened by settlers from many parts of Europe.

- Along the St. Lawrence River, the French founded Quebec and Montreal for the exchange of goods for the *coureurs du bois* – French fur trappers and traders.

- From the Pilgrims' small beginning at Plymouth Plantations (1620), more religious dissenters immigrated to **Massachusetts Bay**. Over 30,000 English **Puritans** spread into surrounding New England by the mid-17th century. In England, Puritans struggled to reform the Anglican Church. In the 1640s, they launched a revolution to gain political power. Those that left the bloody struggles and civil wars in England wanted to start new societies set up according to their own rules. Later, Puritan rule in Massachusetts was challenged by dissenters, and spin-off colonies were founded in Rhode Island and Connecticut in 1636.

Captain John Smith statue at Jamestown, VA
©Paul Stich

- Along the Hudson River, the Dutch founded trading stations at **New Amsterdam** (NYC) and **Ft. Orange** (Albany) by the mid-1600s. **Patroons** received land grants from the government of the Netherlands to establish plantations with slaves and indentured (bonded) servants.

- To Virginia and the Carolinas came second sons of English nobility. **Primogeniture** (preference given to the eldest son and his descendants) barred them from inheriting their fathers' titles and estates in England. Their fathers purchased land grants for them in the New World and from them, they built the plantations of the South with slaves and indentured servants.

From these early beginnings in the 1600s, the British colonies on the Atlantic Coast of North America developed rapidly. From the small farms, lumbering operations, and fisheries of New England to the rice, tobacco, and **indigo** (used to dye cloth) plantations of the Carolinas, the colonies prospered. The prosperity attracted more immigrants. Some came as **indentured servants**. These were people who contracted to exchange their labor for a number of years for their passage to the New World. After their contract was fulfilled, they often purchased land themselves and set up farms. In the South, plantation profits led to an increased demand for slaves.

The first African slaves were brought to Jamestown in 1609. By the 1700s, Portuguese, Dutch, and British slave ships were bringing 2,000 to 3,000 African slaves a year to the southern colonies. Colonial governments set up **Slave Codes** to control the slave population. They denied slaves their rights and defined them not as people, but as property.

There was great religious and ethnic diversity as the colonies developed. English Anglicans remained in the majority, but there was variety, especially as the middle colonies developed. From England came Quakers, from Germany came Lutherans and Amish, from Ireland came Scots-Irish Presbyterians, and from all over Europe came Jews in increasing numbers. New York and New Jersey – originally settled by the Dutch – welcomed many cultures. Pennsylvania and Maryland welcomed all Christian sects, and Rhode Island was open to all religions. By the mid-1700s, settlers of nearly every major religion and many nationalities could be found throughout the English colonies.

Economic activity broadened, too. At first, the majority of settlers were small farmers (yeomen) in the North and plantation owners in the South. Once farms became established, new needs arose. Many merchants, tradesmen (coopers, blacksmiths, millers, wainwrights), fishermen, and lumberjacks emerged. Slowly, new industries developed, especially in the middle colonies. There was iron-making, lumber milling, rum and whiskey distilling, flour milling, shipbuilding, and the making of **naval stores** (pitch, tar, turpentine, varnish) needed by the ship builders. By the 1770s, nearly one-third of all British ships were built in the colonies.

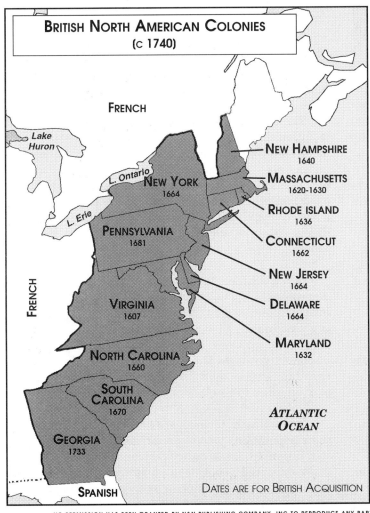

BRITISH NORTH AMERICAN COLONIES
(c 1740)

FRENCH

Lake Huron

L. Ontario

L. Erie

FRENCH

NEW YORK
1664

PENNSYLVANIA
1681

VIRGINIA
1607

NORTH CAROLINA
1660

SOUTH CAROLINA
1670

GEORGIA
1733

NEW HAMPSHIRE
1640

MASSACHUSETTS
1620-1630

RHODE ISLAND
1636

CONNECTICUT
1662

NEW JERSEY
1664

DELAWARE
1664

MARYLAND
1632

ATLANTIC OCEAN

SPANISH

DATES ARE FOR BRITISH ACQUISITION

Old Ship Rigging at Jamestown, VA ©Paul Stich

In the mid-1600s, Parliament in London passed *Navigation Acts* to regulate colonial trade. Yet, as long as the colonies produced wealth for the mother country, Britain was not very strict with them. For the most part, the colonies provided their own goods and services and exported crops and raw material to England. Some settlers grew very rich in the colonies, but the majority remained middle class farmers and tradesmen. As in England and Europe in general, relations between the richer classes and the poorer ones were strained. The poor often blamed the big farmers and shippers when they could not get decent prices for their crops.

Governor's Palace, Colonial Williamsburg, VA
©Paul Stich

The rich usually controlled the colonial governments. In most colonies, white males who were landowners and churchgoers could vote, whether rich or poor. Still, only the rich had the money and time to serve in the colonial governments. Governors were either appointed by the crown or the colony's **proprietors** (owners), or they were voted into office by the well-to-do members of the colonial assemblies. The poor felt the **aristocrats** (rich) in the colonial governments were unsympathetic to their needs. The poor frontiersmen wanted the government to help them fight Native Americans, but the governments shied away from costly military expeditions.

New England communities were small, especially in the 1600s. **Congregational churches** became the community centers. Socially and economically, there was a good deal of interdependence in New England village settlements. The British government did not station many troops in the region. Early settlers lived in stockaded villages for protection, but this led to sharing of land and work. Some fields and pastures were used in common in addition to individually owned farm lands. **Nuclear families** (parents and children) made up the basic social and economic unit.

The social patterns were different in the middle colonies. The farms were bigger and villages far apart. Separated by such distances, settlers did not share land as they did in the New England villages. In the middle colonies, rivers were longer and easier to travel. Rivers such as the Hudson, Mohawk, Delaware, Susquehanna, and Potomac carried vessels and communication.

Religion was still important in the middle colonies. Colonists did come together in Anglican, Presbyterian, Quaker, and Dutch Reformed services. Because church congregations were more diverse than in New England, no single group exercised the degree of political or social control that the Congregational churches did in New England.

Up to the 1660s, the **Dutch West India Company** sold land grants in New Netherland (New York and New Jersey) to rich investors. The Holland-based patroons set up large estates as plantations almost as if they were medieval manors. Few of these patroons came to America. They sent agents who tried to rule tenant farmers and collect the rents. Unless a patroon came to the colony and managed the estate (as did the **Philipses** and **Van Rensselaers**), this absentee landlord system failed. It was already weak when the British took the colony from the Dutch in 1664.

The good farmlands and forests of middle colonies drew a greater diversity of European cultures. While the English dominated the region, there were large settlements of Dutch, Germans, and Scots-Irish.

The diversity sometimes led to social and political isolation of groups. However, economic survival often meant sharing of work and services – barn building is an example. In larger settlements, the need for each others' skills led to economic interdependence. For example, wheat farmers brought their produce to a miller to convert it into flour. This interaction opened doors to more social acceptance of non-English groups.

In the 18th century, commercial towns in the middle colonies grew rapidly. New York City, Albany, Philadelphia, and St. Mary's grew as buying and selling expanded. Life in these towns was bustling. Prosperity grew as shippers and traders distributed imported goods to the farm families of the interior. Iron ore, grains, and forest products were produced and exported to England and to other colonies.

In the South, towns were fewer, farther apart, and their populations were smaller. Norfolk (VA), Edenton (NC), and Charleston (SC) were shipping centers. They exported plantation cash crops (rice, tobacco, and indigo). Like medieval manors, plantations

GENERAL PATTERNS OF COLONIAL POLITICAL POWER

	ROYAL	PROPRIETARY	CHARTER
Ownership & Power	• Crown owned land • Monarch & Parliament ruled through royal governors • All colonial laws need British Privy Council approval	• Land granted by monarch to an individual or group • Proprietors ruled through appointed governors • All colonial laws need Privy Council approval	• Land granted by monarch to a company • People's power specified in a charter
Executive Branch	• Governors appointed by monarch • Governor must approve every legislative act	• Proprietors appointed governors • Governor must approve every legislative act	• Governor elected by the colonists • Governor could veto colonial laws
Legislative Branch	• Bicameral • Upper house appointed by monarch • Lower house elected by colonists	• Bicameral • Upper house appointed by the lower house • Lower house elected by colonists	• Bicameral • Both houses elected by the colonists
Judicial Branch	Court systems in all the colonies followed the British model. Generally, this branch was of lesser importance than the other two.		

became communities in themselves, with great houses and out buildings to provide for the settlers, their extended families, and their slaves.

There were small farms sprinkled throughout the South, especially in the uplands of the western coastal mountains. However, the large plantations and their aristocratic owners' families dominated the political, economic, and social life. Small farmers and tradesmen were not always treated equally by the aristocratic plantation owners. The Anglican Church had the strongest influence in the South, but it played a less powerful role in Southern culture than the Congregational churches played in the life of New England settlers. Aristocratic plantation owners dominated Southern church life as they did social and political life.

UNIT 2

MULTIPLE CHOICE

Directions: Base your answer to question 1 on the time line below and on your knowledge of social studies.

TIME LINE

```
        1450      1550      1660      1750
___A___/___B___/___C___/___D___/___E___
```

1   Using the letters on the timeline above, during which time period were the first English colonies in America founded?
    1   *A*   3   *C*
    2   *B*   4   *D*

2   A major factor encouraging European exploration and discovery was the
    1   establishment of medieval manors
    2   end of Turkish control of routes to the east
    3   downward trend in trade in Europe
    4   development of new navigational aids

3   A disadvantage of the Columbian Exchange for Native Americans was the
    1   arrival of new infectious diseases for which they had no immunity
    2   inability to export tobacco to European countries
    3   lack of new products and animals imported from Europe
    4   failure of the Spanish to develop the mineral wealth of the Americas

4   What role did religion play in the settlement of the American colonies?
    1   Protestant groups failed to spread their beliefs in the New World.
    2   Roman Catholics settled primarily in the New England colonies.
    3   European religious persecution led many groups to come to the New World.
    4   Religion was not an issue for most early settlers in the colonies.

5   A person who sold his labor for a specified number of years in exchange for passage to the New World was called a(n)
    1   slave   3   indentured servant
    2   free immigrant   4   serf

Directions: Base your answer to question 6 on the quotation below and on your knowledge of social studies.

PASSAGE

"In order to win the friendship and affection of that people, and because I was convinced that their conversion to our Holy Faith would be better promoted through love than through force; I presented some of them with red caps and some strings of glass beads which they placed around their necks, and with other trifles of insignificant worth that delighted them and by which we have got a wonderful hold on their affections."

Christopher Columbus, October 12, 1492, San Salvador, Bahamas

6   What did Columbus do to "win the friendship and affection" of the people?
    1   converted them to the Holy Faith
    2   gave them red caps and strings of glass beads
    3   presented them with valuable gifts
    4   used force to convince them of his power

MAP

Directions: Base your answer to question 7 on the map below and on your knowledge of social studies.

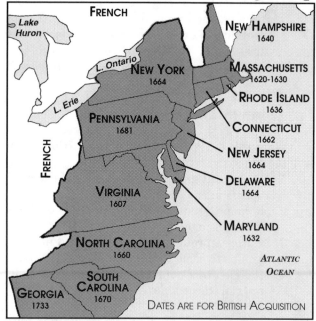

7   Which set shows the correct order of British acquisition from earliest to latest?
    1   Massachusetts, Connecticut, Georgia
    2   Pennsylvania, Virginia, South Carolina
    3   New York, New Jersey, New Hampshire
    4   Maryland, Delaware, Virginia

8   The goal of the *Navigation Acts* was to
    1   prohibit colonial trade with France
    2   eliminate class differences
    3   limit the production of raw materials
    4   regulate colonial trade

Directions: Base your answer to question 9 on the diagram below and on your knowledge of social studies.

New England Colonies
- small communities
- interdependence among inhabitants

Both
- wealthy controlled gov't
- _____

Middle Atlantic Colonies
- large farms
- often socially isolated because of distance between farms

9   Which best completes the Venn diagram?
    1   large British garrisons present
    2   absentee landlords predominated
    3   little cultural diversity
    4   only white males could vote

10 Which is the most accurate statement about economic development in the 18th century American colonies?
    1   The farms of the Middle Atlantic states produced rice, tobacco, and indigo.
    2   In the South, large plantations dominated economic life.
    3   Towns such as New York and Philadelphia grew very slowly.
    4   There was no slave trade in New England towns.

CONSTRUCTED RESPONSE

SET 1

Directions: Base your answers to questions 1 and 2 on the information in the chart at the right and on your knowledge of social studies.

1 What were TWO (2) economic goals of European colonial expansion?

_____

_____

2 What were TWO (2) negative consequences of these economic goals?

_____

_____

_____

EUROPEAN COLONIAL EXPANSION (1487-1609)

Causes
- Growth of urban population and wealth generated markets
- Desire for spices and luxury goods (silks, jewels)
- Need for sea routes to Asia (Ottomans and Turks blocked overland routes)
- Development of better navigational techniques
- Development of better geographic knowledge and maps
- National monarchs needed wealth to consolidate power and compete with other powers
- Desire to spread Christian faith

Effects
- Europeans exploited the wealth of the Americas, Africa, India, Southeast Asia
- Colonial empires and political competition grew
- Slavery and the slave trade spread globally
- Forced labor systems emerged on colonial plantations in the Americas and Southeast Asia
- Mesoamerican civilizations destroyed (Aztec, Inca)
- European diseases killed many indigenous (native) people
- Cultural diffusion accelerated
- Capitalism expanded
- Large numbers of Europeans migrated to other regions (especially the Western Hemisphere)

SET 2

Directions: Base your answers to questions 3 and 4 on the map below and on your knowledge of social studies.

3 What nation controlled the ocean routes around Africa to the Far East? _____

4 What was a consequence of this control for other European nations interested in finding an all-water route to the Far East?

_____

_____

_____

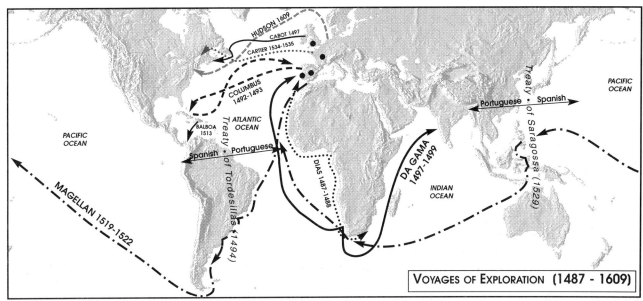

VOYAGES OF EXPLORATION (1487 - 1609)

PRACTICE SKILLS FOR DBQ

Directions: The following task is based on the accompanying documents. The documents may have been edited for the purposes of this exercise. The task is designed to test your ability to work with historical documents. As you analyze the documents, take into account both the source of the document and the author's point of view where relevant.

Historical Context: The settlement of the American colonies began in the 17th century. The reasons for establishing colonies often varied depending on the background of the person or people involved.

Part A - Short Answer

The documents that follow give reasons why people were interested in establishing colonies in America. Examine each document carefully, then answer the question(s) which follow it.

Document 1

1 What are TWO (2) reasons that the Plymouth settlers give for coming to the New World?

> "IN THE NAME OF GOD, AMEN. We, whose names are underwritten, the Loyal Subjects of our dread Sovereign Lord King James, by the Grace of God, of Great Britain, France, and Ireland, King, Defender of the Faith. ...Having undertaken for the glory of God, and Advancement of the Christian Faith, and the Honour of our King and Country, a Voyage to plant the first Colony in the northern parts of Virginia. ..."
> – *Mayflower Compact*, Agreement among the settlers at Plymouth, 1620

Document 2

2 What are TWO (2) ways Hakluyt thinks the colonization of America could help people in England?

> "The known abundance of fresh fish in the rivers, and the known plenty of fish on the sea-coast there (America), may assure us of sufficient food...
>
> "Since great waste woods be there of oak, cedar, pine, walnuts, and other sorts, many of our waste people may be employed in making of ships and boats, and in making of rosin, pitch, and tar...
>
> "Moreover, we shall not only receive many precious commodities besides from thence, but also shall in time find ample use for the labour of our poor people at home, by sale of hats, bonnets, knives, fish-hooks, and a thousand kinds of other wares that in short time may be brought in use among the people of that country (America) to the great relief of the multitude of our poor people and to the wonderful enriching of this realm (nation)."
> – Richard Hakluyt the Elder, A 16th century English promoter of colonization of America

Part B - Essay Response

Task: Write a one paragraph discussion on the reasons for the English colonization of America.

Be sure to note the difference in reasons given by the Plymouth settlers and Hakluyt. (State your thesis in the introduction.)

ADDITIONAL SUGGESTED TASK

From your knowledge of social studies, make a list of additional reasons for English colonization of America. Be sure to indicate which reasons might by given by people who came and what reasons might be given by those in England.

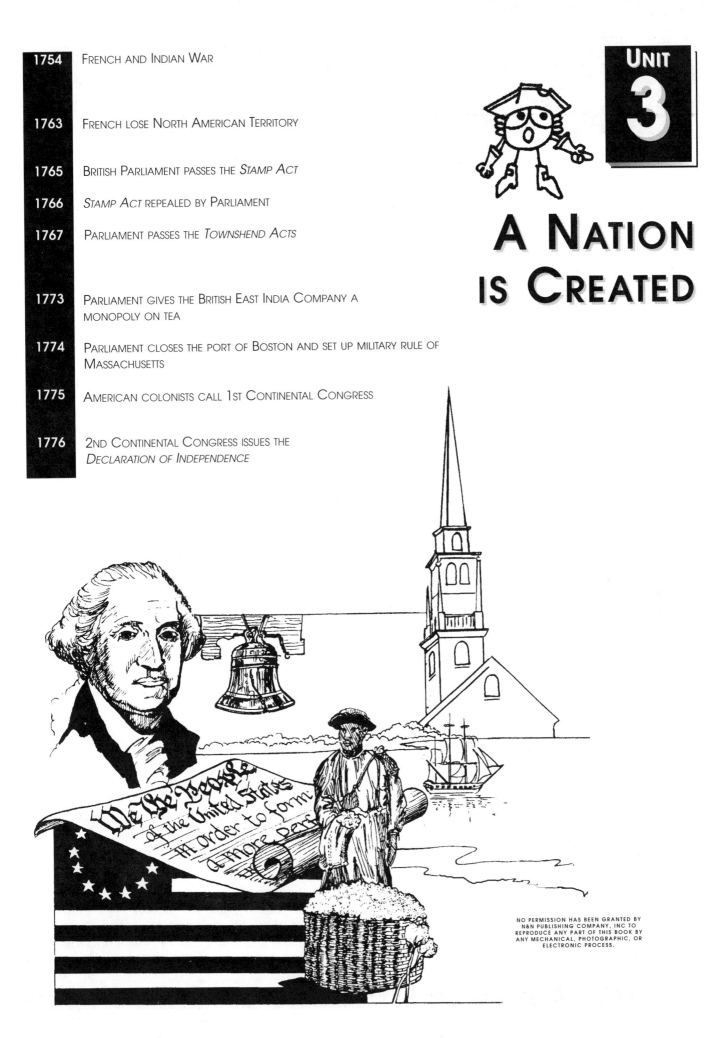

UNIT 3

A NATION IS CREATED

A Nation is Created

Mercantilism was the economic system popular with 17th and 18th century European powers. Its goal was to accumulate national wealth. Under mercantilism, acquiring colonies was an important way to build wealth. The mother country was supposed to protect the colonies while the colonies' raw materials added to its riches. In such a "closed market," colonies were supposed to purchase goods from the mother country.

After the expense of the **French and Indian War**, the British national treasury was low on funds. Off and on for nearly a hundred years, the British fought the French for colonies all over the world. The wars were a financial drain. Since Britain had helped and protected the American settlers, Parliament felt it had a right to tax the colonists to rebuild the national treasury.

Parliament chose to tax colonial business activities to rebuild England's treasury. This especially hurt the richer merchants of New England and elsewhere along the coastal regions. The business class had grown in power and wealth in the 160 years since the founding of the colonies. Prior to this time, the British had never tried to control these merchants very much.

ROAD TO REVOLUTION
Actions and Reactions of the 1760s

Parliamentary Act	Purpose	Colonial Reaction
Navigation Acts (18th century)	The *Acts* forced colonists to trade with Britain and its possessions.	Colonists engaged in smuggling, importing foreign items, and bribing colonial officials.
Writs of Assistance 1760	The *Writs* gave British officials general warrants to search colonial homes and businesses for smuggled goods.	Massachusetts colonists sent protests to officials in London.
Proclamation of 1763	The *Proclamation* banned white settlement west of the Appalachian Mountains.	Colonists defied the order, and continued westward.
Stamp Act 1765	The *Act* imposed an "internal tax" on goods bought and sold within the colonies requiring colonists to purchase specially stamped paper for documents, licenses, papers, and pamphlets.	Mobs destroyed the houses of tax officials in Massachusetts; riots and threats of mob violence spread to other colonies; convened a Stamp Act Congress that issued a declaration of grievances.
Quartering Act 1765	The *Act* forced colonists to provide supplies, rations, and shelter for the troops needed for conflicts between colonists and Native Americans.	Colonists wrote protests against the tyranny of a standing army in peacetime.
Townshend Acts 1767	The *Acts* imposed new import taxes on glass, lead, paint, paper, and tea, with a board for enforcement and levying fines.	Colonists boycotted British goods to pressure merchants to halt their importation of goods.

A tradition of freedom had built gradually in the colonies. For a century and a half, events in Britain reinforced this colonial sense of freedom. From the 1640s to the 1660s, Parliament overthrew and executed a king (Charles I) who would not share power in the English Civil Wars and the Puritan Revolution.

After Parliament restored the monarchy in 1660, it overthrew another king (James II) who would not share power in the **Glorious Revolution** (1688). Before inviting new monarchs to the throne, Parliament proclaimed the English *Bill of Rights* in 1689. Also in the late 1600s, the writings of **Enlightenment** thinkers popularized democratic ideals. **John Locke**'s works proclaimed the right of revolution and the people's power over their own government.

As English citizens, the colonists were part of this democratic heritage. When added to the "**benign neglect**" by Parliament in managing the colonies, the sense of democracy became even stronger. When the British tried to tighten their rule in the 1760s, they found out how powerful the sense of freedom was.

The colonists had been nearly left on their own for more than a century. Their assemblies had made rules and kept order. The new British policies antagonized many in America. In Virginia's House of Burgesses, **Patrick Henry** claimed that Parliament could not tax Virginians, because they were not represented in Parliament. A chain of actions and new tax policies met opposition from the 1760s.

After protests and boycotts of the 1760s, some ministers in Britain saw the colonists as misbehaving children needing discipline. The British began sending more troops to the colonies and pressed the royal governors to enforce order more strictly. The colonists, however, grew more angry as this pressure was applied.

In the 1770s, colonial leaders claimed all the rights of British subjects. Clashes in Boston between colonists and British troops escalated. In 1773, Bostonians disguised as Native Americans raided a cargo ship and dumped tea into the harbor to protest its price. Prime Minister **Lord Frederick North** reacted angrily to this "Boston Tea Party." He closed the port and took over the government of

©Wildside Press

Massachusetts. Other colonies came to the support of Massachusetts. The colonial leaders called a general meeting to air their differences. The **First Continental Congress** met in Philadelphia in September of 1774. It called on the colonists to stop all trade with Britain. It also urged the colonies to arm themselves for defense of their rights.

Unofficial groups began to gather arms and hold regular military drills throughout the colonies. Tension continued to mount until the British commander of Massachusetts tried to arrest **Samuel Adams** and **John Hancock** and destroy their group's supplies in Lexington in April of 1775. Patriot Minutemen skirmished with British General Gage's troops as they retreated to Boston, beginning the **American Revolution**.

The **Second Continental Congress** met in Philadelphia in May of 1775. It selected **George Washington** of Virginia as Continental Army commander, and it sent a petition to **King George III** asking him to stop Parliament's tyranny. The British refused to negotiate with the Congress. In June, British General Gage tried to disperse the rebel forces in Boston. In the **Battle of Bunker Hill**, the British drove the rebels from the field, but lost forty percent of their troops.

In 1775, the Continental Army's forces won skirmishes near Lake Champlain (NY) and Norfolk (VA). They briefly held Montreal, but the patriot invasion of Canada failed at Quebec. To draw more people to the patriot cause, **Thomas Paine** published *Common Sense*, a call to arms that convinced many to fight for the cause.

©Wildside Press

IDEAS OF THE DECLARATION OF INDEPENDENCE

Statement of Democratic Principles	Statement of Grievances	Concluding Statement
The main ideas of this part are: • all men are created equal • all men have certain rights to life, liberty, and the pursuit of happiness • government gets its authority from the people • government can be altered or replaced by the people	This section listed accusations that King George III violated the colonists' rights.	This section declared the colonists' formal break with Great Britain.

©Wildside Press

DECLARATION OF INDEPENDENCE

In June of 1776, the Second Continental Congress formed a committee to make a dramatic statement to say why the Patriots fought. With **Benjamin Franklin** and **John Adams** contributing, twenty-four year old **Thomas Jefferson** combined the committee's thoughts with those of the great thinkers of history, especially John Locke. Jefferson's *Declaration of Independence* is one of the most inspiring and best known documents in human experience. It was signed on July 4th, 1776, a date now known as the birthday of the United States of America.

Fighting moved southward into the middle colonies in 1776. In New York, the British handed the Continental forces serious defeats on Long Island and White Plains and forced Washington to retreat across New Jersey. Washington turned and routed the British at Trenton and then at Princeton.

In 1777, the British attempted to separate New England from the rest of the colonies by a Canadian-Hudson invasion. Continental forces broke this attack at **Saratoga** (NY). The victory was enough to convince the French to form an alliance with the American Patriots and send money, troops, and ships to support them.

In 1779, the British shifted their attention to the South. They took Savannah (GA), Port Royal (SC), and later captured Charleston (SC) and Wilmington (NC). In 1781, General Washington felt he had enough support from the French. He marched his Continental troops from New York and Pennsylvania to challenge the British forces in Virginia.

The American-French force and the French fleet converged on Yorktown. By September 10th, the French fleet drove off the British naval support. This left British **General Charles Cornwallis** isolated and under siege. Without an escape from Yorktown, Cornwallis surrendered to Washington on October 18th. Washington marched back to challenge the British in New York. However, in London, the Prime Minister was ousted, and the new British government offered a truce. In September 1783, Henry Laurens, Ben Franklin, John Adams, and John Jay negotiated the *Treaty of Paris* – the final peace.

THE TREATY OF PARIS 1783

By *The Treaty of Paris* (1783), Britain recognized:

• the independence of the United States of America

• geographic boundaries that made the Mississippi the new country's western boundary

• U.S. fishing rights in the Atlantic

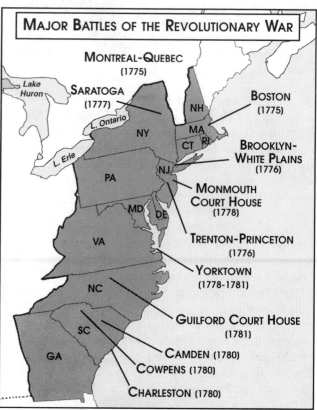

MAJOR BATTLES OF THE REVOLUTIONARY WAR

MONTREAL-QUEBEC (1775)
Lake Huron
SARATOGA (1777)
L. Ontario
NH
BOSTON (1775)
NY
MA
RI
L. Erie
CT
BROOKLYN-WHITE PLAINS (1776)
PA
NJ
MONMOUTH COURT HOUSE (1778)
MD
DE
TRENTON-PRINCETON (1776)
VA
YORKTOWN (1778-1781)
NC
GUILFORD COURT HOUSE (1781)
SC
CAMDEN (1780)
COWPENS (1780)
GA
CHARLESTON (1780)

UNIT 3

MULTIPLE CHOICE

Directions: Base your answer to question 1 on the statements below and on your knowledge of social studies.

Colonies must sell raw materials to the mother country.
Colonies must buy finished products from the mother country.
Accumulation of national wealth is the goal.

1 The three statements best describe
  1 slavery   3 mercantilism
  2 free trade   4 Puritan beliefs

2 The French and Indian War marked a change in British policy toward the colonies because it
  1 resulted in a complete withdrawal of British troops from the colonies
  2 led to a demand that the colonists help pay for their defense
  3 increased the French threat to the colonies
  4 led to an alliance between the Indians and the colonists to end British control

Directions: Base your answer to question 3 on the illustration below and on your knowledge of social studies.

CARTOON

JOIN or DIE

3 This cartoon indicates that the colonies will have to
  1 strike the British as a snake would to win
  2 combat French and Indian invasions
  3 unify if they are to win their independence from Britain
  4 be led by the New England colonies in the fight for independence

4 Which statement about colonial reaction to the actions of the British Parliament is most accurate?
  1 Colonists supported the actions and obeyed the new laws.
  2 No attempts were made to protest the actions peacefully.
  3 Reactions ranged from peaceful protest to mob violence.
  4 Colonists accepted the trade restrictions, but opposed the taxes.

Directions: Base your answer to question 5 on the quotation below and on your knowledge of social studies.

"Can any reason be assigned why 160,000 electors in the island of Great Britain should give law to four millions in the states of America, every individual of whom is equal to every individual of them, in virtue, in understanding, and in bodily strength."

– Thomas Jefferson, *A Summary View of the Rights of British America*, 1774

5 In this statement, Thomas Jefferson's main point is that
  1 Americans are the equal of the British and should have the same say in making laws
  2 Americans and British are equal in virtue, understanding, and bodily strength
  3 laws made in Britain only apply to the British
  4 only the physically strong, virtuous, and intelligent should make laws

6 The Puritan Revolution and the Glorious Revolution indicated that the British
  1 preferred an absolute monarch
  2 opposed citizen participation in the government
  3 would not revolt for freedom of religion
  4 desired limited power for the monarch

Directions: Base your answer to question 7 on the quotation below and on your knowledge of social studies.

"Men being ... by nature all free, equal, and independent, no one can be put out of this estate and subjected to the political power of another without his own consent."

– John Locke, *Two Treatises of Government*, 1690

7 The influence of the thinking of John Locke can be most clearly seen in the
  1 *Mayflower Compact*
  2 *Fundamental Orders of Connecticut*
  3 *Declaration of Independence*
  4 *Navigation Acts*

Directions: Base your answer to question 8 on the map below and on your knowledge of social studies.

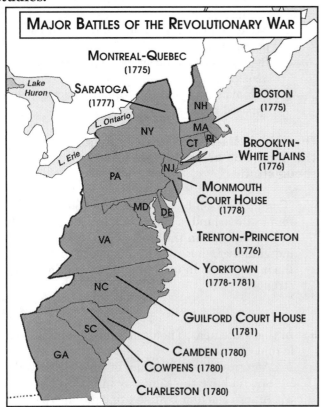

MAJOR BATTLES OF THE REVOLUTIONARY WAR

MONTREAL-QUEBEC (1775)
Lake Huron
SARATOGA (1777)
BOSTON (1775)
L. Ontario
L. Erie
NH
NY
MA
RI
CT
BROOKLYN-WHITE PLAINS (1776)
PA
NJ
MONMOUTH COURT HOUSE (1778)
MD
DE
TRENTON-PRINCETON (1776)
VA
YORKTOWN (1778-1781)
NC
GUILFORD COURT HOUSE (1781)
SC
CAMDEN (1780)
GA
COWPENS (1780)
CHARLESTON (1780)

Directions: Base your answer to question 10 on the map below and on your knowledge of social studies.

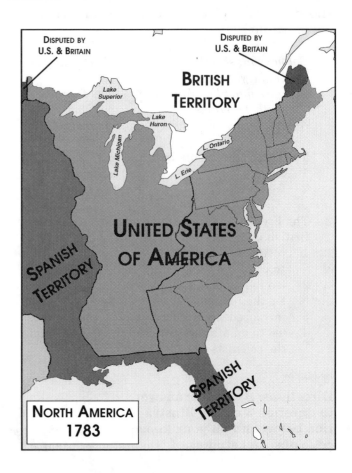

DISPUTED BY U.S. & BRITAIN
DISPUTED BY U.S. & BRITAIN
BRITISH TERRITORY
Lake Superior
Lake Huron
Lake Michigan
L. Ontario
L. Erie
UNITED STATES OF AMERICA
SPANISH TERRITORY
SPANISH TERRITORY

NORTH AMERICA 1783

8   According to the map, the British initially focused their military attempts to regain control of the American colonies on
1   land west of the Appalachians
2   the tobacco growing Carolinas
3   the revolutionary leaders in Virginia
4   populous colonies of the northeast

9   The Battle of Saratoga can be considered a major turning point in the American Revolution because it
1   ended the American invasion of Canada
2   led the French to send aid to the American patriots
3   forced General Washington to cross the Delaware
4   divided New England from the rest of the colonies

10   The presence of European powers on this map meant that
1   nearly all coastal trade was blocked
2   no new states could be added to the union
3   Americans had to learn French
4   Americans needed to be concerned about security

CONSTRUCTED RESPONSE

SET 1

Directions: Base your answers to questions 1 through 3 on the drawing at the right and on your knowledge of social studies.

1   What are TWO (2) ways that the English protected their rights?

_____

_____

2   What are TWO (2) ways that Americans protected their rights? _____

_____

3   What can be concluded about the attitudes of the British and Americans toward protection of rights?

_____

_____

SET 2

Directions: Base your answers to questions 4 through 6 on the graph at the right and on your knowledge of social studies.

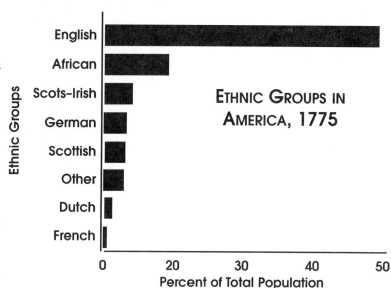

4   What was the largest ethnic group in the colonial population in 1775?

_____

5   What was the second largest ethnic group in the colonial population in 1775?

_____

6   Why were there so many Africans in the colonial population in 1775?

_____

_____

PRACTICE SKILLS FOR DBQ

Directions: The following task is based on the accompanying documents. The documents may have been edited for the purposes of this exercise. The task is designed to test your ability to work with historical documents. As you analyze the documents, take into account both the source of the document and the author's point of view where relevant.

Historical Context: In 1776, the Continental Congress declared the thirteen colonies independent of Britain. In the Declaration of Independence, the Congress gave the reasons for declaring independence and its justification for revolution.

Part A - Short Answer

The documents that follow give reasons why Americans declared their independence. Examine each document carefully, then answer the question(s) which follow it.

Document 1

1a To what were American colonists denied admission?

_____

_____

1b What right did the colonists think was violated by the denial shown in the drawing?

_____

_____

_____

_____

No Admittance To Colonists

British Parliament

Document 2

2a What country was the "old lady" who was "an island queen?"

_____

2b Who did the "daughter" represent?

_____

2c What reaction did the "daughter" have to the demand for the tax on tea?

_____

_____

_____

REVOLUTIONARY TEA

There was an old lady lived over the sea
And she was an island queen.
Her daughter lived off in a new country
With an ocean of water between.
The old lady's pockets were full of gold
But never contented was she,
So she called on her daughter to pay her a tax
Of three pence a pound on her tea,
Of three pence a pound on her tea. – Anonymous Author(s)

Task: Discuss the reasons why the American colonies revolted against Britain in 1776. (State your thesis in the introduction.)

ADDITIONAL SUGGESTED TASK

From your knowledge of social studies, make a list of additional reasons why the colonies declared their independence from Great Britain in 1776.

UNIT 4

EXPERIMENTS IN GOVERNMENT

EXPERIMENTS IN GOVERNMENT

FORMER COLONIES SETUP NEW GOVERNMENTS

After the Revolution, the thirteen new states set up new constitutional governments and began reforms. In many states, they gave all classes voting rights in free elections. They created strong, bicameral (two-house) legislatures, stronger courts, and protections of individual rights. Several states emancipated slaves and gradually abolished slavery (MA, NH, PA, CT, and RI).

After declaring independence, New York's Provincial Congress set up a new state government. John Jay played a major part in creating the state constitution of 1777. The legislature was bicameral – the Senate and the Assembly checked each other. The court structure remained the same as in the colonial era. Voting was restricted to those owning property worth £100 (British pound sterling) or more.

The new New York state constitution showed that distrust of executive power was strong. The governor's power was restricted. While the governor was commander of the militia, the term of office was only three years. The governor could not veto laws; a special council had that power. Non-elected posts were not appointed by the governor; another special council had that power. Also, there was a special Court of Errors and Impeachment to keep watch on government officials.

CONGRESS SETS UP A NATIONAL GOVERNMENT

During the Revolution, the Second Continental Congress set up a national government for the United States called the ***Articles of Confederation*** (1781). This new government:

- ended the war
- got the states to drop their claims to western territories
- set up a frame of government to create new western states (*Northwest Ordinance*)
- sent diplomats to other countries.

However, this national **confederation** government was very weak. Having struggled and overthrown harsh central rule from Britain, the new states were very suspicious of any national government. Under the *Articles of Confederation*, there was a legislative branch (Congress), but it could only pass laws with a 2/3rds majority. There was no executive to enforce the national laws, and there were no central courts to interpret those laws and settle disputes between states.

Historians often refer to the era under the *Articles of Confederation* as the **Critical Period** in American history. Problems arose even before the Revolution ended. Raising money and keeping order were difficult. Congress could not regulate trade among states and along the coastal waters. It could tax, but the states collected the taxes. Congress issued money, but states could also issue money, causing confusion as to value. A unanimous vote was needed to make any changes in the national government.

During the Critical Period, incidents of economic and political instability became more common. Disputes among states led to them blocking commerce with tariffs and other regulations. A depression hit the country in 1786, and a taxpayers' revolt (**Shays' Rebellion**) erupted in Massachusetts that turned bloody. By 1787, these events made it clear to many citizens that the government needed reform if the country was to survive. Delegates in Congress tried to offer proposals for reform, but the proposals could not get unanimous votes. Finally, an interstate commerce meeting in Maryland led to a call for a special national convention to revise the *Articles*.

Independence Hall Philadelphia, PA, where the Constitutional Convention met in 1787 ©PhotoDisc

COMPROMISES OF THE CONSTITUTIONAL CONVENTION

NAME	PROBLEM	COMPROMISE
The Great Compromise	How was the number of votes in Congress per state to be determined? (Large states wanted population to be used. Small states wanted all to have equal number.)	Bicameral (2 houses) legislature – one based on population, the other based on equal representation for all states.
The Three-Fifths Compromise	How were slaves to be counted in determining the number of votes per state in Congress? (Southern states wanted them counted. Northern states opposed counting them.)	Every five slaves would equal three persons in determining a state's population.
The Slave Trade Compromise	Those against slavery wanted trade abolished. Most Southern states wanted to preserve it.	The importation of slaves would end after 1808 (slavery itself was allowed to continue).
The Tariff Compromise	Northern businesses wanted imports taxed to equalize competition. Cotton and tobacco exporting Southerners feared U.S. tariffs would cause foreign countries to retaliate with high tariffs against their exports.	Congress could not tax exports, only imports.

THE CONSTITUTION:
A NEW FRAMEWORK OF GOVERNMENT

Fifty-five delegates met in Philadelphia from May through September of 1787. This group held its meetings in secret. Instead of revising the *Articles*, they decided to draft a whole new framework for the national government. Throughout the summer, the Constitutional Convention delegates debated and compromised on a new, stronger constitution. Some stayed the whole time; some came and went; and, some stormed out in anger, never to return.

By September, the Convention delegates created a new government for the United States of America. All parties had to change their thinking as the new government took shape. This meant there had to be many compromises along the way (see chart above).

When the Constitutional Convention finished its work, the document it released to the states for ratification (approval) created a new, and much stronger, national government. At its heart were six important principles:

- **Limited Government** – the *Constitution of the United States* specifically lists what the national government can do and cannot do.

- **Federalism** – the *Constitution of the United States* divides power between the central government and the state governments (see diagram below).

- **Representative government** – the *Constitution of the United States* allows the people to elect the people who make decisions (at least indirectly).

- **Separation of Power** – the *Constitution of the United States* strictly subdivides power within the central government into legislative, executive, and judicial branches (see chart on next page).

- **Checks and Balances** – the *Constitution of the United States* makes sure the three branches stay within their limits by giving each branch the power to watch and limit the other two branches.

U.S. CONSTITUTION LIMITS POWER BY DIVIDING IT BETWEEN THE NATIONAL AND STATE GOVERNMENTS.

FEDERALISM

Delegated Powers
(national government only)
interstate & foreign commerce
foreign relations
declares war
coins money
immigration
postal service

Implied Powers
Congress can stretch
the delegated powers.

Concurrent Powers
(both governments)
pass laws
taxation
borrowing
court systems
penal systems
law enforcement agencies
general welfare of citizens
charter banks and
corporations

Reserved Powers
(state governments only)
intrastate commerce
local governments
public health
voter qualification
supervise elections
supervise education
license occupations

AMERICANS ARE CITIZENS UNDER TWO GOVERNMENTS:
NATIONAL (U.S. FEDERAL) GOVERNMENT AND THE STATE IN WHICH THEY RESIDE.

THE RATIFICATION STRUGGLE

	Federalists (supporters)	Antifederalists (opponents)
Who	merchants, shippers, plantation owners, upper classes	rural farmers, lower classes
Why	wanted stability and order	feared too much power; no guarantee of individual rights; thought power would go to a small, aristocratic group
Where	coastal trading towns, middle states, and south	New England, frontier areas in all states

- **Provision for change** – the *Constitution of the United States* allows Congress to meet new situations by stretching its power (elastic clause) and allows formal change through amendments.

To become the new law of the land, the new constitution had to be ratified by 9 of the 13 states. In the months after its release, some of the states approved the document quickly, but bitter struggles erupted in several states, including Virginia, New York, North Carolina, and Rhode Island. Supporters became known as **Federalists** and opponents became known as **Antifederalists**.

By July 1788, Rhode Island had rejected the new constitution, but ten states had ratified it. The new government was approved. Still, New York and North Carolina struggled over ratification. Without New York especially, the country would be badly divided.

In July 1788, New York delegates gathered at a convention in Poughkeepsie. Alexander Hamilton and John Jay led the Federalists, and Governor George Clinton led the upstate opponents. Hamilton and Jay had written the **Federalist Papers** along with Virginia's James Madison. These were powerful newspaper essays defending the constitution. Jay and Hamilton persuaded key neutrals to support the new constitution, while promising to support a bill of rights. New York ratified by a slim 30-27 vote.

North Carolina ratified in August, 1788. (Later, Rhode Island reconsidered and ratified in January, 1790). After elections in early 1789, George Washington was chosen first President, and John Adams was chosen as the first Vice President. The new government was launched in New York in April 1789, but moved to Philadelphia in late 1790. (It did not permanently settle in the District of Columbia until 1800.)

SEPARATION OF POWERS
Branches of Government and Functions (Responsibilities)

Legislative Congress	Executive President	Judicial Supreme Court & Federal Courts
Passes Laws	**Enforces Laws**	**Interprets Laws**
Levies taxes	Approves or vetoes laws	Hears cases and appeals involving federal law
Prints & coins money	Collects taxes	Reviews constitutionality of Congressional law
Creates federal courts	Spends government money	Reviews constitutionality of Presidential actions
Approves President's appointments	Appoints ambassadors, dept. heads, federal judges	Interprets treaties
Declares war	Commands Armed Forces	
Supports Armed Forces	Negotiates treaties	
Ratifies treaties		
Sets trade regulations		

Constitution of The United States

Preamble

We the people of the United States, in order to form a more perfect union, establish justice, insure domestic tranquility, provide for the common defense, promote the general welfare, and secure the blessings of liberty for ourselves and our posterity, do ordain and establish this Constitution of the United States of America.

Original Constitution

Article I: Establishes Congress as a bicameral legislative branch (House of Rep. & Senate); how members are chosen and terms; lists 17 specific powers plus the "elastic clause;" presidential veto and override; actions prohibited

Article II: Establishes executive branch with President and Vice President; duties of office; how elected; appointment power; checks on power, including impeachment procedure

Article III: Establishes judicial branch, with Supreme Court and its jurisdiction; how Congress sets up lower Federal courts; defines treason

Article IV: Declares equality among the states, extradition, admission of new states, Congress' authority over territories; requires republican form of government in all states

Article V: Establishes procedure for amending the Constitution

Article VI: Declares Constitution the Supreme law of the land

Article VII: Establishes procedure for the 13 states to ratify the new Constitution

Constitutional Amendments

Bill of Rights (1791)

1st Amendment - freedom of speech, press, assembly, free exercise of religion

2nd Amendment - right to bear arms

3rd Amendment - forbids government from quartering of troops in peacetime

4th Amendment - protects against unwarranted search

5th Amendment - protects rights of accused to due process; eminent domain

6th Amendment - protects rights to fair trial & counsel

7th Amendment - right of jury trial in civil cases

8th Amendment - protects against cruel punishment & excessive bail

9th Amendment - rights not specifically mentioned still exist

10th Amendment - powers not specified in Constitution left to states and people

---

Subsequent Amendments

11th Amendment (1795) - suits by citizens of one state against a particular state must be heard in the latter's courts not in Federal ones

12th Amendment (1804) - electors must use separate ballots for President and Vice President

13th Amendment (1865) - abolishes slavery

14th Amendment (1868) - defines citizenship, application of due process, and equal protection

15th Amendment (1870) - defines citizens' right to vote

16th Amendment (1913) - allows Federal income tax

17th Amendment (1913) - direct popular election of United States Senators

18th Amendment (1919) - manufacture, sale, importation, & transportation of alcoholic beverages forbidden in U.S. (repealed by 21st Amend.)

19th Amendment (1920) - right of women to vote

20th Amendment (1933) - redefines term of President & sessions of Congress

21st Amendment (1933) - repeal of prohibition amendment (18th)

22nd Amendment (1951) - limits Presidential term

23rd Amendment (1961) - provides presidential electors for District of Columbia

24th Amendment (1964) - abolishes poll taxes for Federal elections

25th Amendment (1967) - defines succession to presidency & disability of president

26th Amendment (1971) - eighteen year-old citizens may vote in Federal elections

27th Amendment (1992) - sitting Congress may not raise own salary

UNIT 4

MULTIPLE CHOICE

Directions: Base your answer to question 1 on the time line below and on your knowledge of social studies.

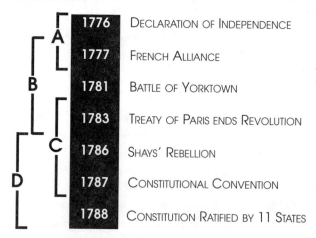

1776	DECLARATION OF INDEPENDENCE
1777	FRENCH ALLIANCE
1781	BATTLE OF YORKTOWN
1783	TREATY OF PARIS ENDS REVOLUTION
1786	SHAYS' REBELLION
1787	CONSTITUTIONAL CONVENTION
1788	CONSTITUTION RATIFIED BY 11 STATES

1   During which time period were the *Articles of Confederation* adopted?
   1 *A*   3 *C*
   2 *B*   4 *D*

2   According to the New York State Constitution adopted in 1777, the governor could only serve three years, could not veto laws, and could not appoint non-elected officials. This indicates that
   1 the governor had powers similar to those of the President of the U.S.
   2 there was concern about an executive with too much power
   3 most of the power was in the hands of the judicial branch
   4 actions of King George III of England had little effect on the Provincial Congress

Directions: Base your answer to question 3 on the cartoon at the right and on your knowledge of social studies.

3   Which weakness of the *Articles of Confederation* is shown in this cartoon?
   1 lack of a bill of rights
   2 requirement of a two-thirds majority to pass laws
   3 states had too much power
   4 lack of central courts to interpret laws

4   Shays' Rebellion, the depression in 1786, and states' use of tariffs and trade regulations against each other were factors leading to the
   1 calling of the Constitutional Convention in 1787
   2 writing of the *Articles of Confederation*
   3 establishment of separation of powers in the *Constitution of the United States*
   4 passage of the American *Bill of Rights*

Directions: Base your answer to question 5 on the speakers' comments below and on your knowledge of social studies.

SPEAKER

Speaker A: The *Articles of Confederation* have opened the entire nation to grave danger because the central government lacks the power to deal effectively with crises.

Speaker B: The power the *Constitution of the United States* gives to the President is excessive. He will soon be another George III.

Speaker C: The *Constitution of the United States* lacks a bill of rights to protect the freedoms we just fought to obtain.

Speaker D: The proposed *Constitution of the United States* will provide the stability and order that we lack now.

5   Which two Speakers best state the arguments put forth by the Federalists?
   1 Speakers *B* and *C*
   2 Speakers *A* and *B*
   3 Speakers *A* and *D*
   4 Speakers *C* and *D*

6 The *Constitution of the United States* gives Congress power to pass laws, the President power to veto laws, the Supreme Court power to declare laws unconstitutional, and Congress the power to begin the amendment process. These powers are examples of the principle of
1 representative government
2 federalism
3 separation of power
4 checks and balances

7 According to the *Constitution of the United States*, the President can
1 declare laws unconstitutional
2 command the Armed Forces
3 print and coin money
4 establish trade regulations

8 Only the national government can declare war and coin money; only the state governments can regulate trade within their borders and license certain occupations; but both governments establish court systems and have law enforcement agencies. The principle involved in this division of power is called
1 checks and balances
2 separation of power
3 federalism
4 representative government

9 At the Constitutional Convention, the Three-Fifths Compromise was adopted to solve the problem of how to
1 divide Congressional representation between large and small states
2 count the slave population toward representation and taxation
3 tax the exportation of agricultural products
4 amend the *Constitution of the United States* through state conventions

Directions: Base your answer to question 10 on the chart below.

CHART

State Votes for Ratification of the *Constitution of the United States*	
State	**Vote** (for – against)
Northeast States:	
New Hampshire . . 57 - 46	
Massachusetts . 187 - 168	
Connecticut . . . 128 - 40	
Rhode Island . . . . 34 - 32	
Middle Atlantic States:	
New York . . . . 30 - 27	
Pennsylvania . . . . 46 - 23	
New Jersey . . . . . . 38 - 0	
Delaware . . . . 30 - 0	
Maryland . . . . 63 - 11	
Southern States:	
Virginia . . . . 89 - 79	
North Carolina . . 184 - 77	
South Carolina . . 149 - 73	
Georgia . . . . 26 - 0	

10 Using the information in this chart, it is possible to conclude that
1 support for the *Constitution of the United States* was overwhelming in all areas
2 opposition to the *Constitution of the United States* was apparent only in the south
3 only Delaware and New Jersey had unanimous votes
4 there was substantial opposition to the *Constitution of the United States* in New England

CONSTRUCTED RESPONSE

SET 1

Directions: Base your answers to questions 1 through 3 on the chart and on your knowledge of social studies.

1 What are TWO (2) groups in the population that supported the Federalist position?

_____

_____

2 What is ONE (1) class difference between those who supported the Federalists and those who were Antifederalists?

_____

_____

3 Why was it especially important that New York ratify the *Constitution of the United States*?

_____

THE RATIFICATION STRUGGLE		
	Federalists (supporters)	**Antifederalists** (opponents)
Who	merchants, shippers, plantation owners, upper classes	rural farmers, lower classes
Why	wanted stability and order	feared too much power; no guarantee of individual rights; thought power would go to a small, aristocratic group
Where	coastal trading towns, middle states, and south	New England, frontier areas in all states

> "I doubt, too, whether any other Convention we can obtain may be able to make a better Constitution. For when you assemble a number of men to have the advantage of their joint wisdom, you. . .assemble. . .all their prejudices, their passions, their errors of opinion, their local interests, and their selfish views..."
>
> – Benjamin Franklin, speech to the Constitutional Convention, 1787

4   According to Franklin, what are TWO (2) problems that may occur when you assemble a group of men to take advantage of their wisdom when writing a document such as the *Constitution of the United States*?

_____

5   Based on this quotation, was Franklin probably a Federalist or an Antifederalist? Explain why.

_____

PRACTICE SKILLS FOR DBQ

Directions: The following task is based on the accompanying documents. The documents may have been edited for the purposes of this exercise. The task is designed to test your ability to work with historical documents. As you analyze the documents, take into account both the source of the document and the author's point of view where relevant.

Historical Context: In 1787, the Continental Congress met to write a new constitution to replace the weak *Articles of Confederation*. During those meetings, several key issues became subjects of heated debate and division among the delegates. Eventually, compromises were reached which were included in the *Constitution of the United States*.

Part A - Short Answer

Document 1

1*a* What issue faced by the delegates is shown in this chart?

one figure = 50,000 slaves

Counted for representation and taxation   **Not counted for representation and taxation**

_____

1*b* What compromise on this issue was adopted in the *Constitution of the United States*? _____

_____

Document 2

2*a* What issue concerns this delegate? _____

> "To proclaim a national legislature with representation based on population is to proclaim tyranny for New Jersey and small states like it."
>
> – Anonymous delegate, Constitutional Convention, 1787

2*b* What compromise on this issue was adopted in the *Constitution of the United States*?

Part B - Essay Response
Task: Identify at least TWO (2) issues that caused disagreement among the delegates to the Constitutional Convention in 1787. For EACH issue identified, explain the compromise solution adopted in the *Constitution of the United States*. (State your thesis in the introduction.)

ADDITIONAL SUGGESTED TASK
From your knowledge of social studies, make a list of additional areas of disagreement among the delegates to the Constitutional Convention in 1787.

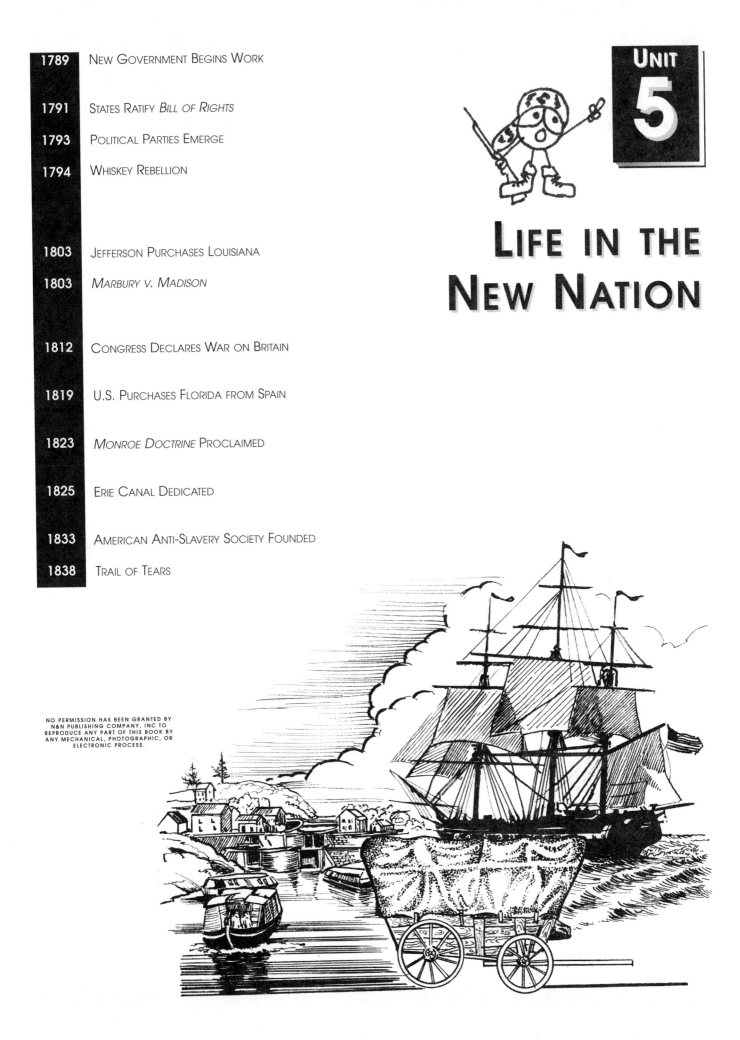

UNIT 5

LIFE IN THE NEW NATION

LAUNCHING THE NEW GOVERNMENT
SETTING PRECEDENTS

President Washington and the new Congress began work immediately in April 1789. The new Constitution was a theoretical outline of how government was to work. It was not a precise guide. Each law and policy was a new step – a **precedent** (a model for those who followed). Some of these precedents became such strong influences on government that historians began calling them an "**unwritten constitution**." They include the cabinet, political parties, and judicial review.

When they ratified the Constitution, five states attached instructions to pass amendments insuring individual rights. The first Congress sent twelve amendments to the states for approval. Ten were ratified in 1791 and became known as the *Bill of Rights*. The first Congress also set up the federal judiciary. It organized the Supreme Court with a Chief Justice and five associate justices. (There now are eight associates.) Congress also set up thirteen district courts, three circuit courts of appeal, and an Attorney General's office to deal with federal cases.

In the summer of 1789, Congress also authorized the first administrative departments to assist President Washington in administering the laws: State (foreign affairs), Treasury, War, and the Post Office. The President appointed heads of the departments (State – Thomas Jefferson; Treasury – Alexander Hamilton; War – Henry Knox; Post Office – Samuel Osgood). Washington also appointed Edmund Randolph as Attorney General – the government's prosecutor and lawyer.

THE CABINET EMERGES

President Washington routinely called the department heads together to consult on issues and policies. Sitting as a group, the department heads became known as the President's **Cabinet**. It had no official status, but Presidents have used the Cabinet members as advisors ever since. As a result, Washington set one of his first precedents and this powerful group became part of the "unwritten constitution."

Washington appointed John Jay as the first Chief Justice and five other associate justices to the Supreme Court of the United States. These judges also had to "ride circuit" – they traveled about the country serving in other federal courts.

HAMILTON'S ECONOMIC PLAN

President Washington and his advisors then began work on straightening out the financial problems of the country. The government and the states owed nearly 80 million dollars to citizens, lenders, and other countries from the Revolution. Treasury Secretary Alexander Hamilton proposed several actions to Congress. He wanted to get the country on solid financial footing and raise its credit in world markets.

CURRENT DEPARTMENTS OF THE EXECUTIVE BRANCH

1 State - 1789
2 Treasury - 1789
3 Justice (Attorney General) - 1789
4 Interior (federal lands) - 1849
5. Agriculture - 1889
6 Commerce - 1903
7 Labor - 1913
8 Defense - 1947
9 Housing & Urban Development - 1965
10 Transportation - 1966
11 Energy - 1977
12 Health & Human Services - 1977
13 Education - 1979
14 Veterans Affairs - 1989

HAMILTON'S FINANCIAL PLAN

Secretary Hamilton's proposals included:

- absorbing all state and national debt and issuing new bonds to refinance

- levying excise taxes on luxuries such as jewelry and liquor to raise money

- levying tariffs on imports to raise money

- creating a national bank to handle government accounts and distribute coin and currency – The Bank of the United States

Not everyone agreed to this strategy. James Madison and Thomas Jefferson led the opposition to Hamilton's plan. They attacked it as favoring the rich and the speculators (high risk investors). Speculators bought old bonds from owners at a low price and resold them to the government at a higher price. Some states had paid the war debts and did not want to have to join in paying those of others. There were compromises on many points, but Hamilton negotiated successfully. He convinced Congress that getting the government on solid financial footing was worth the expense.

POLITICAL PARTIES EMERGE

The political struggles over Hamilton's financial plan gave birth to another part of the "unwritten constitution" – the first major **political parties**. Political parties have a number of purposes:

- electing officials
- influencing the public
- conducting campaigns
- framing solutions to political issues
- monitoring the other groups in power

During Washington's administration, the different ideas of the **Federalists** and **Democratic-Republicans** built up followings. The parties began to offer candidates in elections. Influential newspapers emerged that supported one party's views and criticized the other's.

EXERTING FEDERAL AUTHORITY

One of the major tests of the new government came over collection of the excise tax on whiskey. In frontier regions, farmers distilled their grain into whiskey. It was easier to transport barrels across the rugged country to market than bulky raw grain in bales and bags. As a finished product, it also brought higher income. The excise tax was very unpopular. By 1792, opponents began resisting collection agents.

First, Washington issued a proclamation backing the agents. However, mobs in western Pennsylvania ignored the order. The resistance became known as the **Whiskey Rebellion**. Sometimes, mobs tarred and feathered the tax collectors.

Washington could not tolerate this challenge to federal authority. In 1794, he set another precedent. He called out the militia from Virginia, Maryland, and New Jersey. The 13,000-man force captured the Pennsylvania mob leaders and the "rebellion" was over. The government tried the leaders for treason. However, the President later pardoned them.

COMPARISON OF THE FEDERALISTS AND THE DEMOCRATIC-REPUBLICANS	
THE FEDERALISTS	**THE DEMOCRATIC-REPUBLICANS***
Leaders:	Leaders:

Alexander Hamilton John Adams	Thomas Jefferson James Madison
Supported: • loose construction of the U.S. Constitution • stronger central government • central control of economic affairs, pro-national bank & protective tariffs	Supported: • strict construction of the U.S. Constitution • stronger state government • less central control of economic affairs; against a national bank & high tariffs
Supporters: Wealthy & propertied groups – merchants & manufacturers	Supporters: "Common People" - small farmers, city labor, frontier people
Foreign Affairs: pro-British	Foreign Affairs: pro-French
Photos: ©Wildside	*For a while after 1800, the group was called "Republicans," but is no relation to the modern Republican Party which formed in the 1850s. By the 1830s, the group took the permanent name of "Democrats."

Washington had upheld the authority of the new government. The event demonstrated the power of the federal government to enforce the law.

PROBLEMS WITH THE FRENCH

In foreign affairs, Washington also had challenges. France had helped the colonists in the American Revolution. The new French revolutionary government requested American aid against the British. Secretary of State Jefferson supported the idea. Secretary Hamilton advised neutrality, saying the new U.S. was too weak to be drawn into a war.

The French sent Edmond Genêt to the United States as their ambassador. Citizen Genêt toured the United States recruiting privateers. (A privateer is a privately owned ship authorized by a government during wartime to attack and capture enemy vessels.) Genêt's activities irked President Washington who asked the French to recall the ambassador.

In 1793, Washington chose to issue the **Proclamation of Neutrality**. He proclaimed that the U.S. should stay out of alliances in the future. He negotiated treaties to solve boundary and debt problems with Britain and Spain. With these policies, Washington set another precedent – the U.S. followed neutrality in foreign affairs for more than 100 years. Setting a two-term precedent, Washington left office in 1796. He had placed the country on a strong, practical course for the future.

In the election of 1796, Washington's Vice President, Federalist John Adams, received the most votes. The second largest vote-getter, Democratic-Republican Thomas Jefferson, became the new Vice President. Relations with the revolutionary government of France were stormy under Adams. The French wanted bribes to set up a commercial treaty and the United States refused. Some of Hamilton's Federalist followers in Congress wanted to declare war on France. However, Adams managed to work out the problem peacefully when Napoleon Bonaparte came to power in 1800.

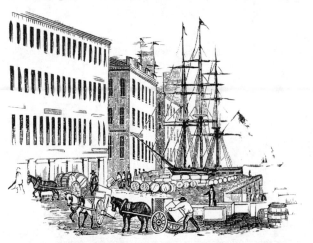

While he avoided a war, Adams became unpopular. The problems with France, the raising of taxes, and British harassment of U.S. shipping all hurt him. In the election of 1800, Federalist President Adams placed third in electoral votes.

Democratic-Republican Thomas Jefferson was tied with his running mate, Aaron Burr. According to the Constitution, the House of Representatives had to break the tie. Democratic-Republican congressmen wanted Jefferson, but some Federalist congressmen favored Burr. However, Federalist leader Alexander Hamilton disliked Burr more than he disliked Jefferson. After 36 ballots, Hamilton rallied the Federalists to choose Jefferson. To avoid future ties, the states ratified the Twelfth Amendment to the Constitution in 1803. It required separate electoral votes for President and Vice President.

JEFFERSON AS PRESIDENT

In Thomas Jefferson's first administration (1801-1805) two events changed the course of American history – the **Marbury v. Madison** decision and the **Louisiana Purchase**. The Marbury decision gave the Supreme Court the power of judicial review. The Louisiana Purchase doubled the size of the United States.

Judicial review is the power of the Supreme Court to determine if local, state, and federal laws or governmental actions violate the *United States Constitution*. The power of judicial review grew out of a Supreme Court decision involving job appointments by President John Adams.

Just before leaving office in 1801, President Adams appointed a number of federal judges. However, he did not have his Secretary of State deliver written notices of the appointments to the appointees. The new Democratic-Republican President was Thomas Jefferson. He would not allow his new Secretary of State, James Madison, to deliver Adams' appointments. One of Adams' Federalist appointees, William Marbury, sued in federal court. He wanted the court to force Secretary Madison to deliver his job appointment.

Most hearings before the Supreme Court come to it on appeal from cases tried in lower state or federal courts. A lower federal court passed the Marbury issue to the Supreme Court in 1803. In *Marbury v. Madison*, the Supreme Court decided for Madison. However, the Court really decided for itself in the long run.

In *Marbury*, the most important outcome was that the Supreme Court checked the power of Congress. It overturned a Congressional law for the first time. In the *Judiciary Act of 1789*, Congress had given the

John Marshall (1755-1835) , Revolutionary soldier, historian, congressman, diplomat, Secretary of State. His 35 years as Chief Justice established the Supreme Court as a powerful branch of the federal Government. ©Wildside

power. In *Marbury*, the Court declared that portion of the *Judiciary Act of 1789* **unconstitutional**. The judicial branch could not order the executive branch to do something. Therefore, the Court could not order Madison to give Marbury his appointment.

In this decision, Marshall set the precedent for judicial review. He clarified the Supreme Court's most important power. This power is not mentioned in the Constitution, so Marshall created another part of the "unwritten constitution." Marshall served as Chief Justice from 1801 to 1835. During that long period, he strengthened this power of judicial review in a number of famous cases. To this day, judicial review remains the Supreme Court's most important power.

THE LOUISIANA PURCHASE

Another constitutional question arose over expansion of territory. Jefferson sent diplomats to negotiate for trade rights for western farmers through the French port of New Orleans. France's First Consul, Napoleon Bonaparte, needed money for his plans in Europe and offered to sell the whole Louisiana Territory.

This unexpected offer from Bonaparte created a dilemma for the government. Nowhere in the Constitution is any branch given the power to expand U.S. territory. As a Democratic-Republican, Jefferson believed in limited power for the national government

Supreme Court the power to give orders to the President. In *Marbury v. Madison*, Chief Justice Marshall said Congress could not do this because it violated the constitutional principle of separation of

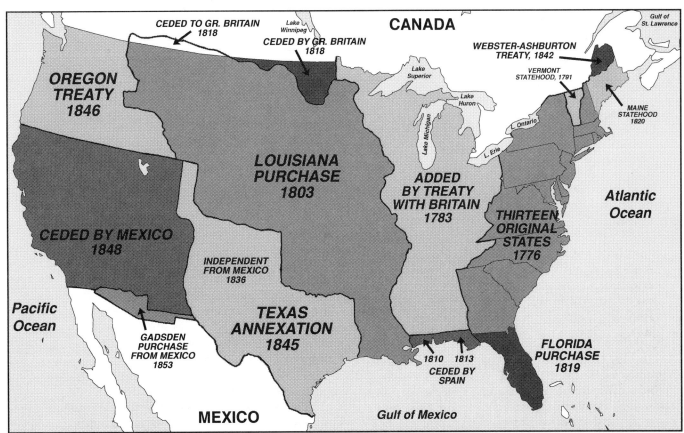

and he was against assuming any new power. He wanted the territory, but was a purchase constitutional? In 1803, he finally decided to stretch his treaty-making power and buy Louisiana for 15 million dollars. There were some objections, but the Senate quickly approved the deal.

The 800,000 square miles of the Louisiana Territory doubled the size of the United States. The Louisiana Purchase gave the U.S. control of the Mississippi River. It extended the western boundary of the nation to the Rocky Mountains. President Jefferson desired information about the new land. He directed **Meriwether Lewis** and **William Clark** to lead an expedition into the new territory. During their 1804-1806 trip, **Sacajawea** (1784-1812), a Shoshone Native American, helped the explorers. Stories of the trip sparked added interest in western lands. However, large scale settlement was still decades away.

The new western lands offered opportunities for settlement and investment. In the next decade, surging nationalism and the War of 1812 increased Americans' interest in the west.

THE WAR OF 1812

In the first decade of the 19th century, the Napoleonic Wars broke out in Europe. Following President Washington's warnings, Presidents Adams, Jefferson, and Madison struggled to keep the country neutral.

Britain blockaded the European continent and choked off supplies to France. Both pestered U.S. ships, and the British impressed American sailors – kidnapping them and forcing them to serve in the British Navy. At the same time, the French launched their own blockade of the British Isles.

U.S. trade across the Atlantic and in the Caribbean suffered. President Jefferson took drastic action to avoid war. He pressed Congress to pass an *Embargo Act*. From late 1806 to early 1809, this act forbade all U.S. foreign trade. The embargo was extremely unpopular with trading interests. The New England states strongly protested. Congress repealed the *Embargo Act* in less than two years. In its place, it passed another law that restricted trade only with warring Britain and France.

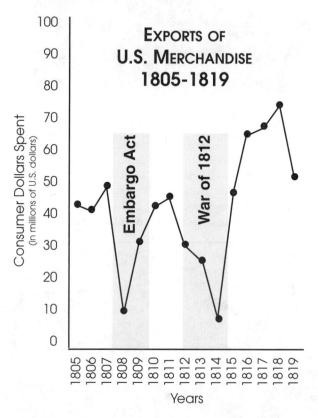

James Madison became President in 1809. He inherited the neutrality problems from Jefferson. The European powers took advantage of the neutral United States. The British set up an effective naval blockade. They forced all neutral trade to Europe through their ports. The French condemned any neutral ships that obeyed British regulations. Caught in the middle, Madison protested that they were both violating neutrals' rights on the seas. However, he failed to keep the United States from being drawn into the European conflict.

Some Americans wanted a declaration of war. In Congress, a group of fiery young Westerners and Southerners blamed the British for inciting the

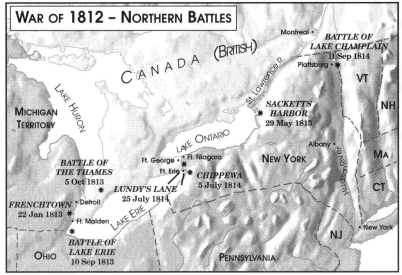

WAR OF 1812 – NORTHERN BATTLES

CANADA (BRITISH)

- Montreal
- **BATTLE OF LAKE CHAMPLAIN** 11 Sep 1814
- Plattsburg
- VT
- NH
- St. Lawrence R.
- **SACKETTS HARBOR** 29 May 1813
- LAKE ONTARIO
- Albany
- MA
- NEW YORK
- CT
- Ft. George • Ft. Niagara
- Ft. Erie
- **CHIPPEWA** 5 July 1814
- **BATTLE OF THE THAMES** 5 Oct 1813
- **LUNDY'S LANE** 25 July 1814
- LAKE HURON
- MICHIGAN TERRITORY
- Detroit
- **FRENCHTOWN** 22 Jan 1813
- Ft. Malden
- LAKE ERIE
- NJ
- New York
- OHIO
- **BATTLE OF LAKE ERIE** 10 Sep 1813
- PENNSYLVANIA
- Hudson R.

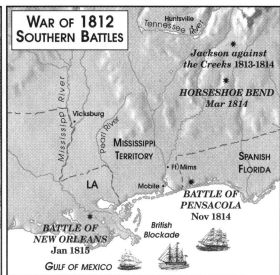

WAR OF 1812 SOUTHERN BATTLES

- Huntsville
- Tennessee River
- **Jackson against the Creeks 1813-1814**
- **HORSESHOE BEND** Mar 1814
- Mississippi River
- Pearl River
- Vicksburg
- MISSISSIPPI TERRITORY
- LA
- Ft. Mims
- Mobile
- **BATTLE OF PENSACOLA** Nov 1814
- SPANISH FLORIDA
- **BATTLE OF NEW ORLEANS** Jan 1815
- British Blockade
- GULF OF MEXICO

Indians in their region. These young **"War Hawks"** (**John C. Calhoun**, SC and **Henry Clay**, KY) patriotically called for war. There was an underlying desire to take British lands from Canada. Federalists in New England opposed the drive toward war, claiming a war would totally destroy the economy. The War Hawks persuaded Congress to declare war in June, 1812.

Madison was forced to follow through and conduct a war for which the country was unprepared. American hopes of conquering Canada collapsed in catastrophic campaigns in 1812 and 1813. The armed forces were ill equipped and the attacks were uncoordinated. In 1812, American commanders surrendered Detroit in August and gave up control of Lake Champlain in November.

In 1813, U.S. ships under Captain Oliver Hazard Perry destroyed the British fleet on Lake Erie. On the oceans, American ships won a series of battles, but the British tightened a blockade around America's coasts, ruining American trade.

In 1814, the British defeated Napoleon in Europe. They began to transfer large numbers of troops to the fighting in America. In August, they marched into Washington, D.C. and burned most of the public buildings. President Madison fled into the countryside.

Peace came with the *Treaty of Ghent* late in 1814. The treaty declared the War was a draw, but it addressed none of the causes. The War had officially ended but neither the British nor the American commanders knew yet. In January 1815, the British attacked New Orleans. General Andrew Jackson won a decisive victory over the British forces. In the years that followed, relations with Britain improved and negotiations solved some of the earlier problems.

"We have met the enemy and they are ours."
Oliver Perry defeats the British on Lake Erie, September 1813 – ©Wildside Press

THE MONROE DOCTRINE

During this early national period, President **James Monroe** (term 1817-1825), set another major foreign policy precedent. In 1823, Imperial Russia intruded on U.S. territorial claims in the Oregon region. In addition, an alliance of European powers (The Holy Alliance – Austria, France, Prussia, and Russia) wanted to reclaim Latin American colonies that became independent during the Napoleonic Wars.

Monroe's Secretary of State, John Quincy Adams (1767-1848), urged the President to take action. Monroe's statement:

- warned Europe that there would be no more colonization of the Western Hemisphere
- pledged the U.S. would not interfere with existing colonies
- vowed the U.S. would remain neutral in European affairs

This policy later became known as the *Monroe Doctrine*. Britain wanted to keep its trade with the new American republics and quietly backed Monroe. The policy discouraged the European alliance. The *Monroe Doctrine* became a cornerstone of United States foreign policy throughout the 19th and 20th centuries.

THE ERA OF GOOD FEELINGS

While the young U.S. won nothing in the War of 1812, the experience fired the patriotism of the country. The War became a forge that shaped a new American spirit.

During the War, the Federalist Party attacked Madison and the Democratic-Republicans. The Federalists were strongest in mercantile New England and the coastal trading towns – places that suffered financially before and during the War. Some of the Federalists were so critical of the war effort that they gave their party an anti-patriotic reputation. After the War, the Federalist Party gradually lost support and disappeared.

With little opposition, the Democratic-Republicans ruled the country in harmony for almost a decade. One newspaper proclaimed it was an "Era of Good Feelings" – but it was more than that. There was a new feeling of energy. Problems with Europe declined. Negotiations settled boundary problems with Britain and gained Florida from Spain.

The old Revolutionary leaders faded. The new generation was ready to build on the older generation's firm foundation. As a new, vibrant nation, there was desire to break new ground in the western lands and foreign powers were no longer in the way. There was a desire to break new ground with technology, too. Small mills and factories, running first on water power then on steam, began to multiply.

Henry Clay, the young leader of the House of Representatives, sponsored a national development program. He called it the **American System**. Its main components were:

- federally financed roads to link east and west
- tariffs to protect new manufacturing
- rechartering of the Bank of the United States to regulate the money supply

Henry Clay (Chicago Historical Society)

Congress rechartered the Bank, and tariffs remained high; but, it never acted fully on Clay's ideas for roads. However, the states undertook vigorous road and canal building programs, and steamboats became more common. On the Hudson, the Ohio, the Missouri, and the Mississippi Rivers, they hauled large loads. They were fast and far more comfortable than wagon travel.

As the Era of Good Feelings ended, the first railroads were coming into existence. All of this transport development meant there was an **infrastructure** being created that would transform America as industrialization picked up speed.

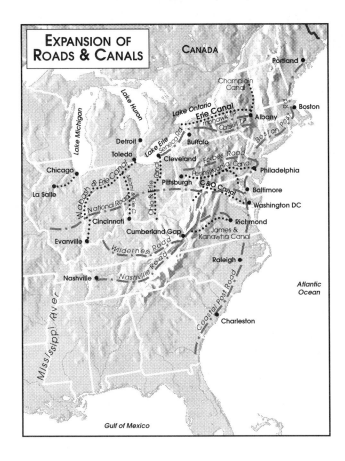

EXPANSION OF ROADS & CANALS

THE MISSOURI COMPROMISE

Amid all the grand developments of this period, there was still the issue of **slavery**. By the early 1800s, most states north of Maryland had abolished slavery. New states such as Ohio, Indiana, and Illinois banned it, too. In the South, slavery was important to the plantation economy. New states such as Louisiana, Alabama, and Mississippi entered the Union as slave states.

Antislavery arguments became stronger after the War of 1812. Rural, southern slave states were losing the power in the House of Representatives, because the northern states populations were growing faster. There was an equal balance of 11 free and 11 slave states represented in the Senate. Antislavery legislation could always be blocked there – if the balance remained.

In 1820, Missouri applied for statehood with legalized slavery. There was an outcry that all the rest of the west would become slave states. Henry Clay offered a compromise. His *Missouri Compromise* said:

- new states would always be admitted in pairs – one free, one slave (Maine and Missouri in 1820)

- territories north of 36° 30' N. latitude would henceforth be considered free, those to the South would allow slavery

The *Missouri Compromise* quieted the slavery controversy for that time. Later, when more new territory was added, the issue came back even stronger. Eventually, it tore the nation apart.

THE AGE OF JACKSON

While there was no organized political opposition after the Federalists faded from the scene, there were differences of opinion in the Era of Good Feelings. The North, South, and West developed different economic patterns. What people wanted from the government changed, too. Looking at issues primarily from a regional view is called **sectionalism**. As the 1820s progressed, sectional views became the dominant force in American political life (see map on following page).

Even in colonial days, the North was more of a shipping and commercial region. The slowdown of foreign trade in the War of 1812 pushed business people toward setting up their own factories. Textile mills emerged in the New England and Middle States.

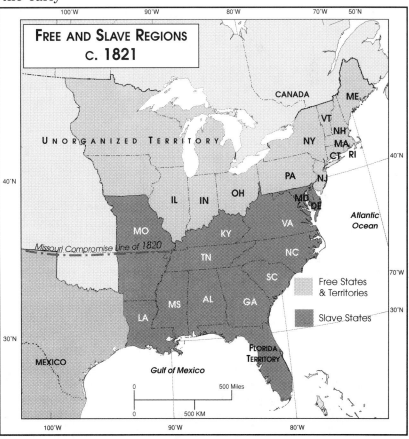

FREE AND SLAVE REGIONS C. 1821

Free States & Territories

Slave States

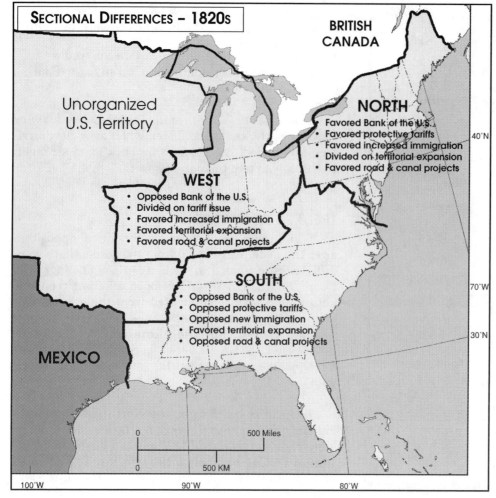

SECTIONAL DIFFERENCES – 1820s

BRITISH CANADA

Unorganized U.S. Territory

NORTH
• Favored Bank of the U.S.
• Favored protective tariffs
• Favored increased immigration
• Divided on territorial expansion
• Favored road & canal projects

WEST
• Opposed Bank of the U.S.
• Divided on tariff issue
• Favored increased immigration
• Favored territorial expansion
• Favored road & canal projects

SOUTH
• Opposed Bank of the U.S.
• Opposed protective tariffs
• Opposed new immigration
• Favored territorial expansion
• Opposed road & canal projects

MEXICO

0 ___ 500 Miles
0 ___ 500 KM

100°W   90°W   80°W   70°W   40°N   30°N

The Southern economy was split between Europe and America. Large, cash-crop plantations were a long tradition in the South. Rice and tobacco were grown and exported on a large scale. Inventions such as the cotton gin (1793) made cotton a profitable crop in the South.

During the War of 1812, new Northern mills bought raw cotton from the Southern planters. After the War, demand for cotton by Europe returned. Mills in England were more advanced than those in the United States. The English mills could outbid U.S. Northern mills for the Southern cotton. Southern planters often made more money shipping cotton overseas than they did supplying Northern textile mills. Although Southern planters traded with Europe and imported manufactured goods, the money they needed for land, seed, animals, and equipment was often borrowed from the bankers of the North.

In the new Western states of Ohio, Indiana, and Illinois, large grain farms developed. Farmers shipped their food to the North to feed the manufacturing population that was not able to grow its own food. They traded mainly with the North for manufactured or imported goods, and they borrowed money

for land, seed, animals, and equipment from the bankers of the North. The North-West connection strengthened as the 19th century progressed.

DEMOCRACY EXPANDS

Sectional views altered politics, but so did another change – a broadening of participation in politics. From the colonial days, a person needed property to qualify to vote. As a result, the politics of the older states were dominated by the rich and big landholders. Frontier settlers were remote from the centers of life where political decisions were made.

As new states entered the Union, the poor settlers became the main population, and they became the voters. Democracy changed. Social position and wealth did not count as much as in the 18th century. Any white male over age 21 qualified to vote. This new, open spirit was felt in the older states, too. By the 1830s, reformers in almost every state extended suffrage rights to all white males. (Still, females, Native Americans, and slaves could not vote. Except in some parts of New England, the 32,000 free African American males [1830 estimate] could not vote, either.)

New political parties emerged from struggles in the Era of Good Feelings. The Democratic-Republicans split into two groups. Conservative, eastern business interests formed the National Republicans or **Whigs**. Farmers and industrial workers made up the **Democrats**. These new parties were more democratic in several ways. In the past, caucuses (small groups of key leaders) picked candidates. The new parties held **nominating conventions** where party members chose who would be the candidates and party leaders.

ANDREW JACKSON AND THE COMMON MAN

Democrat Andrew Jackson, the self-made man of the frontier, became the hero of the common man. In 1824, the frontier hero of the Battle of New Orleans lost a tied election to John Quincy Adams. The conser-

Andrew Jackson (Library of Congress)

vative Adams was a favorite of the eastern business interests. Some claim Henry Clay's vote to break the tie in the House of Representatives robbed Jackson of the presidency. (Adams made Clay his Secretary of State.) Jackson's Democrats became better organized. They worked hard for the next four years and made sure their man won the election of 1828.

Jackson swept Adams' appointees out of office and replaced them with his own. In what came to be known as the **Spoils System**, he rewarded his party followers with government jobs. Some were not qualified for the jobs, but there were no qualifications specified in those days.

NATIVE AMERICAN REMOVAL

Jackson was famous as a frontier Indian fighter in the Creek Wars (1814-1820). As President, Jackson sided with white settlers. In 1828, he supported Georgia's claim to govern the Cherokee Nation and buy and sell land guaranteed the Cherokee people by treaties with the U.S. government. While John Marshall and the Supreme Court upheld the treaties in *Cherokee Nation v. Georgia*, Jackson refused to enforce the Court's decision. Jackson's supporters in Congress passed the *Indian Removal Act* in 1830. Under the Act, the government sent troops to escort more than 70,000 people of the Cherokee and Creek nations out of Georgia and Alabama and the Chicasaw and Choctaw nations out of Mississippi to a new Indian Territory in what is now Oklahoma. The tragic journey of 1838-1839 became known as the "Trail of Tears." Hundreds of elderly and children died enroute.

In Florida, the Seminole people resisted removal and began the Second Seminole War (1835). They were finally defeated by the U.S. Army in 1842. The government deprived the Seminoles of their lands. They were forced onto reservations in Oklahoma, with only a few staying in southern Florida.

THE TARIFF ISSUE

In 1828, Congress passed a very high protective tariff (Southerners called it the **"Tariff of Abominations"**). Its aim was to protect infant Northern industries from foreign competition. Southerners traded much of their cash crops with Europe. Southerners felt the high tariff would ruin their economy. They claimed foreign nations would retaliate by raising their tariffs against Southern exports.

Vice President John C. Calhoun, secretly wrote the *South Carolina Exposition and Protest*. It denounced the *Tariff of 1828*. In the *Exposition*, Calhoun spelled out the **doctrine of nullification**. He claimed that, like the Supreme Court, individual states could proclaim acts of the federal government unconstitutional. He claimed states did not have to enforce federal laws they nullified. Other national leaders rejected Calhoun's arguments. They claimed Article VI of the Constitution says that states cannot pass laws that contradict federal law.

The doctrine of nullification began a great debate in the U.S. Senate in 1830. Senator **Robert Y. Hayne** (SC) championed the state's rights or state supremacy position. Senator **Daniel Webster** (MA) argued that only the Supreme Court could declare laws unconstitutional. He said that if the states could nullify federal laws, the Union would become a mere "rope of sand."

Anger grew against the tariff. Congress passed the Jackson-backed *Tariff Act of 1832*. It substantially

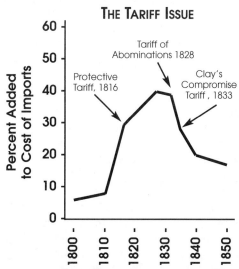

reduced tariff rates, but South Carolina officially declared the tariff "null and void" and refused to abide by it. If the federal government tried to enforce the tariff law, South Carolina declared it would **secede** (leave the Union).

South Carolina's actions angered President Jackson. He prepared to send federal troops to enforce the law. Once again, Senator Henry Clay offered a compromise and avoided armed confrontation. Clay introduced a bill to gradually reduce the tariff to levels acceptable to both the North and the South. Congress passed Clay's compromise and the constitutional crisis subsided.

THE BANK WAR

Jackson was popular with the common man because he attacked the Bank of the United States. He claimed the Bank was a tool of the eastern commercial interests supported by the Whigs. He said the government-sponsored Bank controlled lending and was unfair competition for small state-sponsored banks and hurt small farmers.

In 1832, Senator Clay and Jackson's Whig rivals in Congress tried to renew the Bank's charter. The President vetoed the Bank bill, claiming the Bank was a tool of the rich. Jackson had the Secretary of the Treasury remove federal funds from the Bank and deposit them in small state banks. Eventually, this ruined the Bank of the United States and caused a depression. However, the action made Jackson even more popular with the common people.

THE AGE OF HOMESPUN 1790-1860s
THE AGRICULTURAL SOCIETY

Between the Revolution and the Civil War, trade flourished and small industries emerged. On the whole, however, America was a farming nation. From 1784 to 1821, the amount of improved farmland rose from 1 million acres to more than 5 million. A steady stream of pioneers moved west. Eastern farmers moved to more open, fertile lands. Also, the hope of large tracts of fertile land in a free country attracted immigrants.

Setting up a farm on the frontier was an enormous undertaking. Clearing the forested lands east of the Mississippi was hard work, all done by hand. A skilled woodsman took a week to clear an acre. Even with neighbors' help, early pioneer farmers rarely cleared and planted 5 acres in their first year. After that, few settlers cleared more than 3 or 4 acres per year. Fencing had to be made to keep animals under control. Felled trees were used to make a primitive cabin, a barn, and fence rails until there was enough

income from the farm to buy boards, and other building materials.

COMMUNITY LIFE

Neighbors often helped new families clear a small plot to get established and plant enough acreage to survive. Some communities helped new families build shelters and barns. Frontier churches brought people together and made them aware of their needs. They even set up community schools for the children to learn basis skills.

Time was at a premium on the early farms. When surplus grain was finally produced, time had to be taken to load it and haul it to a flour mill miles away. Logs were plentiful, but boards were only available if logs were taken to a sawmill, taking more time away from the farm chores. Often, this hauling was done in winter by sleigh for easier travel. Several families often joined forces on these hauling expeditions so that less time was consumed.

FAMILY PATTERNS

The frontier farmers were self-sufficient, but far from free. They were locked into a struggle for survival. Keeping the frontier family and farm animals supplied with food was a full-time job for everyone. First year crops were often sparse. Preserving the food was difficult and time-consuming. Hunting in fall and winter took much time. Every tool and dwelling, all clothes, and all food had to be made or processed by hand. Childhood was not carefree. Children provided the extra hands needed for many tasks, so families were large. Many women died in childbirth. Most families endured drudgery and poverty for years, and prosperity came only to a few.

TECHNOLOGICAL CHANGE

It took farmers many years – sometimes decades – to reach a point where they could produce a surplus (food beyond the basic necessity thay they could sell). It was not until the 1850s that the better plows of **John Deere** and early machines such as **Cyrus McCormick**'s reaper began to filter into family farms.

Production of more than was needed for survival meant surplus (excess) could be sold – if it could be transported to market. Often, there was no nearby market for the crops grown. With only trails or rutted roads, transport was difficult and worse, time consuming. Even in the 1820s, few farm families had extra income of more than thirty dollars annually.

Not until after the War of 1812 were improved roads and canals begun. The **Erie Canal**, the foremost engineering feat of the age, took eight years to complete (1817-1825). Once done, western New York farmers could drive cattle to the Canal and on to slaughter houses in Albany and Troy. If they could haul their produce a short distance over land to the Canal, they could send it by barge to Albany and then in steamboats down the Hudson to New York City. More cities emerged along the bustling Canal (Utica, Rome, Syracuse). Buffalo became a major port, a transfer point between the Great Lakes and the Atlantic.

EARLY INDUSTRIALIZATION

Between the War of 1812 and the Civil War, industry grew rapidly in America. Better roads, steamboats, canals, and later railroads connected the western lands with the coasts. Raw materials and finished goods criss-crossed the country. In the 1840s, **Samuel Morse**'s telegraph sent news and messages zipping back and forth in hours. More important, the telegraph sent orders for goods and services zinging between producers and markets.

The small, water-powered mills of the early 1800s in Massachusetts became textile factories as new steam technology developed power looms and sewing machines. Steam power meant factories did not have to locate by fast-flowing rivers. Factories could go closer to arteries of transportation or be located in port cities.

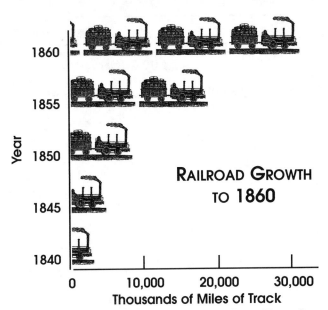

RAILROAD GROWTH TO 1860

Ready-made clothes were a major product. Even farm families bought them, freeing people to do other tasks. Broad-based markets developed. Mechanics, carpenters, and working people in towns and cities bought clothes and food made in other towns.

Working conditions changed as factories multiplied. Laborers worked 10-12 hour days, six days a week in dimly lit, poorly ventilated mills with dangerous machines. There was little workers could do about poor conditions. Any protesters were fired quickly. In almost every state, strikes were illegal. Some workers with skills that owners needed formed **trade unions** and negotiated better wages. Unskilled workers, often immigrants, had no power. Owners cut their wages at will and made unfair rules. Not until after the Civil War did unions form for less skilled workers, and even they were not very strong.

SOCIAL CHANGES

To outside observers, such as French writer **Alexis De Tocqueville** (*Democracy in America*, 1835), everyone in America seemed to be in motion. Movement changes life. As life changes, ideas flow freely in religion, education, and literature. With people exposed to new ideas, there were those who saw room for improvement. The first half of the 19th century produced a variety of reform movements. Reformers wanted to:

- discourage alcohol consumption
- abolish slavery
- promote women's rights
- improve treatment of the mentally ill

RISE OF AMERICAN CULTURE

During the early national period. Creative individuals from New England and New York produced a vigorous new national literature.

EDUCATION

Major changes took place in education. Schools put all ages in one room. Physical punishment was common and teachers were poorly trained. The rich sent their children to private schools or even to Europe.

Reformers **Horace Mann** and **Henry Barnard** pushed for public school change. They wanted the states to pay for schools with separate grades. They called for a longer school year, standard texts, and teacher training schools. Improvements in education swept from New England to the Midwestern states, but the South resisted the change.

ABOLITION

Efforts to abolish slavery in the early 1800s focused on letting it die out gradually. The Constitution forbade importing slaves after 1808. The **American Colonization Society**, founded in 1817, wanted to return freed African Americans to Africa. It helped to establish the nation of Liberia in West Africa (1822) for this purpose. Few actually gained freedom, however, and even fewer freed African Americans returned to Africa.

In the 1830s, abolitionists became more militant and

Frederick Douglass

Sojourner Truth

radical. Boston editor **William Lloyd Garrison** led the movement for immediate emancipation. Others included **Angelina** and **Sarah Grimke** who lectured throughout the North for the American Anti-Slavery Society. Former slaves such as **Harriet Tubman**, **Frederick Douglass** (photo above), and **Sojourner Truth** (photo at left) worked with abolitionists to form the "underground railway" – a secret network of operatives and "safe houses" to smuggle escaped slaves to Canada in the 1850s.

WOMEN'S RIGHTS

Militants in the early women's rights movement, included **Lucretia Mott, Elizabeth Cady Stanton,** and the Grimke sisters. In 1848, leading American women met at Seneca Falls (NY) to issue twelve resolutions demanding equality and the *Declaration of Sentiments*. Patterned after the *Declaration of Independence*, it declared that all men and women are created equal.

TREATMENT OF THE INSANE

Dorothea Dix led a crusade to improve the horrible treatment of the insane and mentally ill. Her 1846 report to the Massachusetts legislature described the horrible conditions of the insane. It persuaded state lawmakers to allot money for public mental institutions and provide more humane conditions.

Dorothea Dix

TEMPERANCE

Concern over alcohol abuse led to the rise of the temperance movement. Its followers sought to limit, and later ban, alcohol consumption. **Reverend Lyman Beecher** (1775-1863) of Connecticut, called for total prohibition of alcohol in 1825. The **American Temperance Society** was founded in 1826. It urged total abstinence. The Northern and Midwestern states were strongly for these efforts.

RELIGION

Religious reformers created a movement that challenged more traditional religions, such as Congregational, Presbyterian, and Episcopalian. New preachers held emotional religious revivals. In Rochester (NY), **Charles Grandison Finney** preached free will and that people could choose not to sin. During this revival era, denominations such as the Baptists and Methodists grew rapidly.

Two new religions were the Mormons and the Shakers. **Joseph Smith** of Fayette, NY founded the Mormon Church of Jesus Christ of Latter-day Saints in the 1830s. Many Americans condemned the Mormons' new scriptural revelation and their practice of polygamy. In 1846, under **Brigham Young**, they set up cooperative, strictly ruled communities near the Great Salt Lake in Utah territory.

The **Shakers** (the United Society of Believers in Christ's Second Appearing), were Quaker reformers from England who settled in upstate New York in the 1770s. Under **Mother Ann Lee**, they practiced celibacy and believed the world would soon end. Through revivals, membership increased. Prior to 1860, membership peaked at 6,000 and began to decline afterwards. Shakers founded small, self-sufficient agrarian communities supported through sales of craft items.

AMERICAN LITERATURE – 1800s

- **Henry Wadsworth Longfellow** wrote historical poems such as *Evangeline* (1847) and *Song of Hiawatha* (1855) that celebrated the uniqueness of the American experience.

- **Ralph Waldo Emerson** (1803-1882) promoted thought through lectures and essays (*Nature, Representative Man*).

- **Henry David Thoreau** criticized American government and supported an individual's right to disobey unjust laws in *Civil Disobedience* (1849) and *Walden* (1854).

- **Washington Irving** wrote of New York's Hudson River and created the mythical lives of Rip Van Winkle and Ichabod Crane in his *Sketch Book* (1820).

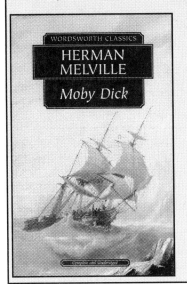

- **James Fenimore Cooper** wrote the "Leather AStocking Tales" – novels of the colonial American frontier including *The Last of the Mohicans* (1847), *The Deerslayer* (1841). and *The Spy* (1847).

- **Edgar Allan Poe** spent a tumultuous life writing and editing in New York, Virginia, and Baltimore. His poems (*The Raven*, 1845) and *The Bells*, 1849) and short stories (*The Pit and the Pendulum*, 1842, *The Fall of the House of Usher*, 1845), gave American literature a rich heritage.

- **Walt Whitman** wrote poems that described and praised the energy of American life (*Leaves of Grass*, 1855).

- **Nathaniel Hawthone** wrote novels that posed ethical questions about American life (*The Scarlet Letter*, 1850 and *The House of the Seven Gables*, 1851).

- **Herman Melville** wrote the novel *Moby Dick*, (1851) that explored themes of pride, leadership, tolerance, free will, and more.

UNIT 5
MULTIPLE CHOICE

CONCEPT

1   Precedents became models for future generations and led to the "unwritten constitution." Which is an example of the above statement?
    1   Washington's use of department heads as advisors
    2   power of the President as Commander-in-Chief
    3   establishment of the Supreme Court
    4   ratification of the Bill of Rights

2   Alexander Hamilton's financial plan provoked opposition from
    1   European creditors of the U.S.
    2   states without war debts
    3   speculators in bonds
    4   bankers and investors

3   During the wars of the French Revolution period, Washington's government
    1   aided the French king, Louis XVI
    2   sided with the British
    3   announced a policy of neutrality
    4   sent aid to the French revolutionary governments

SERIES

Directions: Base your answer to question 4 on the events list below and on your knowledge of social studies.

- **Establishment of a naval blockade**
- **Impressment of American sailors**
- **Interference with U.S. foreign trade**

4   The above actions led the U.S. to
    1   announce the *Monroe Doctrine*
    2   declare war against Britain in 1812
    3   revoke the *Embargo Acts*
    4   seize control of Louisiana

Directions: Base your answer to question 5 on the graph below and on your knowledge of social studies.

LINE GRAPH

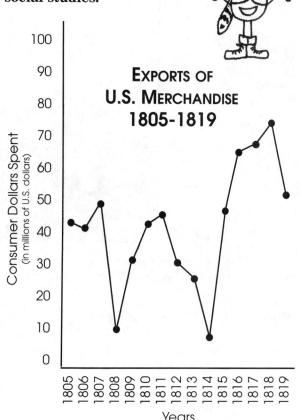

EXPORTS OF U.S. MERCHANDISE 1805-1819

Consumer Dollars Spent (in millions of U.S. dollars)

Years

Directions: Base your answer to question 8 on the map below and on your knowledge of social studies.

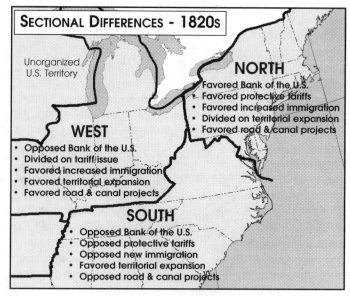

SECTIONAL DIFFERENCES - 1820s

Unorganized U.S. Territory

NORTH
• Favored Bank of the U.S.
• Favored protective tariffs
• Favored increased immigration
• Divided on territorial expansion
• Favored road & canal projects

WEST
• Opposed Bank of the U.S.
• Divided on tariff issue
• Favored increased immigration
• Favored territorial expansion
• Favored road & canal projects

SOUTH
• Opposed Bank of the U.S.
• Opposed protective tariffs
• Opposed new immigration
• Favored territorial expansion
• Opposed road & canal projects

5   Which is the most accurate conclusion about U.S. exports between 1805 and 1819??
1   Events in Europe had no impact on U.S. exports.
2   The Tariff of Abominations led to a steep drop in U.S. exports.
3   The high level of exports in 1807 was the result of record wheat crops.
4   The *Embargo Act of 1808* resulted in a drop in exports.

6   In the case of *Marbury v. Madison*, the Supreme Court established the principle of
1   separation of powers
2   judicial review
3   separate, but equal facilities
4   equal education for all

7   The period immediately after the end of the War of 1812 was known as the "Era of Good Feelings" because
1   the U.S. won military victories over Spain
2   western expansion was completed
3   political party disagreement was less apparent
4   the evils of industrialization ended

8   Which is the most accurate conclusion about the West and North after the War of 1812?
1   They held the same positions on the Bank of the U.S. and the tariff issue.
2   Their positions were largely based on similar economic interests.
3   Both areas were highly industrialized and wanted protective tariffs.
4   Neither wanted involvement of the federal government in their economic affairs.

Directions: Base your answer to question 9 on the cartoon below and on your knowledge of social studies.

Americas

9   The cartoon emphasizes that the Monroe Doctrine was a
1   pledge that the U.S. would not invade Europe
2   declaration of war against existing European colonies in the Americas
3   warning to European nations not to seek new colonies in the Americas
4   blockade of European trade to the Americas

Directions: Base your answer to question 10 on the quotation below and on your knowledge of social studies.

"The first of September was fixed as the time for a part (of the Cherokee population) to be in motion on the route. At noon all was in readiness for moving; the teams were stretched out in a line along the road through a heavy forest, groups of persons formed about each wagon, others shaking the hand of some sick friend or relative who would be left behind. ...In all the bustle of preparation there was a silence and stillness of the voice that betrayed the sadness of the heart."
– William Shorey Coodey, August 28, 1838,
witness to the first drive along the Trail of Tears

10 This reading indicates that William Shorey Coodey
1 felt that the Cherokee population was well treated
2 fully supported the policy of the U.S. government
3 approved of the arrangements for travel
4 sympathized with the feelings of the Cherokees

Directions: Base your answer to question 11 on the outline below and on your knowledge of social studies.

I _____
  A. Family Patterns
    1. frontier farms self-sufficient
      a produced own food
      b made clothes, tools, dwelling
    2. large families

B. Community Involvement
  1. helped clear land
  2. raised houses and barns

11 The most suitable title for this outline is
1 Life on the Frontier
2 An Industrial Town
3 Life on an Indian Reservation
4 New England Farm Life

Directions: Base your answer to question 12 on the quotation below and on your knowledge of social studies.

"We hold these truths to be self-evident: that all men and women are created equal; ...

"The history of mankind is a history of repeated injuries and usurpations on the part of man toward woman, having in direct object the establishment of an absolute tyranny over her. To prove this, let facts be submitted to a candid world.

"He has never permitted her to exercise her inalienable right to the elective franchise (vote).

"He has taken from her all rights in property, even to the wages she earns."

12 This quotation is most associated with the ideas of
1 Harriet Tubman
2 Mother Ann Lee
3 Dorothea Dix
4 Elizabeth Cady Stanton

CONSTRUCTED RESPONSE

SET 1

Directions: Base your answers to questions 1 and 2 on the chart at the right and on your knowledge of social studies.

1 List TWO (2) groups which supported the Federalists.

_____

_____

2 Select ONE (1) of the positions supported by the Federalists and explain why the groups indicated above would benefit from the policy.

COMPARISON: FEDERALISTS & DEMOCRATIC–REPUBLICANS	
FEDERALISTS	**DEMOCRATIC–REPUBLICANS**
Leaders: Alexander Hamilton & John Adams	Leaders: Thomas Jefferson & James Madison
Supported: • loose construction of the U.S. Constitution • stronger central gov't. • central control of economic affairs, pro-national bank & protective tariffs	Supported: • strict construction of the U.S. Constitution • stronger state gov'ts. • less central control of economic affairs; against a national bank & high tariffs
Supporters: Wealthy & propertied groups, merchants, and manufacturers	Supporters: "Common People" - small farmers, city labor, frontier people
Foreign Affairs: pro-British	Foreign Affairs: pro-French

_____

_____

SET 2

Directions: Base your answers to questions 3 through 5 on the maps below and on your knowledge of social studies.

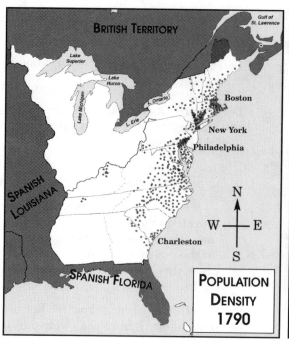

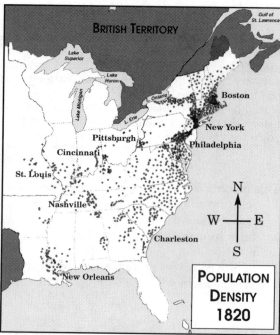

3   In which area of the country was the heaviest population density located in 1790?

_____

4   To where did people begin to move between 1790 and 1820?

_____

_____

5   What caused the movement of population indicated in the answer above?

_____

_____

_____

PRACTICE SKILLS FOR DBQ

Directions: The following task is based on the accompanying documents. The documents may have been edited for the purposes of this exercise. The task is designed to test your ability to work with historical documents. As you analyze the documents, take into account both the source of the document and the author's point of view where relevant.

Historical Context: In 1803, President Thomas Jefferson purchased the Louisiana Territory from Napoleon Bonaparte of France. At the time of the purchase the area was largely unknown. As a consequence, Jefferson commissioned William Clark and Meriwether Lewis to explore the Territory and report back their findings.

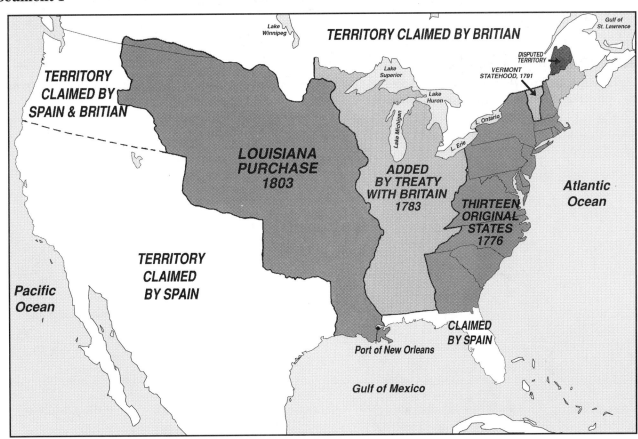

1   What is ONE (1) way that the Louisiana Purchase changed the United States?

_____

_____

_____

Document 2

2   Why might some of the descriptions of the Louisiana Purchase by Lewis and Clark encourage people to move west?

"We camped in the plains, one of the most beautiful plans I ever saw, open and beautifully diversified with hills and valleys all presenting themselves to the river covered with grass and a few scattering trees, a handsome creek running through.

"As we continued on our way we passed several rapids all of them great fishing places.

"We killed some ducks and geese and gathered some blackberries."

- Excerpts from the Journals of Lewis and Clark

_____

_____

_____

_____

Part B - Essay Response

    Task: Explain why the Louisiana Purchase was an important addition to the United States. (State your thesis in the introduction.)

ADDITIONAL SUGGESTED TASK

From your knowledge of social studies, make a list of other reasons why the Louisiana Purchase was important to the young United States.

1846	U.S.-MEXICAN WAR
1853	*UNCLE TOM'S CABIN* PUBLISHED
1854	*KANSAS NEBRASKA ACT*
1855	REPUBLICAN PARTY FOUNDED
1861	CIVIL WAR
1865	RECONSTRUCTION BEGINS
	PRESIDENT LINCOLN ASSASSINATED
1877	RECONSTRUCTION ENDS

UNIT
6

DIVISION
& REUNION

DIVISION & REUNION

UNDERLYING CAUSES OF THE CIVIL WAR

MANIFEST DESTINY

During the 1840s, New York newspaper journalist John O'Sullivan wrote about the idea of **"Manifest Destiny."** O'Sullivan meant that it was United States' "divine mission" to spread democracy from "sea to shining sea." This meant Americans wanted to expand to the Pacific. The ideal was to spread democracy, but many expansionists saw profits from trade and rich agricultural lands.

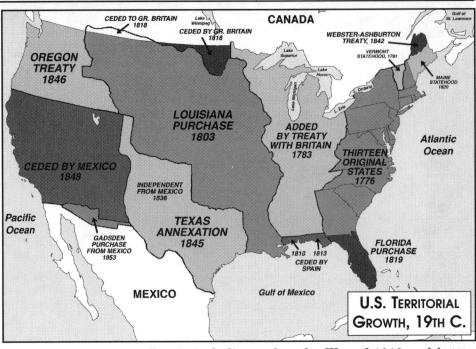

U.S. TERRITORIAL GROWTH, 19TH C.

The map at the right shows the rapid territorial growth of the United States in the first half of the 19th century. Expansion was almost an obsession with many Americans at the time.

Patriotic feelings after the War of 1812 and better transportation pushed many Americans westward. New farm machines meant farms could be bigger, and the western prairies offered opportunities. However, western movement brought up the question of extending slavery into the new territories.

TERRITORIAL EXPANSION AND SLAVERY

Territorial expansion began with the purchase of Louisiana in 1803. However, few settlers crossed the Mississippi until the middle of the 19th century.

In the 1820s, **Stephen Austin** of Virginia arranged with the Mexican governor to settle 1200 American families in Texas. In a decade, 50,000 American settlers arrived. Cultural and religious differences led to prob-

UNITED STATES TERRITORIAL EXPANSION

Territory	Acquisition
1803 Louisiana	Purchased from France for $15 million; doubled U.S. territory, secured port of New Orleans.
1818 Northern Border	Negotiation with British set western U.S.-Canadian border at 49th parallel; exchange of territory in the Minnesota – Montana region.
1819 Florida	After an Indian uprising quelled by General Andrew Jackson, the U.S. claimed Spanish lands; Under the Adams-Onis Treaty, the U.S. paid $5 million for Florida Peninsula and gave up claim to Texas.
1842 Northern Maine	Webster-Ashburton Treaty settled disputed boundary with Great Britain.
1845 Texas	An independent republic after 1836, Congress agreed to Texas' request to be annexed.
1846 Oregon	Treaty with Britain extended the 49th parallel border from the Rockies to the Pacific.
1848 Mexican Cession	War broke out with Mexico over Texan boundary; U.S. paid $15 million for southwest region which included New Mexico, Arizona, California, Utah, Nevada, and Colorado.
1853 Gadsden Purchase	Bought from Mexico to complete a southern transcontinental rail line.

lems with the Mexican government. War broke out in 1835. The American settlers declared Texas' independence in 1836. Early defeats at the Alamo and Goliad were followed by a major victory at San Jacinto. Texan general **Sam Houston** took Mexican dictator Santa Anna prisoner at San Jacinto. This forced the Mexican government to recognize Texas' independence.

In 1845, the Republic of Texas asked to become a state of the United States. Northerners feared Texas would become a slave state and add to Southern influence in Congress. Support for Texas' statehood slowly grew, however. In 1845, Congress admitted Texas, and it became the 28th state.

OREGON

Settlement beyond Texas was slow. Rough terrains and harsh climates discouraged many. The Oregon Trail led settlers to the Northwest, jointly occupied by the United States and Great Britain. As the American population of Oregon grew, some wanted the U.S. to claim all of Oregon – to latitude 54º 40' N. War was avoided when Britain and America compromised on the 49th parallel. This extended the existing boundary between the United States and Canada.

MEXICAN WAR (1846-1848)

By the mid 19th century, a number of disagreements existed between the United States and Mexico:

Battle of Chapultepec, 1847
(*Arms, Armor, Battles*, Wildside Press ©1996)

- U.S. annexation of Texas
- Disputes over the Texas-Mexico boundary
- Increased American settlement in the Mexican territory of California
- Debt disputes between Americans and the Mexican Government

Diplomatic attempts to settle the disputes failed. After a border skirmish near the Rio Grande River in 1846, President Polk asked Congress for a declaration of war. Congress agreed, and the U.S. invaded Mexico. By the end of 1847, Generals **Zachary Taylor** and **Winfield Scott** occupied Mexico City. **Captain John C. Fremont**'s conquests helped to overthrow Mexican rule in California.

Mexico agreed to the *Treaty of Guadalupe Hidalgo* in 1848. The Treaty established the Rio Grande as the border of Texas. It gave up California and the New Mexico Territory. In return, the United States paid Mexico $15 million and agreed to settle any disputed debts.

IMPACT OF WESTERN EXPANSION

The new territory added thousands of Spanish-speaking people to the United

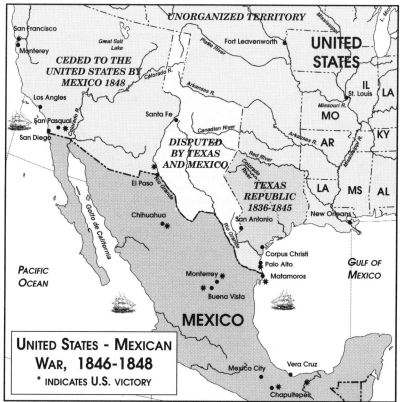

UNITED STATES - MEXICAN WAR, 1846-1848
* INDICATES U.S. VICTORY

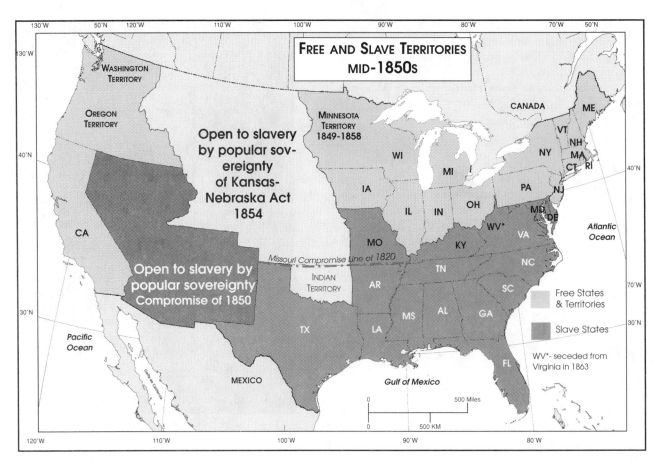

FREE AND SLAVE TERRITORIES MID-1850s

Open to slavery by popular sovereignty of Kansas-Nebraska Act 1854

Open to slavery by popular sovereignty Compromise of 1850

Missouri Compromise Line of 1820

WASHINGTON TERRITORY

OREGON TERRITORY

MINNESOTA TERRITORY 1849-1858

CANADA

CA

INDIAN TERRITORY

Free States & Territories

Slave States

WV*- seceded from Virginia in 1863

Pacific Ocean

Atlantic Ocean

MEXICO

Gulf of Mexico

500 Miles

500 KM

States. Many found the adjustment difficult as more and more Americans moved into the region. Problems of ethnic and economic discrimination arose. There was a lack of respect and understanding of the traditional ways of those of Spanish ancestry. The new territory also included thousands of Native Americans, who lost their hunting grounds and their lands after many battles with U.S. troops through the 1890s.

The expansion of territory magnified the slavery issue. The Missouri Compromise of 1820 quieted the issue for a while. When the great new expanses of territory were added in the 1840s, fears on both sides of the issue broke open. There was more land north of the 36°30' compromise line. California asked for admission as a free state in 1850. More than one-third of California was below the old compromise line. Southerners knew the Senate balance of free v. slave states would be upset.

THE FAILURE OF COMPROMISE

Henry Clay, the aging "Great Compromiser," once again offered a solution. It became the *Compromise of 1850*. California was admitted as a free state. However, the slavery question in the rest of the new southwest territories was up to a vote of the territory's settlers. This became known as known as "**popular sovereignty**." Also, the 1850 compromise included a new *Fugitive Slave Act*. It made it easier

for bounty hunters to track down runaway slaves more rapidly in the North.

Neither the proslavery nor the antislavery people were happy with this new arrangement. Abolitionists were outraged. Moderate abolitionists wanted gradual elimination of slavery. They thought it would gradually fade away with slave labor unable to compete with new machines. The popular sovereignty idea meant slavery could spread west. Extreme abolitionists complained the *Fugitive Slave Act* defeated all their efforts with the underground railway.

The sides in the slavery argument soured on compromise. In the North, the abolitionist crusade gained more power in 1852. In that year, Harriet Beecher Stowe published her propaganda novel of harsh treatment on the plantations, *Uncle Tom's Cabin*.

In 1854, Congress passed the *Kansas-Nebraska Act*. It allowed the slavery issue to be settled by popular sovereignty in all territories. Slavery and antislavery groups rushed to the Kansas Territory. Their five year struggle killed over 200 settlers.

The Democrats and the Whigs tried to avoid losing support. They refused to take a stand on the slavery issue. As a result, abolitionists turned first to a weak **Free Soil Party**. When it failed, in the mid-1850s, they joined a broader based **Republican**

Party. Generally, the Republicans were moderates who opposed the extension of slavery into the new territories, but did not seek full **emancipation** (freedom from bondage and oppression).

In 1857, the Supreme Court tried to resolve the slavery issue. In ***Dred Scott v. Sanford***, the Court ruled that slaves were property. It said the Fifth Amendment to the Constitution forbids Congress from depriving citizens of life, liberty, or property without due process of law. Since it said slaves were property, the *Missouri Compromise* and other actions taken by Congress over the years to forbid slavery were unconstitutional. As a result of the Scott decision, all territories were open to slavery.

John Brown
(Civil War CD, Digital Stock ©1995)

Abolitionists denounced the Scott Decision. In 1859, extreme abolitionists helped **John Brown** of Kansas raid the federal arsenal in Virginia. Brown hoped the arms he captured would start a slave revolt. Brown was captured, tried for treason, and executed. Southerners feared more attacks would come.

By 1860, the Democrats were badly split among those who defended slavery and those who wanted more compromise. In November, the Republicans gained enough electoral votes in the North to elect their candidate, **Abraham Lincoln** (IL).

Abraham Lincoln
(Civil War CD, Digital Stock ©1995)

THE CIVIL WAR
LINCOLN BECOMES PRESIDENT

Lincoln was a moderate, not an abolitionist. He wanted to stop slavery from spreading into the new territories. Still, Southerners feared the Republicans would soon abolish all slavery. In fact, not one Southern state voted for Lincoln. Lincoln would not become President until March, 1861, but things began to fall apart in December. South Carolina announced it would secede from the Union. Six more southern states followed South Carolina. In February 1861, they formed the Confederate States of America. They elected **Jefferson Davis** (MS) as their President. Four more states joined the Confederacy by June.

Jefferson Davis
(Civil War CD, Digital Stock ©1995)

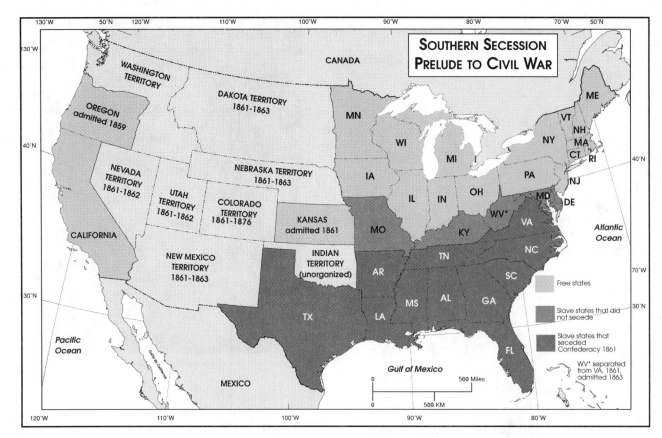

When secession began in December 1860, **James Buchanan** was still President. He declared that actions by the Southern states were unconstitutional. However, he also believed the Constitution did not give him the power to stop the states from seceding. Buchanan let the situation worsen. When Confederate leaders seized federal forts and arsenals, the President took no action to resist.

Lincoln took office in March and called for reconciliation. In April, Confederate forces attacked **Fort Sumter** in Charleston (SC) harbor. The federal forces surrendered the next day. The surrender made Northerners realize that political solutions were impossible and war was necessary. The tragedy of the American Civil War began.

The South's resources were less than half those of the North, but they were in the right places and easier to mobilize (organize). The South had excellent commanders and enough of an army to win a short war in a few decisive battles. However, when the War dragged on for over four years, the South's limited resources added up to defeat.

The African American population served both sides. In all, 68,000 African Americans died in the War. Southern slaves were used in military construction and supply operations. In the North, Congress passed laws allowing African Americans to serve in separate units in the Union Army in 1862. They received less pay and inferior equipment than other units. Nearly 20,000 gave their lives as Union soldiers.

ADVANTAGES AND DISADVANTAGES OF BOTH SIDES

When the War Between the States began in 1861, the North had greater financial and productive resources – on paper. However, the North's population and resources were spread over a vast area that reached westward to the frontier. It had the potential, but not the actual capacity to outproduce the South. The North's productive capacity developed gradually as the War progressed.

Factor	North (% of country's total)	South (% of country's total)
NORTH v. SOUTH: AN 1861 RESOURCE COMPARISON		
Population	22 million (63%)	9 million (37%) (includes 3 million slaves)
Railroads	21,000 miles (71%)	9,000 (29%)
Factories	120,000 (85%)	20,600 (15%)
Industrial Workers	2 million (92%)	111,000 (8%)
Acres of Farmland	105,000 (65%)	56,000 (35%)

At the beginning of the War, the South had important advantages. The Southerners were united in defending their land. They could prepare, dig in, and wait. The Northerners had to take the offensive. Congress and the President had to organize men and supplies to travel into unknown Southern lands. The North had to conquer the South and then occupy the conquered territory. Both sides had good commanders – many had been classmates at West Point and Annapolis. However, the South wound up with many more experienced officers, many of whom were killed or wounded as the War progressed.

As the War stretched into its second and third years, the productive power of the North became organized. The Union's training and supplying of a vast military force stimulated the Northern economy. Manufacturing and farming boomed. The North's naval blockade stopped Southerners from exporting cash crops and Southern wealth dried up.

Early in the War, Great Britain wanted Southern cotton for its textile mills. There were incidents with British ships along the blockade. In 1863, when Lincoln issued the *Emancipation Proclamation*, England stopped trying to trade with the South. England had abolished slavery in the 1830s. Once it became clear that the North was fighting to free the slaves, the British government could not support the Southern cause.

Lincoln planned a long strategy of wearing out the South. The U.S. Navy's Atlantic and Gulf of Mexico blockade choked off the South's trade. Another Union goal was to control the Mississippi River to stop the movement of supplies.

Congress became impatient as the North lost a series of early battles trying to capture Richmond (VA). Congress criticized Lincoln for changing commanders. Finally, victories in the West (Shiloh, Vicksburg, Chattanooga) produced the aggressive commander Lincoln needed – **Ulysses S. Grant**. General Grant organized the men and supplies to move on Richmond. Grant pushed Confederate Commander, General **Robert E. Lee**, into retreat away from his supplies and forced the South's surrender.

The states made major contributions to the war effort. Many volunteered in the first months of the War. When news of the slaughters on the battlefields started arriving, enlistment declined. The Congress set up a draft in 1863, but it allowed the rich to buy exemptions. The poor and new Irish immigrants could not afford exemptions. In New York, anti-draft riots broke out in the summer of 1863 and lasted for three days. Despite this, New York provided the largest number of enlistments. It also provided the largest amount of supplies and bought the most war bonds of any Northern state. (See Civil War Battles on pages 72 and 73.)

RESULTS OF THE CIVIL WAR

The Civil War ended with a human cost of over half a million lives. It was a **total war** in that many civilians lost lives and untold amounts of property. It was a savage and brutal conflict. Reuniting the nation proved to be a long and difficult task.

PRESERVATION OF THE UNION

The North's victory meant that Lincoln's goal of keeping the nation whole was achieved. The President wanted to begin the physical rebuilding of the ruined South. He looked to restore peace and harmony. The struggle had been bitter – forgiveness was hard.

ABOLITION OF SLAVERY

The *Emancipation Proclamation* of 1863 had announced the North would abolish slavery in the rebelling states. With the War over, Lincoln planned to have the rebel states pass laws abolishing slavery as they re-entered the Union. Because the states took no action on slavery, Congress moved. In December 1865, the states ratified the **Thirteenth Amendment** abolishing slavery.

Lincoln Memorial - Washington, DC
(PhotoDisc ©1997)

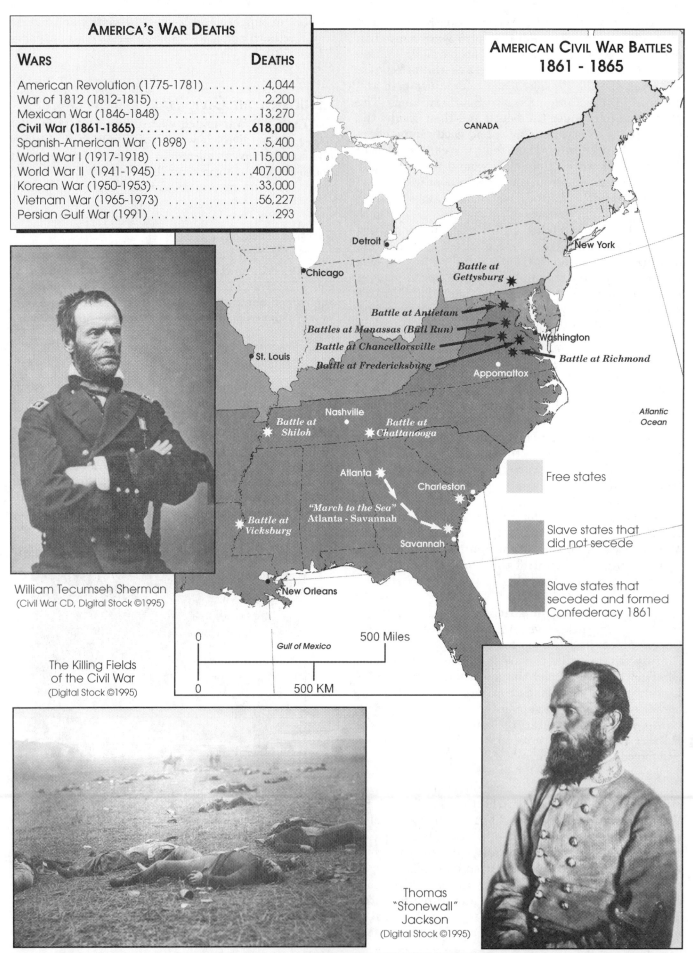

AMERICA'S WAR DEATHS

WARS	DEATHS
American Revolution (1775-1781)	4,044
War of 1812 (1812-1815)	2,200
Mexican War (1846-1848)	13,270
Civil War (1861-1865)	**618,000**
Spanish-American War (1898)	5,400
World War I (1917-1918)	115,000
World War II (1941-1945)	407,000
Korean War (1950-1953)	33,000
Vietnam War (1965-1973)	56,227
Persian Gulf War (1991)	293

AMERICAN CIVIL WAR BATTLES
1861 - 1865

CANADA

Detroit

Chicago

New York

Battle at Gettysburg

Battle at Antietam

Battles at Manassas (Bull Run)

Battle at Chancellorsville

Battle at Fredericksburg

Washington

Battle at Richmond

St. Louis

Appomattox

Atlantic Ocean

Nashville

Battle at Shiloh

Battle at Chattanooga

Atlanta

Charleston

"March to the Sea" Atlanta - Savannah

Battle at Vicksburg

Savannah

New Orleans

Free states

Slave states that did not secede

Slave states that seceded and formed Confederacy 1861

0   500 Miles

Gulf of Mexico

0   500 KM

William Tecumseh Sherman
(Civil War CD, Digital Stock ©1995)

The Killing Fields
of the Civil War
(Digital Stock ©1995)

Thomas
"Stonewall"
Jackson
(Digital Stock ©1995)

Davis, Lee, & Jackson
*Stone Mountain
Confederate Memorial*, Georgia
(W.H. Garnsey ©1999)

Ulysses Simpson Grant
(Civil War CD, Digital Stock ©1995)

Robert E. Lee
(Civil War CD, Digital Stock ©1995)

CIVIL WAR COMMANDERS & BATTLES

North

Ulysses S. Grant
(Shiloh, Vicksburg, Chattanooga, Richmond)

Joseph Hooker (Chancellorsville)

George B. McClellan (Antietam)

George G. Meade (Gettysburg, Richmond)

Philip Sheridan (Richmond)

William T. Sherman (Atlanta)

South

P.G.T. Beauregard (Manassas, Shiloh)

Braxton Bragg (Chattanooga)

John B. Gordon (Richmond)

Thomas "Stonewall" Jackson
(Manassas, Antietam, Fredericksburg, Chancellorsville)

Joseph E. Johnston (Vicksburg, Chattanooga, Atlanta)

Robert E. Lee
(Antietam, Fredericksburg, Chancellorsville, Gettysburg, Richmond)

RECONSTRUCTION

There were many in Congress who wanted the South punished. They were not happy with what Lincoln planned. He believed that the Union had not been broken. He believed the Southern states should not be treated harshly. Under Lincoln's plan, regained Southern states could set up new state governments as soon as 10% of those people who voted in 1860 took an oath of loyalty to the Union. High-ranking Confederates would not be allowed to vote.

Andrew Johnson
(Library of Congress)

After Lincoln's assassination in April 1865 by John Wilkes Booth, conflict deepened between Congress and Lincoln's successor, President **Andrew Johnson**. Congress then took greater authority in Reconstruction planning. President Johnson's plan generally followed Lincoln's. He wanted to grant amnesty to most Southerners who took loyalty oaths to the Union. He outlined steps for new civilian governments. These steps included drawing up new state constitutions that outlawed secession and ratified the Thirteenth Amendment.

Johnson's plan did not work. White pre-war leaders regained power in the Southern states and used the **Black Codes** (segregation laws) to block civil rights for African Americans. Johnson's struggles with Congressional leaders were so stormy that the House of Representatives **impeached** him in 1868. At his trial, the Radical Republicans in the Senate did not have enough votes to remove him. Johnson continued as President until the next election.

In late 1865, Radical Republican leaders in Congress swept aside Johnson's work. They took over Reconstruction. Their goals included establishing democracy in the South, ensuring voting and civil rights for all – including African Americans, and redistributing land ("40 acres and a mule"). The Republican-controlled Congress finally passed the **Military Reconstruction Plan** of 1867. Its provisions included:

* the U.S. Army would have control until new governments could be established
* former slaves would be guaranteed the right to vote in state elections
* each Southern state had to ratify the Fourteenth Amendment (defined citizenship and civil rights for all)
* each Southern state had to ratify a Congressionally approved state constitution

The states ratified three amendments to the *United States Constitution* during the Reconstruction years:

* The **Thirteenth Amendment** (1865) abolished slavery in the United States.

* The **Fourteenth Amendment** (1868) made former slaves citizens. This amendment also cancelled the Confederate debt, and blocked former Confederate officials from holding office, and prevented states from denying individuals their basic civil rights (due process).

* The **Fifteenth Amendment** (1870) prohibited states from denying the right to vote "on account of race, color, or previous condition of servitude."

ECONOMIC PROBLEMS

The North lost more soldiers than the South, but there was not much property damage. In fact, the North's economy was stimulated by war production. War demand helped to improve technology as producers looked for faster and cheaper methods of production. The Bessemer Process, around since the 1850s, was widely adopted to produce better and stronger steel. After the War, American factories continued to export goods. From 1860 to 1880, the value of American exports grew by nearly 500%. More important, by 1880, the dollar value of U.S. exports began to exceed imports. The American economy was selling more overseas than it was buying from other countries. Economists call this a "favorable balance of trade" or a trade surplus.

However, most of the growth was in the North. The South's slavery-based plantation system was gone, as were its railroads and main ports. Southern soldiers returned to wrecked farms and demolished homes. The new agricultural system in the South became tenant farming or sharecropping. **Sharecropping** continued the plantation system. In return for the lease of farm land, a sharecropper agreed to turn over a portion of his crops (usually 1/3 for land and 1/3 for use of tools). By 1920, over 2/3 of Southern farmers, both African American and white, were sharecroppers.

There were also four million freed slaves. They had nothing and there were no jobs for them. Southern states tried to legally bind them to work their former masters' lands. Congress created the **Freedmen's Bureau** in February of 1866 to help. This welfare agency was to provide relief supplies (food, clothing, shelter, and medical supplies) to both African American and white Union refugees. It also protected the newly freed slaves' rights in military courts.

In April of 1866, Congress passed a *Civil Rights Act* giving former slaves citizenship, but their economic status did not improve. Most former slaves remained in agricultural occupations as sharecroppers or tenant farmers. If they applied for jobs in textile mills and other factories, they were often refused.

Southern farmers remained poor. High prices for seed, tools, and fertilizer kept them in debt. They still grew a single cash crop – cotton. As cotton production increased, cotton prices dropped causing further hardship for farmers. They borrowed on their only asset – their expected harvest. They agreed to pay a portion of their crops in return for credit.

END OF RECONSTRUCTION

During Reconstruction, Northerners controlled much of the political process in the occupied Southern states. Southerners called these people "carpetbaggers." They administered the Freedmen's Bureau programs, set up businesses, and engaged in politics. They helped African Americans exercise their power under the "Civil War Amendments" (13th, 14th, 15th). They elected many African American people to public office. This included fourteen Congressmen and two United States Senators.

Helped by the Fourteenth and Fifteenth Amendments, Radical Republican governments tried to minimize the political power of conservative Southern Democrats. Yet, white Southerners quickly regained control. A white **backlash** (vicious reaction) developed. Through terrorism, such groups as the **Ku Klux Klan** sought to "keep African Americans in their place." Federal legislation was passed to outlaw the activities of the Klan.

African Americans usually supported the Republicans ("the party of emancipation"). However, they played a limited role in party politics. The conservative Democratic Party leaders refused membership to African Americans. When Reconstruction ended in 1877, Radical Republican state governments fell. African Americans lost political power.

Congress passed the *Amnesty Act* in 1872, which pardoned most of the remaining Confederates. The new Southern leaders worked with the old planter class. They raised their own economic, social, and political power. At the same time, they took power from African Americans. **Poll taxes** of one or two dollars kept poor sharecroppers from voting. The governments required voting **literacy tests** and most former slaves could not read or write.

Socially, African Americans were segregated. By the 1870s and the 1880s, a number of formal (de jure) segregation laws were passed. These became known as **Jim Crow laws**. They were named after an early minstrel show character. African Americans began leaving the South, but found prejudice and poverty in the North too.

DISPUTED ELECTION OF 1876

By the mid-1870s, Reconstruction was gradually ending, Radical leaders had died or left office, reformers had lost momentum, and others were looking to a new industrial focus. Reconstruction lasted until 1877 when Federal troops were withdrawn from the South. There was no real plan to end Reconstruction. It ended through a political deal.

In the election of 1876, Democrat Samuel Tilden of New York won the popular vote by a slim margin (under 275,000). However, he was one electoral vote short of the needed majority. There were a number of disputed electoral votes in South Carolina, Florida, and Louisiana. However, the Constitution provided no procedure to decide these votes. Congress appointed an election commission. It gave the election to the Republican candidate, **Rutherford B. Hayes**.

No one knows for sure, but some scholars think a compromise was worked out between the Republicans and Democrats. They claim the Democrats agreed to support Hayes if the Republicans agreed to remove federal troops from the South. In any case, Hayes became President in 1877, withdrew the Federal troops from the South, and ended Reconstruction.

REMINDER: For help in handling questions, see ADVICE CHART on page 184.

UNIT 6
MULTIPLE CHOICE

Directions: Base your answer to question 1 on the map below and on your knowledge of social studies.

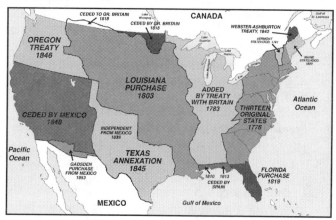

1 Which statement about U.S. expansion is most accurate?
   1 U.S. expansion was primarily achieved by military victories against Britain.
   2 Territories added to the U.S. were gained by a variety of methods.
   3 Most of the territorial acquisitions were purchased from Mexico.
   4 The first areas added to the thirteen original states were on the West Coast.

Directions: Base your answer to question 2 on the illustration below and on your knowledge of social studies.

2 The main point of this illustration is to show
   1 the way the Native Americans and buffalo lived on the prairie
   2 railroad and bridge development during the 19th century
   3 that modern transportation endangered the Native American life style
   4 how accidents with trains endangered buffalo

3 A key issue involved in Texas' request for statehood in 1845 was the
   1 location of railroad lines
   2 concern about its slave status
   3 lack of attraction for settlers
   4 religious differences with Mexico

4 The *Missouri Compromise of 1820* and the *Compromise of 1850* were both attempts to deal with the issue of
   1 slave trade in the South
   2 territories claimed by the Indians
   3 territorial gains from the Mexican War
   4 slavery in territories asking for admission to the Union

5 In the *Dred Scott v. Sanford* case, the Supreme Court said slaves were
   1 free in all federal territories
   2 citizens of the U.S.
   3 allowed to move between states as free persons
   4 the property of their owners

Directions: Base your answer to question 6 on the passage below and on your knowledge of social studies.

"Neither slavery nor involuntary servitude, except as a punishment for crime whereof the party shall have been duly convicted, shall exist within the United States, or any place subject to their jurisdiction."
– Amendment XIII, *Constitution of the United States*

6 This amendment was necessary because the *Emancipation Proclamation* of 1863
   1 only freed slaves in states in rebellion against the United States
   2 affected only slaves who entered the country after 1833
   3 only protected indentured servants
   4 protected people convicted of crimes against work in prison

7 The systems of slavery and sharecropping are alike in that both the slaves and the sharecroppers were
   1 always African American
   2 mostly women
   3 property of landowners
   4 very poor

8 Who controlled much of the political process in the South during Reconstruction?
   1 Ku Klux Klan
   2 Democratic Party
   3 "carpetbaggers" from the North
   4 freed slaves

9 A result of the Civil War for the North was
1 a decline in goods exported
2 an improvement in technology
3 serious destruction of railroads
4 an end to the family farm

Directions: Base your answer to question 10 on the chart at the right and on your knowledge of social studies.

10 Using the information on the comparison chart, it is possible to conclude that the
1 South had more farmland acres available to produce food
2 railroad differences would have little impact on the War's outcome
3 North had a sizable advantage in industrial production
4 slave population would support the efforts of the South

NORTH V. SOUTH: AN 1861 RESOURCE COMPARISON		
Factor	**North** (% of country's total)	**South** (% of country's total)
Population	22 million (63%)	9 million (37% (includes 3 million slaves)
Railroads	21,000 miles (71%)	9,000 (29%)
Factories	120,000 (85%)	20,600 (15%)
Industrial workers	2 million (92%)	111,000 (8%)
Acres of Farmland	105,000 (65%)	56,000 (35%)

CONSTRUCTED RESPONSE
SET 1

Directions: Base your answers to questions 1 through 3 on the the quotation below (Document **A**), the illustration at the right (Document **B**), and on your knowledge of social studies.

Document **A**

"The census and other authentic documents show that, in all instances in which the States have changed the former relation (master and slave) between the two races, the condition of the African, instead of being improved, has become worse. They have been invariably sunk into vice and pauperism. ...while, in all other States which have retained the ancient relation between them, they have improved greatly in every respect - in number, comfort, intelligence, and morals..."
– Letter of John C. Calhoun to Richard Pakenham, April 18, 1844

Document **B**

Based on "After the Sale – Slaves going South from Richmond" Eyre Crowe's painting (1853)

1 Which negative impact of slavery is presented in the picture (Document **B**)?

_____

2 According to the letter (Document **A**), why does Calhoun think that slavery has had positive results?

_____

_____

3 What do the differences between these two documents tell you about attitudes toward slavery in the U.S.?

_____

SET 2

Directions: Base your answers to questions 4 through 5 on the diary quotations below and on your knowledge of social studies.

4   What TWO (2) problems did the Donner Party encountered trying to cross the Sierra Nevada?

_____

_____

_____

_____

_____

Friday Nov. 20th 1846:
Came to this place on the 31st of last month when it snowed – we went on to the pass – the snow so deep we were unable to find the road ... then turned back to this shanty on the Lake ... continuing to snow all the time we were here – we now have killed most part of our cattle having to stay here until next spring & live on poor beef without bread or salt...

Thursday Dec. 25th 1846:
Froze hard last night – Mrs. Murphy says the wolves are about to dig up the dead bodies at her shanty, the nights are too cold to watch them, we hear them howl.

Friday Dec. 26th 1846:
Martha's jaw swelled with the toothache; hungry times in camp, plenty hides but the folks will not eat them – we eat them with a tolerable good appetite.

– The Donner Party, Donner Lake, Sierra Nevada, 20 November 1846 - 1 March 1847

5   Why were people willing to face these dangers? _____

_____

_____

_____

PRACTICE SKILLS FOR DBQ

Directions: The following task is based on the accompanying documents. The documents may have been edited for the purposes of this exercise. The task is designed to test your ability to work with historical documents. As you analyze the documents, take into account both the source of the document and the author's point of view where relevant.

Historical Context: The secession of the Southern states from the federal union in 1860 led to the outbreak of the Civil War. Long simmering issues led to the breakup of the union and the outbreak of hostilities.

COTTON PRODUCTION AND GROWTH OF SLAVERY
(Source: Historical Statistics of the United States)

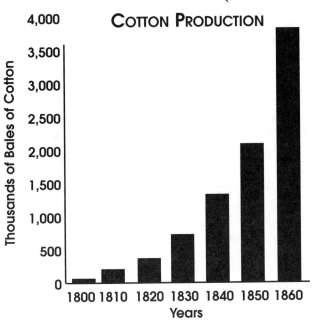

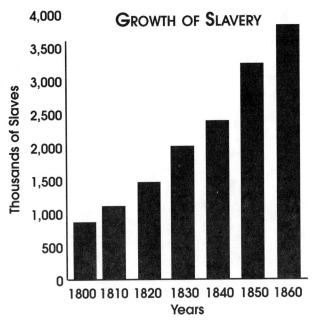

1*a* What is the relationship between the increase in cotton production and the growth of slavery?

_____

_____

1*b* If you were a southern plantation owner, why would the information on these graphs make you concerned about the possible end to slavery?

_____

_____

_____

Document 2 on following page

Document 2

> "... the State of South Carolina having resumed her separate and equal place among nations, deems it due to herself, to the remaining United States of America, and to the nations of the world, that she should declare the immediate causes which have led to this act.
>
> "(The Declaration of Independence, 4 July 1776) established the two great principles asserted by the Colonies, namely, the right of a State to govern itself; and the right of a people to abolish a Government when it becomes destructive of the ends for which it was instituted.
>
> "We affirm that these ends for which the Government (federal) was instituted have been defeated and the Government (federal) itself has been destructive of them by the action of the non-slaveholding States. ... Those States have assumed the right of deciding upon the propriety (correctness) of our domestic institutions (slavery); and have denied the rights of property (ownership of slaves)..."
>
> *– Declaration of the Immediate Causes Which Induce and Justify the Secession of South Carolina from the Federal Union, passed by the South Carolina legislature, 13 November 1860*

2a What are the TWO (2) principles cited from the *Declaration of Independence*?

_____

_____

_____

2b What does this declaration accuse the federal government of doing to the rights of the slave states?

_____

_____

_____

_____

Part B - Essay Response
   Task: Discuss the causes of the Civil War (1860-1865). (State your thesis in the introduction.)

ADDITIONAL SUGGESTED TASK

From your knowledge of social studies, make a list of additional factors that played a role in causing the Civil War.

UNIT 7

AN
INDUSTRIAL
SOCIETY

AN INDUSTRIAL SOCIETY

INDUSTRIAL SOCIETY MATURES IN THE LATER 19TH CENTURY

After the Civil War, the South struggled to rebuild, but the North and the West grew at a very rapid rate. The growth of the North's industrial centers created a huge demand for food. The plains and prairies sprouted large, mechanized farms and cattle ranches. The railroads expanded to haul farm produce to the industrial cities. All of this rapid urban and rural growth changed the country. Every part of American life – social, economic, and political – was altered in the Industrial Age.

THE U.S. DEVELOPED AS AN INDUSTRIAL POWER

To grow on a significant scale industrialization needs several key elements. They are **land**, **labor**, **capital**, **technology**, and **connections**. Without a generous supply of these basic elements and the ability to organize them, a people cannot develop into an industrial society.

American railroads used European steel to build lighter weight, stronger bridges enhancing and accelerating America's industrial development.
(Civil War CD, Digital Stock ©1995)

LAND

Land refers not just to a surface (acreage) for farms, factories, and transport. What is on and under the land, especially minerals, is important. Large deposits of raw materials helped American industry develop. The early railroads and canals brought iron ore, coal, and copper to the developing industrial cities like Pittsburgh, Chicago, and Cleveland.

LABOR

Labor is the human element. Many hands were needed in the early factories. Mechanizing farms in the early and mid-19th century freed up some labor to go into the factories, but foreign shores were the chief source of labor. Immigrants provided the muscle for the factories.

The human factor also included the **entrepreneurs**. These were the people who arranged financing, organized workers and material, operated, and assumed the risk for business firms. Most were honest and energetic, some were ruthless, and a few were dishonest. The entrepreneurs of this age, however, had vision and talent. They thought and acted on a large scale, and drew together the forces that made the United States an industrial giant by the beginning of the 20th century.

Andrew Carnegie was an immigrant entrepreneur. He managed to buy up mines, shipping and construction companies, and manufacturing plants for iron and steel production. He built the Carnegie Steel Company into the largest company in the country by the 1890s.

John D. Rockefeller was an oil entrepreneur. The need for petroleum developed slowly. Oil was first used in lamps for light. But as refining improved, it was used for fuels and lubricants. Rockefeller managed to buy out or out-compete other producers building his Standard Oil Company into a **monopoly** (one company dominating all the production).

CAPITAL

Capital is the money, productive machinery, and the factories themselves. Capital is the means that allows labor to process materials into products. Before the Civil War, small American factories could not produce enough excess profits to finance large expansion.

Most of the funding for early railroads and canals came from European investors.

During the Civil War, demand for arms and supplies by the government provided capital for expansion. Banks risked money to finance new companies. More important, thousands of investors bought small shares (stocks) in new corporations and received dividends for their effort (see chart on page 86). Once the new factories were built and connected to markets, corporations began producing on a large scale. Profits were made and reinvested. This new reservoir of "home-grown capital" fueled the great industrial expansion after the Civil War.

After the Civil War, the industries converted to producing peacetime goods. America even began to export its excess goods overseas.

CONNECTIONS

Connections are key elements in industrial development. Transportation links raw materials, producers, and consumers. Communication includes the postal system and telegraphs that carry messages among suppliers of raw materials, producers, and consumers. Economists call the combined network of

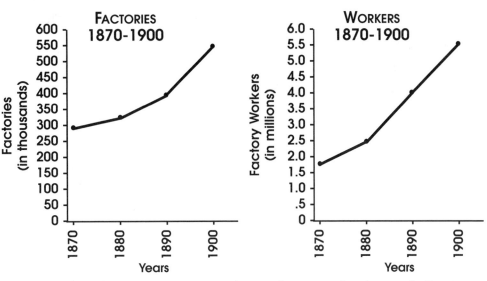

transportation and communication an **infrastructure**. It is the foundation and framework of economic growth.

The waterways, roads, canals, bridges, and railroads developed in the early and middle 19th century provided the vital links for industrialization. Civil War demand stimulated organization of the different types of transportation into a functional system, especially for the North.

The national government aided the expansion of railroads in the period after the Civil War. It made nearly $64 million in loans to the major railroads and it granted 132 million acres for expansion in the western territories by the 1890s. During the Industrial Era, the western states also granted an additional

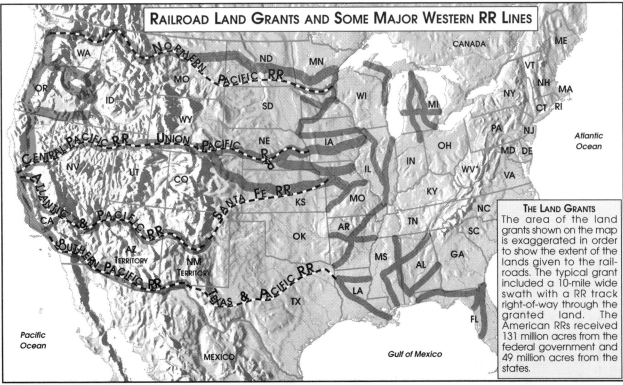

THE LAND GRANTS
The area of the land grants shown on the map is exaggerated in order to show the extent of the lands given to the railroads. The typical grant included a 10-mile wide swath with a RR track right-of-way through the granted land. The American RRs received 131 million acres from the federal government and 49 million acres from the states.

49 million acres. Railroad builders such as Cornelius Vanderbilt and James Hill organized capital and government help to build the New York Central R.R. and the Great Northern R.R.

19TH CENTURY LAND GRANTS TO RAILROADS

RAILROAD	ACRES
Union Pacific	20 million
Santa Fe	17 million
Central and Southern Pacific	24 million
Northern Pacific	44 million

The first telephone systems in the 1870s connected Salem and Boston in Massachusetts and Chicago and Milwaukee. By 1880, there were 148 new telephone companies. In the 1890s, long distance lines connected New York and Chicago. Calls could be made across the country by 1915.

TECHNOLOGY

Technology is the application of science to industrial or commercial uses. Nineteenth century America moved from simple water and steam power for machinery toward turbines, internal combustion engines, and electricity. Thousands of inventions in the nineteenth century helped to mechanize and refine manufacturing processes, making them more efficient and raising productivity.

POLITICAL PROBLEMS IN THE GILDED AGE

As the country changed, all levels of government expanded. This era glittered on the surface, but there was much corruption underneath. As any system gets bigger, there are more people involved, and more opportunity for problems to arise. Corruption became more frequent. Dishonest office holders gave contracts to firms offering bribes. Railroads needed rights of way through public lands. Locally, more public buildings, streetcar lines, roads, sewers, and garbage collections were needed. Nationally, there was more overseas commerce and more tariffs to be collected.

On the federal level, a number of political scandals became public during President Ulysses S. Grant's administration (1869-1877). General Grant himself was an honest man, but some of his advisors were not. Many who surrounded him were put in place by corrupt political bosses.

For example, financial speculators Jay Gould and James Fisk wanted to dominate the gold market. They convinced Grant's brother-in-law to have the President stop the Treasury Department from selling any gold. Grant agreed to the proposal for a time. Gould and Fisk then purchased all available gold they could. With gold scarce, the price rose quickly. However, Grant saw what was happening and changed his mind. As the Treasury Department began selling again, the price of gold fell. It fell so low that it caused a financial panic on 24 September 1869, thereafter known as **Black Friday**. The panic triggered a five year depression.

CROSS-SECTION OF EARLY TECHNOLOGICAL ADVANCES

Inventor	Technological Advance
1830: Peter Cooper	Steam locomotive developer
1840: Samuel F.B. Morse	Telegraph
1850: Elias Howe / Isaac Singer	Sewing machine
1839: Charles Goodyear	Vulcanization of rubber (improves strength & flexibility)
1856: William Kelly	Process for converting iron into steel
1874: Stephen Dudley Field	Electric streetcar
1876: Alexander Graham Bell	Telephone
1879: Thomas Alva Edison	Incandescent electric light bulb
1882: Thomas Alva Edison	Electric power generating plant (NYC)
1884: Ottomar Mergenthaler	Linotype machine (sets printing press type by a keyboard)
1886: Elihu Thomson	Electric welding machine
1897: Adolphus Busch	Patented diesel engines in United States

The Credit Mobilier Scandal (1872): The Union Pacific Railroad contracted with the Credit Mobilier Company to do the construction of the transcontinental railroad. Credit Mobilier swindled over 23 million dollars from the bulk of Union Pacific stockholders. Then it distributed stock to members of Congress and even to the Vice President at ridiculously low prices to block a congressional investigation.

The Salary Grab Scandal (1873): Congress passed an act doubling the pay of the President and raising its own salary by 50% for the previous two years. It was later repealed.

The Whiskey Ring Scandal (1873-1877): Tax collectors and liquor distillers cheated the federal government out of tax revenue in Mid-western cities.

The Indian Service Scandal (1876): A Congressional investigation found that Secretary of War William Belknap had accepted bribes in assigning trading posts in Indian Territory.

Although many U.S. Senators and Representatives were corrupt, there were moves for reform. President James Garfield promised reform, but was assassinated by a disappointed office seeker in 1881. The assassination prodded Congress to act. It passed the ***Pendleton Civil Service Act*** in 1883. The Act required applicants for nearly 15,000 federal jobs to take qualifying tests. Slowly, the new examination system cut down on bribery. A movement began to control the power and influence of the railroads and big business. However, it took nearly 20 years before the Progressive Reform Movement brought major changes.

GROWTH OF THE CORPORATION AS A FORM OF BUSINESS ORGANIZATION

Before the Industrial Revolution, **proprietorships** (single owner) and **partnerships** (small group of owners) were the most common forms of business organization. These forms were basically for small scale business operations.

In the Industrial Revolution, nationwide operations demanded a new form of business organization. The **corporation** was that form. To operate on a national scale, firms needed wider sources of capital and more protection for investors. Corporations allowed for limited sharing of ownership through

AMERICAN CAPITALISM

There was no central agency or program directing America's industrial revolution. This great economic change was driven by **capitalism**. This is a way of making economic decisions. It holds that the means of production must be privately owned. Capitalists believe in **laissez-faire** – that decisions must be made freely by individuals and businesses.

Capitalism is based on continued growth and improvement of living standards. It is fast-moving, but it is not an orderly system. Thousands of businesses are growing at once. Each one makes different decisions daily. The change is fast, uneven, and unpredictable.

As a result, America went through "economic growing pains" in the late 19th century. Some people were hurt in this change. Most Americans saw life change for the better amid the smoke of the factories.

Capitalism works in a **market structure**. Producers and consumers interact freely. Orders and requests go back and forth. Those "market signals" help businesses decide what to produce, who will produce it, how to produce it, and how to distribute the rewards. Consumer demand and cost of resources guide the production decisions. These decisions result in producing a proper supply of goods and services available to meet demand.

For a capitalist system to show progress, production has to be efficient. Production is also linked to borrowing, accumulating, and reinvesting the money (capital) gained in the market. If production expands, the economy as a whole grows. If there is growth, then the quality of life improves.

Before the Civil War, most American businesses were too small to have much excess money for capital investment. Expansion money came from Europeans – especially for railroad development. During the Civil War, demand for war goods generated more profits, and investment capital began to come from Americans themselves. This new reservoir of "home-grown" capital fueled the great industrial expansion after the Civil War.

FORMS OF BUSINESS ORGANIZATION

Form	Advantages	Disadvantages
Proprietorship	• owner close to customers and workers • has total control of management • receives all profits	• owner assumes all risks • limited capital available • one manager's perspective
Partnership	• more capital can be raised • risks are shared • more management perspective	• profits must be shared • unlimited liability for owners • ends if one partner leaves
Corporation	• increased capital through sale of shares (stocks) • losses limited to investment • increased number of managers • ownership transferable • larger growth potential • research facilities possible • risks shared	• state & federally regulated • subject to corporate taxes • management removed from customers & workers

stock sales. Corporations are chartered by state authority and treated as legal persons. Therefore, they can own property, lend and borrow money, sue and be sued, and pay taxes.

GOVERNMENT RESPONSE TO INDUSTRIAL DEVELOPMENT AND ABUSES

The great strides in technology made the remote geographic areas of the United States more accessible to each other. Telephone and telegraph communication, and railroad transportation went beyond state borders. However, in the industrial age, the new interstate commerce required national laws. The new laws made the national government grow increasingly stronger.

There were no laws to stop some companies from forming **mergers** (combinations of several companies) so big that they dominated the market for their product. When one company eliminates all others it becomes a **monopoly** or a **trust**. Once a company controls the market, it can set the design, quality, and quantity of a product. A monopoly can charge high prices because there is no competition to keep it in line by offering the product for a lower price. The trust becomes the dictator of the market.

In the 1870s, farmers of prairie and western states were at the mercy of railroad trusts. Railroad companies formed **pools** to eliminate competition. The group of companies conspired to control prices. Together they acted as a monopoly. Railroad pools charged high prices to get farmers produce to market. The farmers had no alternatives. The public was hurt, too. Food prices rose because it cost so much to bring crops to the market.

The farmers pressed their states to regulate such railroad abuse. However, rich and powerful railroad owners bribed legislators and prosecuters and found ways around the regulations. The Supreme Court of the United States said states could regulate the railroads, but only within their state boundaries. In *Wabash R.R. v. Illinois* decision of 1886, the Court said Congress alone could regulate interstate commerce.

Farmers and the public turned to Congress for action. In 1887, Congress passed the **Interstate Commerce Act**. It regulated railroad rates. It also prohibited railroad pools. Shortly afterwards, Congress passed the **Sherman Anti-trust Act** (1890). It outlawed monopolies in all industries by forbidding *"combinations in restraint of trade."* These acts were a weak start. Neither act was exceptionally strong, and corrupt officials worked to keep them weak. Not until the Progressive Era were strong laws passed to control monopolies.

RESPONSE OF LABOR TO INDUSTRIALIZATION

The pace of industrialization was fast and furious in the late 19th century. Mechanization and assembly lines made work monotonous. Many people worked together in crowded, unsanitary, and unsafe conditions for long hours in **sweatshops**.

Workers had no job security and wages went up and down with economic conditions. If the economy slumped, demand dropped. Businesses slowed or stopped production. There were long depressions in the 1870s (5 years) and 1890s (4 years). There were serious recessions in 1866-1867, 1882-1885, 1890-1891, and 1907-1908. In these periods, layoffs were common; there was no unemployment compensation or government welfare.

When the economy boomed and demand was high, employers sped up production. Machinery broke down and quick repairs made work dangerous. Accidents were frequent. There was no government system of worker's compensation for the injured. Working hours averaged 10 hours per day – 6 days a week. Children and women were employed at wages much lower than those for men.

CHILD LABOR IN THE MINES
Investigators for the National Child Labor Committee photographed a young boy standing outside the Turkey Knob Mine in MacDonald, West Virginia in 1908. Often young children were used in mines to push coal cars and operate tipples used to empty the coal cars at the end of rail piers.
(Library of Congress)

Many factories and mining companies set up company towns. Food, housing, and supplies were bought directly from the company, often at high prices. In the cities, the working class lived in **tenements**. There was widespread poverty. Entire households often worked to bring in enough money for essentials. Working women made up 20% of the work force. The number of working women grew from 2.5 million to 8 million between 1880 and 1910. The working class could not afford the new conveniences made possible by industrialization, (washing machines, telephones, electric lighting).

INCREASE IN THE SIZE OF THE INDUSTRIAL WORK FORCE, 1860-1900 (Source: U. S. Bureau of the Census) AVERAGE NUMBER OF WORKERS PER ESTABLISHMENT		
Industry	1860	1900
Cotton goods	112	287
Iron and steel	65	333
Carpets and rugs	31	213
Meat packing	20	61
Agricultural implements	8	65

As industry grew, owners demanded more of their workers. To deal with the problems, workers formed organizations called **unions**. Workers realized that they had strength if they acted together. Unions wanted the right to **collective bargaining**. This means workers representatives negotiate employment conditions with representatives of management in a contract. Only a small percentage of the work force was unionized. By 1900, less than 1% of workers belonged to unions.

EARLY NATIONAL LABOR UNIONS
Unions became stronger and larger after the Civil War. **Uriah Stephens** and **Terence Powderly** organized the **Knights of Labor** in 1869. The Knights admitted all workers, from skilled to unskilled. In the 1880s, the Knights campaigned for basic reforms. These included an eight hour day, no child labor, and equal pay for men and women. The Knights of Labor supported workers during the McCormick Reaper strike in Chicago in 1886. At one rally, a bomb went off and violence broke out. The Knights were not part of the **Haymarket Riot**. However, authorities blamed them for the violence, public opinion turned against them, and the Knights lost membership.

In 1881, **Samuel Gompers** founded the **American Federation of Labor** (AFL). Gompers concentrated on higher wages, insurance, and better working conditions. The AFL organized only skilled workers along craft lines (i.e., carpenters, masons). Local AFL craft unions set their own course of action. The national AFL lobbied for legislation in Washington and coordinated state lobbying. By 1900, AFL membership had grown to one million workers.

MAJOR STRIKES
The main weapon of the unions was the **strike**. When workers walked off the job as a group, factory

and mine production stopped. If production stopped, owners lost money. The unions hoped the owners would give in to their demands in order to get production started again. Violence sometimes erupted if the owners tried to break the strike by bringing in new workers that unions called **scabs**.

One AFL-connected union, the Amalgamated Association of Iron and Steel Workers, went on strike at Carnegie Steel's Homestead, PA plant in 1892. The company called in a private security agency. Violence erupted, and the governor called out the state militia. The **Homestead Strike** collapsed and the union was smashed. Other steel mills refused to recognize unions in the steel industry.

In 1893, the country went into a depression. The Pullman Palace Railroad Car Company cut wages 25-40%. However, the company would not lower rents or the prices it charged workers for supplies in the company store.

Under the leadership of **Eugene V. Debs**, the American Railway Union (ARU) organized a nationwide boycott. Railroad workers would not handle trains with Pullman cars. As the boycott spread, it stopped the delivery of the federal mail. Pullman lawyers used the *Sherman Anti-trust Act* ("no combinations in restraint of trade") to get a federal court to order the union to stop the boycott. **President (Stephen) Grover Cleveland** ordered federal troops to get the mails moving. Violence erupted, and Debs and ARU leaders were jailed for six months.

The violence of the strikes hurt the unions. People did not sympathize with workers. Unions also kept certain groups out. Immigrants and women were shut out of many unions, because both groups were seen as too willing to accept lower wages. African Americans were usually excluded from union membership during this time period. They were sometimes employed as scabs, but let go after the strike.

Although unions worked hard to make the public aware of poor working conditions in the Industrial Era, they met with little success. Not until the reform spirit of the **Progressive Era** in the early 1900s (see pages 92-95), did enough political pressure arise to get laws to change workers lives.

RESPONSE OF THE FARMER TO INDUSTRIALIZATION

Population grew remarkably in the late 19th century, especially in the cities. The increases were due to both an increasing birth rate and decreasing death rate. Changes in diet and changes in medicine caused these population trends. Immigration rose, too, and most of the newcomers remained in the industrial centers. By 1900, almost half the population was living in the cities.

In response to the demand of the cities for food, farming expanded in the period after the Civil War. People moved west and set up more farms. In 1862, the *Morrill Land Grant Act* provided for the sale of federal land to fund agricultural colleges and quicken the pace of scientific agricultural development.

Also in 1862, Congress passed *The Homestead Act*. It granted a plot of 160 acres of public land in the West to any 21-year old citizen who was head of a family. The homesteader had to file a declaration and pay a small filing fee, then live on the land for 5 years and make certain improvements to receive clear title. The better lands quickly came under the control of the railroads and speculators. Settlers had to buy from them rather than accept the poorer government lands. By 1900, about 600,000 farmers received clear title under the *Homestead Act* to nearly 80 million acres.

The prairie sod encountered by homesteaders on the Great Plains was difficult to plow and plant. There was little lumber. The sod they peeled from the prairie became the primary building material. Homesteaders stacked the sod to build the walls of their houses. For heat, they burned buffalo and cattle manure. Windmills provided much needed water. Harsh Sun, blizzards, drought, flooding, insects, and high winds brought the settlers many problems.

Still, the farmers made headway. Unlike colonial times, the prairie farms were large. They were commercial enterprises. While many failed, those that succeeded were more productive because of mechanization. Cultivators, reapers, combines, and later, steam tractors raised productivity.

Cattle ranching reached its peak in the late 1880s. Overgrazing, disease, severe winters, and falling prices took their toll. Only a few giant ranches remain today. Disputes over land rights occurred between the homesteaders and the ranchers. Violence erupted frequently over land and mining claims. **Vigilantes** (unauthorized secret citizen groups) were sometimes organized to maintain order.

POWERFUL WEAPONS USED ON BOTH SIDES

Unions	Employers
strike	lockout (refusing to let workers in)
boycott	hiring scabs (strikebreakers)
strike fund - $	injunction (court order to stop strikes)
for strikers	yellow-dog contract - workers agree not to
picketing	unionize as condition of employment
publicity	blacklist

LIVESTOCK EXPANSION

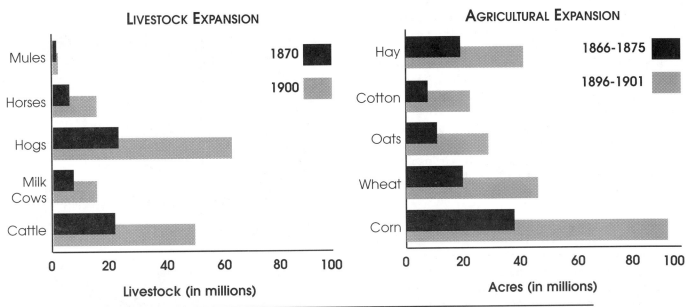

Livestock (in millions)

■ 1870
▨ 1900

Mules
Horses
Hogs
Milk Cows
Cattle

0 20 40 60 80 100

AGRICULTURAL EXPANSION

■ 1866-1875
▨ 1896-1901

Hay
Cotton
Oats
Wheat
Corn

0 20 40 60 80 100

Acres (in millions)

The cash crop farmers paid high charges for storage and transport of their grains. There was foreign competition especially from Canada (grain) and Argentina (cattle). Railroad rates were high; cheating was common. Crop failures made banks cautious about granting loans to farmers. When they did, they charged high interest rates. Transport costs from eastern cities meant farmers paid high prices for goods, credit, and supplies.

The farmers began to organize and demand action from the government on their problems. Through the **Grange** movement (the National Grange of the Patrons of Husbandry, 1867), farmers became politically active. They elected their own candidates for state and local political office. Midwestern states passed state laws to regulate railroads (Grange laws).

The Grange fought the railroads in the courts, too. In 1886, the Supreme Court upheld the Grange laws (*Munn v. Illinois*). However, in 1886 the Court changed its mind. It said that states could regulate the railroads only within their boundaries (*Wabash, St. Louis, and Pacific R.R. v. Illinois*). It held that only Congress could regulate interstate commerce. The Grange helped farmers form **cooperatives** to purchase major equipment. Grain elevators (moving and storage of grain) operated by the Grange achieved some success. In the late 1880s, the Grange movement declined.

In 1892, a new political party emerged to champion farmers' causes. The **Populist Party** came out of the Midwest to champion the causes of the farmers and tried to unite with industrial workers. It made headway in the Midwestern states, and elected some governors, and it had many good reform ideas. However, its popularity challenged the Democratic and Republican Parties. The two major parties began to adopt Populist ideas. When they did, the Populists began to fade.

THE POPULIST PARTY PLATFORM
• more government control of the railroads • graduated income tax • secret ballot • direct election of Senators • 8-hour work day • government ownership of telephone and telegraph • restriction of immigration • free and unlimited coinage of silver at the rate of 16:1

The factory workers that populated the cities needed food, clothing, and shelter. (In the old agricultural society, they used to produce all that for themselves. They could not do this as factory workers and middle class managers.) Interdependence characterized the new urban life. Urban dwellers became a society of consumers. New businesses grew up in the cities to provide for the needs of workers. Examples include A&P food stores, Sears and Montgomery Ward for catalog mail order merchandise, and the building of thousands of **tenement houses** for shelter.

INDUSTRIALIZATION ALTERED AMERICAN LIFE

Industrialization changed American life in many ways. First and foremost, it was a major economic change. Industrialization altered the way goods were produced. At the beginning of the 19th century, goods were mainly produced in the home and distributed locally. By the end of the Civil War in 1865, a great number of goods were being produced in factories and distributed over long distances. The **assembly-line factories** used new machinery, new power sources, and workers that were more unskilled than skilled.

Expansion of factories drew new workers to the cities. With new farm machines, more food could be produced with fewer workers. New workers came from overseas, too. Railroads and other industries advertised in Europe and attracted millions of immigrants to the cities of the United States.

WAVES OF IMMIGRANTS

The United States has been called "a nation of immigrants." The desire for a better standard of living and to leave unemployment, crop failures, or a depressed economy have been the major motivation for immigration. Economically, the large numbers of immigrants who came during the Industrial Era provided the country's labor force.

In the early years of the new nation, the majority of immigrants came from Northern and Western European countries. The largest numbers came from Germany, Ireland, and Scandinavia. These immigrants supposedly **assimilated** (blended) into the existing English-dominated (Anglo-Saxon) culture since their customs and traditions were similar. They also trickled into the country in small numbers, and many pushed on to the new farming regions of the frontier.

In the 1840s, there was a change. A great wave of immigrants swept into the country. Repeated failure of the potato crop in Ireland led to a wave of Irish immigration that exceeded 2 million. By 1850, nearly a quarter of a million Irish were flowing into the U.S. Revolutions and political upheaval pushed nearly 4 million Germans toward America. Millions of others sought economic opportunity. Not all the newcomers were from Europe. Between 1860 and 1900, over quarter of a million left depressed economic conditions in Asia and came as contract laborers.

Socially, this increased immigration caused problems. When large numbers of newcomers come into a society all at once, difficulties arise. For fear of economic competition for jobs or just intolerance of cultural differences, some groups (called **nativists**) opposed the newcomers. Before the Civil War, the **American Party** (or "Know-Nothings") opposed the Irish. They wanted to restrict immigration and office-holding by **naturalized citizens**. To this day, much nativist reaction is connected to fear of economic competition, because impoverished immigrants often take jobs at low pay to survive.

EXAMPLES OF IMMIGRANT CONTRIBUTIONS	
Field	**Group**
Building of transportation systems	Chinese, Irish, Italians, Slavs (railroads, roads, canals)
Mining	Welsh, Poles, Slavs
Textiles/garment trades	English, Jews
Optical equipment	Germans
Chemical industry	French
Stone masons / sculptors	Italians

ETHNIC AND GEOGRAPHIC DISTRIBUTION CIRCA 1870
• Total Continental U.S. Population - 39,818,440
• Almost even male-female split (slight male edge)
• Almost 5 million non-whites (4.8 million African Americans, Indians, Chinese, and very few others)
• 12.3 million people in the Northeast, 13 million in the North Central States, 12.3 million in the South, and approximately 1 million in the West
• Vast majority of Americans (approx. 82%) of Northern and Western European ancestry

As the Industrial Era went on, a new wave of immigrants swept into America. This time, the countries that immigrants came from were different. Southern and Eastern Europeans fled high taxes, poor soil, and high land rents. Poles fled the wars and politics that led their country to be divided by foreign powers.

Other Eastern Europeans fled harsh imperialist governments. Jews fled religious, economic, and political persecution. Although they wanted farms in the west, poverty forced the new immigrants to settle in cities, especially in the Northeast. They formed ethnic neighborhoods and enclaves which became **ghetto** areas ("Little Italys," "Chinatowns," and "Little Polands").

Gradually, immigrants learned the ways of their new home. Street life, work in factories, night school for adults, public and private school for children, immigrant newspapers, and ethnic organizations combined to **acculturate** the immigrants.

The large numbers of immigrants in the cities attracted the attention of the political machines like New York City's **Tammany Hall**. Both the bosses and immigrants benefited from this relationship. The bosses found flats (apartments), food, and jobs for immigrants. The immigrant gave his political loyalty to the boss and political party. Each and every ethnic group has helped to build America, either through hard, physical labor, the use of special skills or aptitudes, or the discovery of a new or different way to operate.

LEISURE ACTIVITIES
REFLECT THE VIEWS OF THE TIMES

Toward the end of the 19th century technology and industrialization began to change life for Americans. They worked long hours, but off the farms, they had more leisure time, too. As leisure time increased, so did the number of ways to spend it. They cycled, swam, and rowed. Many had vacation time. Trains took them to the seashore and to mountain resorts.

Sports became professional entertainment. Professional baseball teams first formed in Cincinnati and Pittsburgh. Teams from eight cities from Boston to St. Louis formed the National League in 1876. The railroads brought circuses, musical comedies, and vaudeville performances to small cities and towns.

Newspapers and magazines expanded for leisure reading. **Yellow journalism** became popular as Joseph Pulitzer's New York *World* and William Randolph Hearst's New York *Journal* exploited lurid scandals, disasters, and crimes to sell papers. Print advertising became a major industry. Dime novels (low-priced, adventure paperbacks) became popular. Stories were primarily about the wild west, detectives, or science fiction.

Hall of Fame pitcher George "Rube" Waddell began his career with the Pittsburgh Pirates in 1897.

Even in the industrial era, most 19th century literature was romantic in nature and flowery in style. "*Rags to riches*" stories were very popular. Writer **Horatio Alger** sold more than 20 million juvenile novels. The themes were usually the same: poor boys bravely rescuing the daughters of a wealthy fathers who help the boys make their fortunes (*Luck and Pluck, Tattered Tom*).

Other popular writers included **Bret Harte** (*The Luck of Roaring Camp*), **Jack London** (*The Call of the Wild*) and **Mark Twain** (*Tom Sawyer* and *Huckleberry Finn*). The realistic and ruthless side of life was also told in **Stephen Crane**'s *Maggie, Girl of the Streets* and **Theodore Dreiser**'s *An American Tragedy*.

INDUSTRIALIZATION CAUSES REFORM:
THE PROGRESSIVE MOVEMENT, 1900-1920

Reform is a part of American life. Americans have always worked on political, social, and economic problems to improve their quality of life. Reform movements have expanded rights, cleaned up the environment, and helped the unfortunate.

The industrial era produced very rapid growth and change. However, people were abused, rights were trampled, competition was ruined, and the environment was ravaged. By 1900, a spirit of reform was on the rise. The new urban middle class were well paid and had the extra time to work on social problems. They were businessmen, lawyers, social workers, doctors, clergy, and educators. They became the core of the Progressive reform movement (1900-1920). Progressives were well-educated, and they had the moral training that stressed a "Christian duty" to help those less fortunate.

Women's rights became a Progressive cause. Much earlier, in 1848, the first women's rights convention met at Seneca Falls NY. It issued the *Declaration of Sentiments* modeled after the *Declaration of Independence*. The Convention called attention to the fact that women were second class citizens, economically, legally, and politically. Women had little legal control of their property or even authority over their own children. The laws gave fathers or other male relatives control over unmarried women's lives. Husbands had legal superiority over wives.

After the Civil War, **Lucy Stone**, **Susan B. Anthony**, and **Elizabeth Stanton** formed organizations to campaign for the ballot. These **suffragists** lobbied in state legislatures and Congress. In 1869, the Wyoming Territorial Legislature gave female residents the right to vote. In 1878, Anthony's group proposed a right-to-vote amendment to the Constitution. In 1890, the major groups merged into the **National American Woman Suffrage Association** (NAWSA).

Woman Suffrage Headquarters, Cleveland, Ohio, 1912
(Library of Congress)

During the Progressive Era, suffragists took more direct action. They staged marches and civil rights demonstrations. Many men began to join the cause. Lobbying and court actions were used up to that time.

In 1913, **Alice Paul** formed the National Woman's Party. She led the party in mass marches and hunger strikes. By 1915, **Carrie Chapman Catt** was leading a more militant NAWSA. **Jeannette Rankin** (MT) became the first female member of the House of Representatives in 1916-1917. Universal suffrage for women was finally achieved in 1920, with the ratification of the Nineteenth Amendment. It forbade denial of voting rights to anyone because of their gender.

THE INFLUENCE OF THE MUCKRAKERS

During the Progressive Era, protests against big business tactics came from many sources. Concerned citizens, churches, and the press prodded all levels of government to take action. Public education made literacy grow in America. As it did, the power of the press grew.

Progressive journalists wrote articles exposing the evils of big business. Because they turned up the dirty side of life, they became known as "muckrakers." Their articles and books often stirred public opinion. In the early 1900s, magazines such as *McClure's* featured muckraking articles. The work of these writers and other Progressive reformers resulted in the passage of many state and Congressional laws.

STATE REFORM EFFORTS

Much of the government reform movement was aimed at abuses on the local and state level. Reformers focused on the cities where the problems of industrialization seemed worse. Reformers called for civil service reform, and the creation of new city commissions and city managers. Reformers wanted affordable services. They wanted government to regulate street cars, electric, gas, telegraph, and telephone companies.

On the state level, reformers had different goals. In the West, they wanted railroad regulation. In the South, they were anti-big-business. In the North, they focused on political corruption and working conditions. In Wisconsin, Republican–Progressive Governor **Robert LaFollette** secured direct primaries, fair taxes, and regulation of railroads. In 1900, Massachusetts limited women's working hours to 60 per week. In 1912, Massachusetts created a commission to recommend minimum wages for women.

States began to protect the health and safety of their citizens. They began factory inspections, offered insurance to cover job accidents, set minimum employment ages and maximum hours for child labor (usually 8–10 hours per day), limited working hours for women, and created old age pensions.

PROGRESSIVE STATE REFORMS
Initiative – process where voters can suggest new laws and amendments
Referendum – people allowed to vote directly on legislation
Recall – process where voters can remove officials from office before their term is up
Secret Ballot – voters could make their choices in privacy

Private individuals and organizations worked for social reform during the Progressive Era. **Jane Addams** founded **Hull House** in Chicago in 1893. It was a model for **settlement houses** in slum neighborhoods. They offered adult education classes, job

MUCKRAKERS	
Writer	**Work**
Ida Tarbell	Wrote a series of exposés on the Standard Oil Company.
Lincoln Steffens	Had a series called *The Shame of the Cities* on urban graft and corruption.
Upton Sinclair	Described unsanitary conditions in Chicago's meat packing plants in *The Jungle* (1906).
Frank Norris	Described railroad abuses against the farmers in *The Octopus* (1901).
Jacob Riis	Wrote about urban problems (immigrant slums in NYC) in *How the Other Half Lives* (1890) and stimulated housing reform.

At the time of her death, *The New York Times* wrote about Jane Addams, "Perhaps the world's best-known and best-loved woman."

(Courtesy of *Ladies' Home Journal* "100 Most Important Women of the 20th Century," Meredith Corp ©1999)

training, clinics, child care, and Americanization classes for immigrants and the poor.

NATIONAL PROGRESSIVE REFORMS

THE SQUARE DEAL

On the national level, political reforms led by Presidents Theodore Roosevelt and Woodrow Wilson answered the muckrakers' calls for action. Theodore Roosevelt's 1904 campaign theme demanded that business and government give consumers a "**Square Deal**."

Using the Commerce Department, President Roosevelt prosecuted over forty trusts (monopolies).

As a result, he was often referred to as "the trust buster." All trusts were not automatically condemned. Instead, their effect on trade was reviewed. In 1904, government action forced the breakup of one of J.P. Morgan's railroad monopolies (*Northern Securities Co. v. U.S.*). In 1911, government prosecutors persuaded the Supreme Court to declare Rockefeller's Standard Oil Company a monopoly and broke it up.

Under the Square Deal, the government assisted in labor disputes. In the 1902 coal miners' strike, Roosevelt called union leaders and mine owners to Washington. When he threatened to use troops to get the mines producing again, owners agreed to settle.

Theodore Roosevelt, 26th President of the U.S.
(White House Historical Association, National Geographic Society)

In 1907, Roosevelt used his presidential powers to add 150 million acres to national forests. He set up plans for natural resource management in the *Newlands Act* (1902); the *Antiquities Act* protected the Grand Canyon and Niagara Falls; and, the *Inland Waterways Act* (1907) improved river systems.

SQUARE DEAL REFORMS	
Action	**Reform**
The Meat Inspection Act (1906)	Inspected (federal) of all meat crossing state lines (first consumer protection law passed by Congress).
The Pure Food and Drug Act (1906)	Forbade the sale of contaminated goods and false labeling.
The Elkins Act (1903)	Expanded powers of the Interstate Commerce Commission (ICC).
The Commerce Department (1903)	Enforcement of anti-trust legislation.
The Hepburn Act (1906)	Authorized Interstate regulation of oil pipelines, railroad terminals, sleeping car companies, and bridges.

NEW FREEDOM REFORMS

Action	Reform
The Underwood Tariff Act (1913)	Reduced import duties and spurred competition and lower prices.
The Clayton Anti-Trust Act (1914)	Strengthened the *Sherman Antitrust Act* of 1890.
The Federal Trade Commission (1914)	Stopped mis-branding and misleading advertising.
The Federal Reserve Banking System (1913)	Set up a government-controlled banking system designed to allow a more elastic currency (adjusts supply as needed).
The Sixteenth Amendment (1913)	Created progressive income tax (tax rate increases as the amount of income increased).
The Seventeenth Amendment (1913)	Directed election of U.S. Senators (meant senators would no longer serve state bosses).

Woodrow Wilson during the 1912 Presidential Campaign against William Howard Taft and Theodore Roosevelt.
(Library of Congress)

THE NEW FREEDOM

President Woodrow Wilson (term 1913-1921) called his Progressive reform program "the New Freedom." Under his program, Wilson viewed trusts as basically evil. He tried to break them and restore free competition in the marketplace. New Freedom reforms came at the end of the Progressive Reform Era. World War I turned the nation's attention away from reform in 1917. After the War, the nation was exhausted with the emotion of fighting for causes, and the spirit of reform faded.

THE SEARCH FOR RACIAL JUSTICE

As the 19th century closed, many African Americans moved to Northern industrial cities to escape poverty, discrimination, and lynchings in the South. In the Progressive Era, several leaders addressed the problems of African Americans.

W.E.B. DuBois   (Library of Congress)

REFORM FOR AFRICAN AMERICANS

Booker T. Washington	W.E.B DuBois	Marcus Garvey
(1856-1915) This former slave called for "realistic accommodation" and a policy of self-help. He founded the Tuskegee Institute, a vocational school for African Americans. He believed African Americans could only achieve equality after they had economic security.	(1868-1963) This New Englander with a Harvard doctorate called for a more militant approach to equality and economic opportunities. In 1905, he helped to form the NAACP (National Association for the Advancement of Colored People) to challenge discrimination in the courts and legislatures.	(1887-1940) This immigrant from Jamaica founded the Universal Negro Improvement Association. The UNIA sought to create free and independent nations in Africa. Garvey hoped that African Americans would help to populate these new nations.

REMINDER: For help in handling questions, see Advice Chart on page 184.

Unit 7

Multiple choice

1 A person who arranges financing, organizes workers and materials, operates a business, and assumes the risk is best known as a (an)
1 labor organizer
2 scab
3 entrepreneur
4 financier

2 To establish Standard Oil Company as a monopoly, John D. Rockefeller
1 gained control of all foreign sources of supply
2 purchased Carnegie Steel Company to make steel pipes
3 bought out J.P. Morgan to finance oil well development
4 lowered oil prices to force competitors out of business

3 A major boost for industrial development after the Civil War came from
1 increased English demand for raw cotton
2 an increase in the availability of domestic capital
3 European investment in canal construction
4 the emergence of the South as an industrial power

Directions: Base your answer to question 4 on the graphs below and on your knowledge of social studies.

4 Based on these graphs (at the bottom of the page), which is an accurate conclusion?
1 Growth in factories and workers occurred between 1870 and 1900.
2 Factories and workers reached their greatest number in 1890.
3 The growth of factories showed a sharper rise than that of workers.
4 Only workers increased in numbers between 1870 and 1880.

5 Which statement best describes the administration of President Grant?
1 President Grant chose qualified and honest advisors.
2 Corruption scandals involved government officials.
3 The U.S. became involved in European wars.
4 Impeachment proceedings against Grant were successful.

6 If an investor wished to limit his risks to the money invested in a business and to be able to sell his investment easily, he would most likely invest in a
1 proprietorship
2 partnership
3 corporation
4 cooperative

7 The Knights of Labor began a decline after the Haymarket Riots because
1 workers refused to join labor organizations
2 working conditions improved making them unnecessary
3 authorities and some of the public blamed them for the violence
4 its goal of equal pay for men and women was achieved

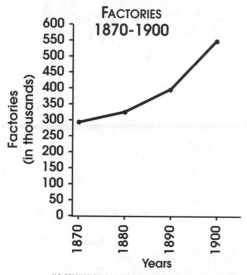

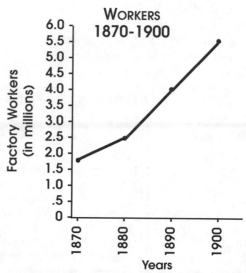

Directions: Base your answer to question 8 on the illustrations below and on your knowledge of social studies.

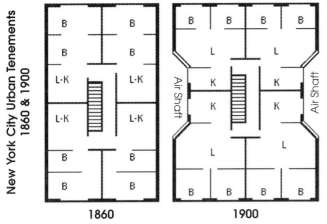

New York City Urban Tenements 1860 & 1900

1860   1900

KEY: **K** = kitchen   **L** = living Room

B = bedroom   ✎ : windows

8   According to the sketches above, the post 1900 tenement was better than that of the 1860s, because it had
   1   better air circulation
   2   more apartments on each floor
   3   more fire escapes
   4   centrally located stairs

Directions: Base your answer to question 9 on the map below and on your knowledge of social studies.

9   The best title for this map would be
   1   "U.S. Acquires New Territories by Treaty with Britain"
   2   "Slavery Expands to New Territories in the West"
   3   "Native Americans Pushed to Reservations in East"
   4   "Settlers Push Frontier to the West"

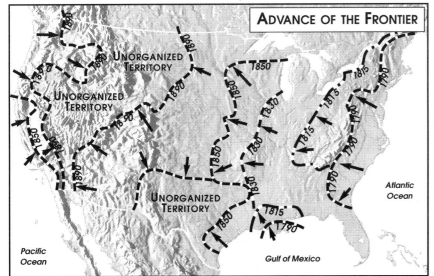

ADVANCE OF THE FRONTIER

UNORGANIZED TERRITORY

UNORGANIZED TERRITORY

UNORGANIZED TERRITORY

Atlantic Ocean

Pacific Ocean

Gulf of Mexico

Directions: Base your answer to question 10 on the cartoon below and on your knowledge of social studies.

10   What is the main point of this cartoon?
   1   Only wealthy people lived in New York City.
   2   Construction of buildings over six stories was limited.
   3   Corrupt politicians controlled New York City.
   4   Physically large men dominated New York City politics.

11   Which headline might have appeared in a newspaper at the time of the Homestead Strike in 1892?
   1   ***Unions Win Right to Represent Steel Workers***
   2   ***Homestead Strike Ends Without Violence***
   3   ***Governor Calls Out State Militia to End Strike***
   4   ***Carnegie Refuses to Hire Private Security Agency***

12   A major factor contributing to the success of prairie farms was their
   1   increased mechanization
   2   small size
   3   self-sufficiency
   4   easily planted soil

13   The new urban middle class was the core of the Progressive reform movement because it
   1   wanted people to move west
   2   believed it was a "Christian duty" to help the less fortunate
   3   thought education should be denied to those in the lower class
   4   supported the interests of big business

Directions: Base your answer to question 14 on the chart below and on your knowledge of social studies.

ETHNIC AND GEOGRAPHIC DISTRIBUTION CIRCA 1870

- Total Continental U.S. Population - 39,818,440
- Almost even male-female split (slight male edge)
- Almost 5 million non-whites (4.8 million African Americans, Indians, Chinese, and very few others)
- 12.3 million people in the Northeast, 13 million in the North Central States, 12.3 million in the South, and approximately 1 million in the West
- Vast majority of Americans (approx. 82%) of Northern and Western European ancestry

14 Which is a correct conclusion about ethnic and geographic distribution around 1870?
1 About 50% of the U.S. population was non-white.
2 Most of the population was concentrated in the Northeast.
3 People of North and West European ancestry were the dominant group.
4 The Irish had not yet entered the U.S. in large numbers.

CONSTRUCTED RESPONSE
SET 1

Directions: Base your answers to questions 1 and 2 on the illustration at the right and on your knowledge of social studies.

1 Identify TWO (2) factors that affected life in the United States after the Civil War.

_____

_____

2 Select ONE (1) of the two items identified in your answer to question 1 and explain how it changed life in the U.S.

_____

_____

_____

_____

Directions: Base your answer to question 15 on the quotation below and on your knowledge of social studies.

"...The coming of Chinese laborers to the United States be, and the same is hereby, suspended; and during such suspension it shall not be lawful for any Chinese laborer to come, or, having so come after the expiration of said ninety days, to remain within the United States."
– *Chinese Exclusion Act*, 1882

15 The point of view expressed in the quotation above would most likely be supported by which group?
1 Progressives
2 Nativists
3 Muckrakers
4 Suffragists

Directions: Base your answers to questions 3 and 4 on the dialog at the right and on your knowledge of social studies.

"I'll be wanting some (railroad) cars of you people before the summer is out," observed Dyke to the clerk... "There'll be a big wheat crop to move this year, and I don't want to be caught in any car famine. ... Suppose we went into some sort of pool, a sort of shippers' organization, could you give use special rates, cheaper rates - say a cent and a half?"

The clerk looked up. "A cent and a half! Say four cents and a half and maybe I'll talk business with you."

"Four cents and a half," returned Dyke, "I don't see it. Why, the regular rate is only two cents."

"No, it isn't," answered the clerk, looking him gravely in the eye, "It's five cents."

– Frank Norris, *The Octopus*, 1901

3 Why is Dyke (the farmer) concerned?

_____

_____

_____

_____

4 What is ONE (1) step taken by farmers and ONE (1) step taken by the government to deal with the problem which is the subject of the reading?

_____

_____

_____

_____

PRACTICE SKILLS FOR DBQ

Directions: The following task is based on the accompanying documents. The documents may have been edited for the purposes of this exercise. The task is designed to test your ability to work with historical documents. As you analyze the documents, take into account both the source of the document and the author's point of view where relevant.

Historical Context: In the period after the Civil War, industrialization in the U.S. progressed rapidly. It brought many positive changes to American life, but in its early stages, many negative impacts were also apparent.

continue with Part A on the next page

Part A - Short Answer

Document 1

1   What is ONE (1) negative impact of the Industrial Revolution shown in this drawing?

_____

_____

_____

Document 2

> "Girls, hand-sewers, earn nothing for the first month, then as unskilled workers they get $1 to $1.50 a week, $3 a week, and (as skilled workers) $6 a week. ... In the general work, men are only employed to do button-holing and pressing (as skilled workers), and their earnings are as follows: 'Pressers,' $8 to $12 a week....
>
> "The average weekly living expenses of a man and wife, with two children, as estimated by a self-educated workman named Bisno, are as follows: Rent (three or four small rooms), $2; food, fuel, and light $4; clothing, $2, and beer and spirits, $1...."
>
> –Joseph Kirkland, *The Poor in Great Cities*

2a   How do the earnings of skilled girls and skilled men workers differ?

_____

_____

_____

2b   Compare the earnings of skilled male workers with the average weekly living expenses for a family of four. Based on this comparison, why was it often necessary for more than one family member to work if the family wished to improve its standard of living?

_____

_____

_____

_____

Part B - Essay Response

Task: Explain how the Industrial Revolution in the U.S. had a negative impact on the quality of life of many Americans of that time. (State your thesis in the introduction.)

ADDITIONAL SUGGESTED TASK

From your knowledge of social studies, make a list of negative impacts of the Industrial Revolution on the quality of life of Americans of that time.

UNIT

8

THE U.S. AS AN INDEPENDENT NATION IN AN INCREASINGLY INTERDEPENDENT WORLD

THE U.S. AS AN INDEPENDENT NATION IN AN INCREASINGLY INTERDEPENDENT WORLD

OVERSEAS TERRITORIAL EXPANSION

IMPERIALIST SENTIMENT BUILDS

In the late 19th century, industrial expansion prompted United States business to look beyond its borders for markets and raw materials. The economic desire to expand pushed America toward **imperialism** – extending national economic or political power over other areas.

In the late 19th century, agricultural and industrial exports grew by more than 300% in value. Merchant and naval fleets were modernized to handle the surplus goods. As the 20th century opened, international commerce became an important part of the American economy.

Internal growth, the Civil War, and Reconstruction kept Americans focused on domestic affairs for much of the nineteenth century. They even ridiculed Secretary of State Seward's desire to purchase Alaska from Russia in 1867 as "Seward's Folly." However, the situation changed as America industrialized. There were economic, military, cultural, and even emotional influences that pushed Americans toward imperialism.

In 1890, a U.S. Navy officer wrote an important book – *The Influence of Sea Power Upon History, 1660-1783*. In it, Captain **Alfred Thayer Mahan**

said that nations with sea power dominated the world. He said that it was time for Americans to "look outward" for naval bases, markets, and raw materials. The increased speed of steam ships made trade more profitable. However, steam ships needed "coaling stations" to refuel on long voyages. Americans took a new view of the islands of the Pacific.

Religion was a factor, too. Christian missionaries also went into Asia and the Pacific to find converts. In *Our Country* (1885), **Rev. Josiah Strong**, claimed that it was the country's "divine mission" to spread democracy, liberty, and Christianity to less civilized people.

There was an emotional side to imperialism, too. At this time, European nations were scrambling to control colonies in Africa, India, and Indochina. They claimed it was the "White Man's Burden" to bring western civilization to less developed regions. A colonial empire also became a status symbol of a "great power."

Starting with the **annexation** (incorporation of a territory into an existing country) of Midway Island in 1867, the U.S. began building an overseas colonial empire. It was not as large as those of European powers, but it was geographically far-flung and it was ethnically diverse. Most Americans supported colonial expansion, but there was opposition to the country's growing global involvement.

New England sent Congregational missionaries to Hawaii early in the 19th century. American sugar cane growers gradually dominated affairs in the islands. In 1893, American settlers overthrew Queen **Liliuokalani** and requested annexation by the United States. President **Grover Cleveland** saw that native Hawaiians opposed annexation and he dropped the idea. Five years later, the Spanish American War convinced the imperialists that Hawaii was needed. It would be a mid-Pacific supply base. **President William McKinley** and Congress quickly approved the annexation of Hawaii in 1898.

The U.S. set up coaling operations in the Samoan Islands in the South Pacific in 1872. Britain and Germany also showed interest in the islands. In 1889, the United States and Germany each annexed part of Samoa.

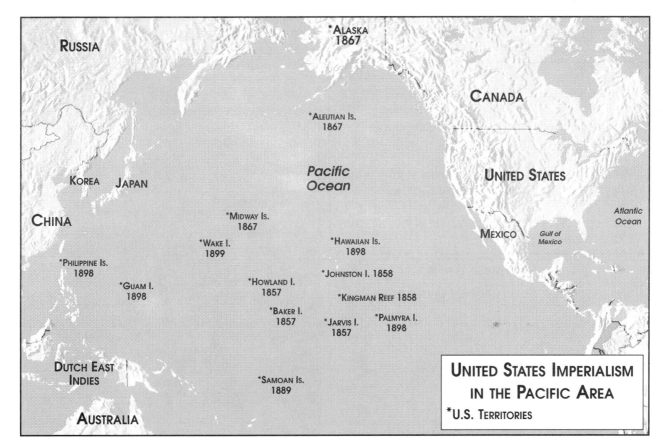

RUSSIA

*ALASKA 1867

CANADA

*ALEUTIAN IS. 1867

Pacific Ocean

UNITED STATES

KOREA   JAPAN

CHINA

Atlantic Ocean

MEXICO   Gulf of Mexico

*MIDWAY IS. 1867

*WAKE I. 1899

*HAWAIIAN IS. 1898

*PHILIPPINE IS. 1898

*JOHNSTON I. 1858

*GUAM I. 1898

*HOWLAND I. 1857

*KINGMAN REEF 1858

*BAKER I. 1857

*JARVIS I. 1857

*PALMYRA I. 1898

DUTCH EAST INDIES

*SAMOAN IS. 1889

AUSTRALIA

UNITED STATES IMPERIALISM IN THE PACIFIC AREA
*U.S. TERRITORIES

SPANISH AMERICAN WAR:
U.S. FOREIGN POLICY CHANGES

In the late 19th Century, Cuba – one of Spain's last colonies in America – was in revolt. By 1895, Cuban rebels had reopened a guerrilla war. (Guerrillas use "hit-and-run" tactics.) In Cuba, the rebels burned sugar fields, ambushed Spanish soldiers, sabotaged railroads, and blew up shipping facilities. To gain sympathy for the rebel cause, exiled leader **José Martí** gave speeches and articles in U.S. newspapers. He was popular in America. When Martí returned to Cuba in 1895, he was killed in a rebel attack. Martí became a martyr. His death aroused Spain's critics in the United States.

The Spanish Governor-General in Cuba was Valeriano Weyler. He placed about 500,000 suspected rebels in concentration camps. About 200,000 persons died in the camps. American newspapers such as Hearst's *New York Journal* and Pulitzer's *New York World* referred to Weyler as a "butcher." Americans contributed funds and guns to the rebels. The U.S. government tried to persuade Spain to negotiate with the rebels.

President McKinley sent the battleship *Maine* to Cuba to protect American citizens from the violence. The *Maine* exploded mysteriously in Havana harbor in February 1898 killing 266 U.S. sailors. Newspapers whipped up American outrage. Congress clamoured

for war. Again, McKinley wanted Spain to compromise with the rebels. Now the rebels demanded independence. Spain would not give up Cuba. Ignored by the Spanish, McKinley finally bowed to Congressional pressure. He asked for a declaration of war and Congress responded with one on 25 April 1898.

THE DISCOMFORT OF IMPERIALISM

The fighting in the Spanish American War lasted only ten weeks. Spain asked for terms on 26 July and signed the *Treaty of Paris* in December 1898. If the Senate ratified the treaty, the U.S. would annex the Philippines and have the status of an imperial power. Some Americans who felt uneasy about having colonies formed the **Anti-Imperialist League**.

The League pressured Senators to vote against the Treaty. League members included social welfare leader Jane Addams, labor leader Samuel Gompers, educator John Dewey, author Mark Twain, and industrialist Andrew Carnegie. They were against taking overseas territories. Imperialism contradicted our Constitution and Bill of Rights by denying inhabitants their liberty. They believed the new territories should be independent.

Pro-imperialists won the treaty fight narrowly. They claimed the new people needed time and education before they could be set free. Business interests did not want to give up the profits the new colonies

Causes

- Harsh treatment of Cubans by Spanish rulers

- American investors loss of profitable agricultural trade (sugar cane, tobacco)

- Yellow journalism – false and exaggerated stories published by American newspapers

- Explosion of the battleship *Maine* (incorrectly blamed on the Spanish)

Results

- Spain gave up Cuba (placed under American supervision)

- Spain gave Puerto Rico and Guam to the U.S.

- U.S. paid $20,000 to Spain for the Philippines

Chief organizer, Lieutenant Colonel Theodore Roosevelt, poses with the Rough Riders who fought in the battle of San Juan Hill, Cuba, 1 July 1898 (Library of Congress)

could generate. The Senate ratified the *Treaty of Paris* in February 1899 by a close vote. In the Philippines, rebels who had fought with the Americans against the Spanish now rebelled. **Emilio Aguinaldo** led a bloody four-year war. The United States lost 4,000 soldiers and nearly 20,000 Filipinos were killed. In a 1902 settlement, the U.S. pledged independence for the Philippines by 1940.

A NEW ROLE IN WORLD AFFAIRS

With a new presence in the Caribbean and the Pacific, the U.S. embarked on a new foreign policy. From the days of George Washington, the U.S. usually kept to itself except for trade with other nations. With a colonial empire, and expanded trade, there would be more situations requiring government decisions. Presidents would have to negotiate treaties or use force to solve problems with other nations. This called for a more active diplomatic role for the President and the need for a larger, more modern navy. Very soon after the Spanish American War, Presidents Theodore Roosevelt, William Howard Taft, and Woodrow Wilson found themselves devoting a great deal of time to a new, more active foreign policy.

ASIA: THE OPEN DOOR POLICY

Gaining colonies in the Pacific put the U.S. into contact with events in Asia. American merchants had traded with China as early as the 18th century. At the end of the 19th century, Foreign powers (Britain, Germany, France, Russia, Japan) carved out exclusive areas of China they called **"spheres of influence."** These were not full colonies. They were local areas where the foreign nations had negotiated exclusive economic rights for themselves. This "sphere" situation made it difficult for U.S. traders to do business in China.

In 1899 and 1900, Secretary of State **John Hay** sent two notes to the major powers with trading interests in China. In them, he outlined the **Open Door Policy**. His first note called for equal opportunity for all nations in trade, investments, and profits. Hay's second note warned the imperialistic nations of Europe and Japan not to annex any Chinese territory. The Open Door Policy sounded impressive. However, the U.S. found it difficult to enforce. Other powers largely ignored it.

In 1900, Chinese groups called "righteous and harmonious fists" rebelled against the foreign powers on their soil. The press nicknamed them "Boxers." The U.S. sent troops to help Germany, Britain, France, Belgium, Russia, and Japan put down this **Boxer Rebellion**. Afterwards, the other powers quietly accepted the U.S. presence, but never officially recognized the Open Door Policy.

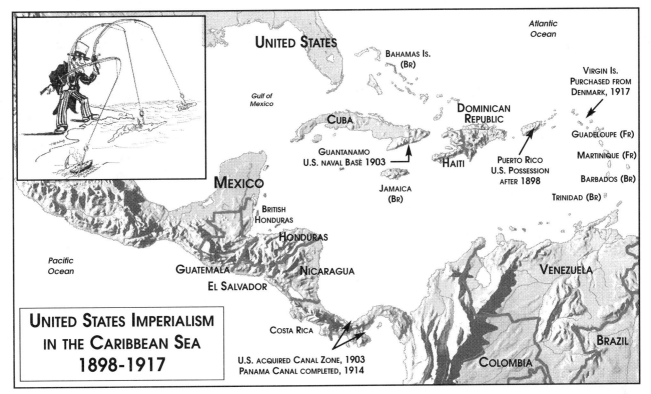

UNITED STATES IMPERIALISM IN THE CARIBBEAN SEA 1898-1917

LATIN AMERICA: THE BIG STICK POLICY

In the early 19th century, the U.S. wanted no conflicts with Europe, and it wanted to trade with the newly independent nations of Latin America. In 1823, President James Monroe stated that European nations must stop any further colonization in the Western Hemisphere. Britain quietly backed Monroe's policy because it wanted trade opportunities in Latin America, too. Britain's backing was enough to keep any other powers from challenging the *Monroe Doctrine* for 40 years. Note: During the American Civil War, France tried to control Mexico through a puppet emperor. The **Maximilian Affair** (1864-1867) was condemned by the United States and eventually abandoned by the French. Maximilian was defeated and executed in 1867.

In the 1890s, U.S. business in the Caribbean increased. American citizens ran into problems with Latin American countries. They wanted more protection from the U.S. government. After the Spanish-American War, the United States began to influence and intervene in the domestic affairs of many Latin American nations. Many Latin American nations resented the increased meddling in their affairs.

After 1900, President Theodore Roosevelt took a strong position in regard to Latin America. He believed the U.S. should wave a "big stick" – make a strong show of force in foreign affairs. He felt this policy would keep Europeans out of the Western Hemisphere and bring the Latin American nations in

PRESIDENT THEODORE ROOSEVELT'S BIG STICK POLICY

Event	Results
Venezuela (1902)	Britain and Germany asked President Roosevelt to mediate debt disputes with Venezuela. The Germans tried to use force, and Roosevelt warned he would use force to protect any Caribbean nation (reinforced the *Monroe Doctrine*).
Dominican Republic (1903-1905)	The Dominican Republic was unable to repay debts to European nations. To keep Europe out of the Americas, the U.S. took over the Dominican economy and supervised the debt repayment.
Panama (1903)	In 1903, the Colombian Senate refused to ratify a treaty giving the U.S. land rights for a canal in Panama. U.S. naval ships helped Panamanian rebels stage a revolt that led to independence. A U.S.-Panamanian Canal Zone treaty was finalized. (Roosevelt later boasted he "took the Canal.") After ten years of construction, the Atlantic and Pacific Oceans were joined in 1914.

Background Causes of World War I

- Economic competition – industrialized nations competed for markets and raw materials.

- **Nationalism** – groups ruled by other nations struggled for independence (e.g., Austria ruled the Serbs).

- Entangling alliances – Groups of nations (**Triple Alliance** = Germany + Austria + Italy v. **Triple Entente** = Britain + France + Russia) allied themselves to balance the power of others.

- Military competition – European nations tried to build bigger and better armies and navies than their rivals (submarines, tanks, poison gas, artillery, machine guns, and airplanes made warfare much more deadly).

- Imperialism – European nations, in need of raw materials, confronted each other for colonies in Asia and Africa.

EUROPE AT THE START OF WORLD WAR I

ALLIED POWERS

CENTRAL POWERS

line with U.S. wishes. The energetic President saw this intervention idea as an extension of the *Monroe Doctrine*. It became known as the **Roosevelt Corollary**.

A NEW GLOBAL ROLE

WORLD WAR I INVOLVEMENT

The United States struggled to stay out of European affairs in the 19th century. However, its change of status to an industrial giant at the end of the century made it more important in global affairs. The expansion of overseas trade increased its contacts with other countries, especially in Europe. By 1914, a complex series of events drew Europe into a general war (see box above). When Europe became involved in World War I, the United States wanted no part of the conflict. In 1914, President Wilson issued a *Proclamation of Neutrality*. However, as neutrals, U.S. merchants wanted to continue trading with both sides.

Eventually, the label of neutrality lost its meaning. American ships were attacked. One side or the other felt the goods Americans supplied were helping the enemy. The British controlled the surface of the Atlantic and blocked American ships from trading with Germany. The Germans' submarines threatened shipping to Britain from under the waves. President Wilson protested, and the attacks stopped for a while.

Despite neutrality, the U.S. was still a nation of immigrants. There were many who were emotionally

supporting one side or another in the European conflict. Wilson urged the people to keep a neutral outlook. Still, there were cultural forces at work. America's heritage was English. The belief in democracy shifted sympathy toward Britain and France as opposed to the autocratic **Central Powers**. There was greater trade and investment with the Allies than with the Central Powers. All these factors combined to influence the nation's thinking.

By 1916, the War in Europe stalemated (no decisive victories for either side). The loss of life and the economic costs mounted, but no one could win. Desperate, the British resumed seizing American ships, but the Germans' U-boats stepped up the torpedoing of American ships. The killing and destruction by the Germans finally drove Wilson to ask Congress for a declaration of war in April of 1917.

The U.S. was unprepared to wage war. Congress had not seen much reason to build up the armed forces while the nation was neutral. The army was small and short of supplies. In 1916, Congress authorized a slight increase in manpower and equipment. Men volunteered, but nearly 4 million were drafted under the *Selective Service Act* of May 1917.

Congress granted President Wilson emergency powers to set up the economy for wartime. Wilson created boards and agencies that made key economic decisions, making it a partial **command economy**. (The basic U.S. economic system is a **market economy**. In

KEY ELEMENTS OF WILSON'S FOURTEEN POINTS

Early in 1918, President Wilson announced America's war aims and proposed a plan for world peace included were the following ideas:

- An end to secret diplomacy

- Freedom of the seas

- Free and open trade

- Reduction of armaments

- Consideration for native populations in colonial areas

- **Self-determination** (independence) for subject nationalities of Europe, including Poland, Czechoslovakia, and Alsace-Lorraine

- A general association of nations to protect the political independence and territorial integrity of all nations

a market economy, the combined daily decisions of consumers and businesses run the economy with little governmental interference.) In a command economy, the government plans and makes the basic economic decisions for the public.

For those that did not serve in uniform, there were high-paying defense plant jobs. Women, immigrants, and African Americans easily found work. Because labor was in short supply and demand was high, wages rose. There were some strikes, but if they slowed the war effort, the strikers were arrested. Socialists and other opponents of the War were treated harshly. Some Americans, such as Socialist Party leader Eugene Debs, were arrested, fined or imprisoned. In *Schenck v. the U.S.*, the Supreme Court upheld the government's treatment of war protesters. It said the government could suppress freedom of speech when there was a "clear and present danger" to the society.

General **John J. Pershing** began organizing, equipping, and training 42 divisions. Pershing and some administrative units of the **AEF** (American Expeditionary Force) arrived in Europe in June, only two months after the declaration of war. Earlier in 1917, civil war and revolutions rocked Russia and forced the Tsar to **abdicate** (abandon the throne). Later in 1917, the communist Bolsheviks under Lenin came to power. They surrendered to Germany and dropped out of the War just as America was coming into it.

With Russia out of the War, German commanders shifted troops from the Eastern Front to the Western Front in France. They began pressing Britain and France. However, the American forces tipped the balance for the Allies. By the spring of 1918, the AEF helped to stop the German advances. America suffered 115,000 war deaths and 204,000 wounded. The Great War took 8.5 million lives worldwide, and twice as many were wounded. Germany surrendered as the Allies neared its border in November 1918.

U.S. GOVERNMENT COMMAND DURING WW I

Federal Agencies	Economic Sectors Managed
War Industries Board	Allocated raw materials; supervised war production
War Labor Board	Mediated labor disputes to prevent strikes
Shipping Board	Built transports for men and materials
Railroad Administration	Controlled and unified R.R. operations
Fuel Administration	Increased production of coal, gas, and oil; eliminated waste
Food Administration	Increased farm output; public campaigns to conserve supplies

Raising Funds For The War Effort: Increased income and excise taxes; "Liberty Bond" and "Victory Bond" Drives

Peace Negotiations

In 1919, the major powers gathered for an international peace conference that took place at the Versailles Palace outside Paris. In attending the conference, Wilson was the first President to leave the country while in office. President Wilson, David Lloyd George (Britain), Georges Clemenceau (France), and Vittorio Orlando (Italy) controlled the conference.

President Wilson hoped to negotiate a fair and just peace based on his **Fourteen Points** (see chart on page 107). However, rivalries among the European nations stood in his way. He discovered that secret treaties dividing territory had been made at the start of the War. Wilson did achieve his most important goal, the creation of a **League of Nations**. However, the President could not get the other nations to adopt other points of his plan.

After several months at Versailles, a treaty was completed. The ***Treaty of Versailles*** dissolved the German, Austro-Hungarian, and Ottoman Empires. In the Treaty, the European powers demanded huge **reparations** (financial payments for damages) from Germany. They demanded German disarmament. France also demanded German territory. Germany's colonies were put under the League of Nations' authority.

Returning home, the President knew the Senate had to ratify any treaty he signed in Paris. Yet, he barely consulted with the Senate during the negotiations. The nation was weary of war and reform. There were Senators such as William E. Borah and Henry Cabot Lodge, who opposed the League of Nations. They said the people did not want any more involvement in Europe. Wilson stubbornly refused to compromise. He toured the country trying to get the people to put pressure on their isolationist Senators. Wilson suffered a stroke during the tour. It crippled the President for the rest of his life. In the end, the Senate rejected the *Treaty of Versailles*. Later, to end the war, the United States signed separate peace treaties with different countries of the Central Powers.

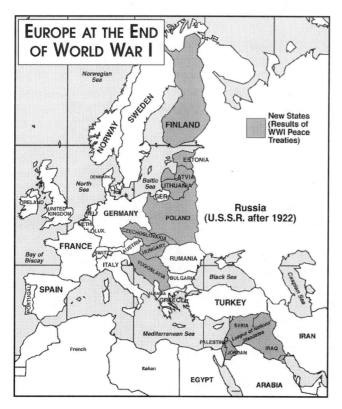

REMINDER: For help in handling questions, see ADVICE CHART on page 184

UNIT 8
MULTIPLE CHOICE

Directions: Base your answer to questions 1 and 2 on the quotation below and on your knowledge of social studies.

"Whether they will or not, Americans must now begin to look outward. The growing production of the country demands it. The position of the United States, between the two Old Worlds and the two great oceans, makes the same claim, which will soon be strengthened by the creation of the new link joining the Atlantic and Pacific, by the advancing civilization of Japan, and by the rapid peopling of our Pacific states."

– Alfred Thayer Mahan, "The United States
Looking Outward," *Atlantic Monthly*, 1890

1 In this quotation, what position does Mahan take in regard to U.S. imperialism?
   1 The U.S. should remain in isolation.
   2 The U.S. should halt European immigration.
   3 There are numerous reasons why the U.S. should expand.
   4 Geography should have no impact on U.S. expansion.

2 Which argument does Mahan's statement: "The growing production of the country demands it" best support?
   1 need for international markets
   2 "White Man's Burden"
   3 need for military bases
   4 goal of limiting British expansion

3 The U.S. sought to protect its trade with China by
   1 proclaiming the Roosevelt Corollary to the *Monroe Doctrine*
   2 announcing the Open Door Policy
   3 aiding rebels in the Boxer Rebellion
   4 removing all tariff barriers for Chinese products

4 Which headline was the result of the other three?
   1 ***Americans Lost At Sea When Ship Sunk by German U-Boat***
   2 ***British Searching Neutral American Ships***
   3 ***U.S. Enters World War I***
   4 ***Russia Freed from Tsarist Control***

Directions: Base your answer to question 5 on the maps below and on your knowledge of social studies.

5 These maps indicate that the participants in the Paris Peace Conference wished to
   1 expand Russian influence in Eastern Europe
   2 provide self determination for subject peoples
   3 establish a German-Russian common border
   4 increase the size of the German Empire

6 Much of the initial U.S. expansion in the Pacific can be attributed to the
   1 need to import raw materials from the islands
   2 pressure from the islanders for annexation
   3 end of trade relations with China
   4 desire to establish coaling and supply bases

Directions: Base your answer to question 7 on the items below and on your knowledge of social studies.

- Harsh treatment of Cubans
- Yellow journalism
- Explosion of Maine

7 All of the above are correctly associated with the
  1 Open Door Policy
  2 outbreak of World War I
  3 beginning of the Spanish American War
  4 Boxer Rebellion

8 In the early 20th century, a number of Latin American countries became the object of possible intervention because they
  1 were unable to repay debts owed to European creditors
  2 refused to allow European imports
  3 revolted against their European colonial masters
  4 threatened to force the removal of European armies

Directions: Base your answer to question 9 on the graph below.

WORLD WAR I COMBAT LOSSES
(Central & Allied Powers)

NUMBER KILLED (in millions of lives)

Germany	1.8
Austria-Hungary	1.2
Ottoman Empire	0.325
Russia	1.7
France	1.39
British Empire	0.98
Italy	0.5
U.S.	0.115

Central Powers   Allied Powers

Source: Larousse, *Dictionary of World History*, 1987

9 According to the information in the graph above, which statement is most accurate?
  1 The losses of the Allied Powers exceeded those of the Central Powers.
  2 Only Germany and Russia had over one million combat losses.
  3 U.S. and British Empire losses were almost identical.
  4 Russian army losses were low, because Russia quit fighting in 1917.

Directions: Base your answer to question 10 on the cartoon below and on your knowledge of social studies.

10 An appropriate caption for this cartoon is
  1 "U.S. Leaves League of Nations"
  2 "Senate Blocks U.S. Entrance into League of Nations"
  3 "U.S. Supports League Intervention in China"
  4 "U.S. Senate Provides League Financial Support"

11 Prior to American involvement in World War I in 1917, the U.S. position might best be described as
  1 one of strict neutrality with no trade with either side
  2 officially neutral, but with extensive trade with the Allies
  3 watchful waiting with a balanced trade relationship with both sides
  4 one of embargo with no ships allowed to leave American shores

12 Both Wilson's *Fourteen Points* and the *Treaty of Versailles* contained provisions for
  1 reduction of armaments for all nations
  2 an end to secret diplomacy
  3 freedom of the seas
  4 self determination for many subject peoples

BAR GRAPH

CONSTRUCTED RESPONSE

SET 1

Directions: Base your answers to questions 1 through 3 on the chart at the right and on your knowledge of social studies.

U.S. EXPORTS TO THE MAJOR WARRING NATIONS, 1914-1916 (IN MILLIONS OF DOLLARS)			
Nations	**1914**	**1915**	**1916**
Major Allied Powers: France, United Kingdom, and Tsarist Russia	785.0	1,314.8	2,465.6
Major Central Powers: Germany, Turkey, and Austria-Hungary	370.7	30.9	0.3

1 What happened to U.S. trade with the major Allied Powers between 1914 and 1916?

_____

_____

2 What happened to U.S. trade with the major Central Powers between 1914 and 1916?

_____

_____

3 What does the difference in the answers to questions 1 and 2 tell you about the status of U.S. neutrality before its entrance into World War I?

_____

_____

SET 2

Directions: Base your answers to questions 4 through 6 on the quotation at the right and on your knowledge of social studies.

4 What does Du Bois say about the attitude of African-American soldiers toward fighting in World War I?

_____

_____

> "We (African American soldiers) are returning from war! *The Crisis* and tens of thousands of black men were drafted into a great struggle. ...We fought gladly and to the last drop of blood; for America and her highest ideals...
>
> But today we return!
> We sing: This country of ours ... is yet a shameful land.
> It lynches.
> It disenfranchises (denies the right to vote) its own citizens.
> It encourages ignorance.
> We return. We return from fighting. We return fighting.
>
> Make way for Democracy! We saved it in France, and ... we will save it in the United States of America, or know the reasons why.
> – W.E.B. Du Bois, *The Crisis* (an NAACP publication), 1919

5 What THREE (3) accusations does Du Bois make about American treatment of African Americans?

_____

_____

_____

6 What does Du Bois say African American soldiers will do on their return to the United States?

_____

_____

PRACTICE SKILLS FOR DBQ

Directions: The following task is based on the accompanying documents. The documents may have been edited for the purposes of this exercise. The task is designed to test your ability to work with historical documents. As you analyze the documents, take into account both the source of the document and the author's point of view where relevant.

Historical Context: In the period after the Civil War, the U.S. joined many of the European powers in expansion abroad. Those who favored expansion cited many different reasons for imperialism including advantages for the imperialist power and the people who became subjects of another government.

Document 1

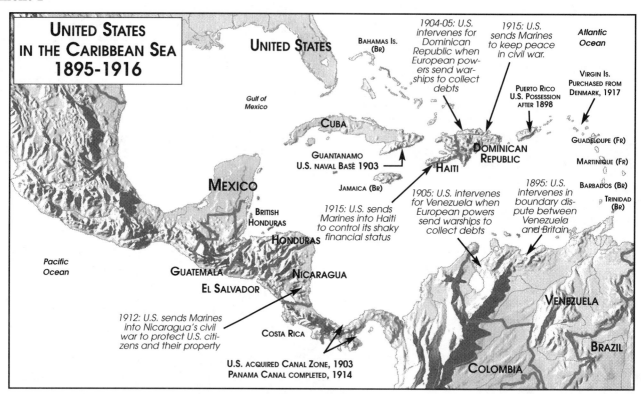

1a What are TWO (2) reasons why the United States intervened in the affairs of Caribbean countries?

_____

_____

_____

1b Why was a naval base in Guantánamo Bay, Cuba, important for carrying out U.S. policy?

_____

_____

_____

_____

Document 2

2a According to McKinley, what are
   TWO (2) reasons why the United
   States should annex the Philippines?

_____

_____

_____

> "The truth is I didn't want the Philippines and when they
> came to us as a gift from the gods, I did not know what to do
> about them. ...
>   "And one night late it came to me this way: (1) that we could
> not give them back to Spain - that would be cowardly and dishon-
> orable: (2) that we could not turn them over to France or
> Germany, our commercial rivals in the Orient - that would be
> bad business; (3) that we could not leave them to themselves -
> they were unfit for self-government and they would soon have
> lawlessness and misrule over there worse than Spain's was; and
> (4) that there was nothing left for us to do but to take them all
> and educate the Filipinos, and uplift and civilize and
> Christianize them."
>
> – U.S. President William McKinley, 1901

_____

_____

2b According to McKinley, what are TWO (2) advantages the Filipino people might gain from a U.S. annexation?

_____

_____

_____

_____

Part B - Essay Response
   Task: Discuss at least THREE reasons why the U.S. became an imperialist power in the period after the
   Civil War. Include SPECIFIC examples of U.S. imperialism to back up the reasons you cite. (State your
   thesis in the introduction.)

ADDITIONAL SUGGESTED TASK

   From your knowledge of social studies, make a list of additional reasons for U.S. imperialism and for each
   reason cited, give a specific example as proof.

Unit 9

The United States Between the World Wars

THE UNITED STATES BETWEEN THE WORLD WARS

THE ROARING TWENTIES:
THE REPUBLICAN DECADE

As 1918 ended, Americans were emotionally drained. Crusades take great energy. The Progressive Reform Era was a crusade that went on for two decades. In addition, World War I was a crusade to "make the world safe for democracy." Yet, for many Americans World War I was a bitter crusade. They had made great sacrifices of lives and national wealth, and Europe ignored them and went right back to its old, corrupt power politics.

Americans' exhaustion deepened in 1919. A great influenza epidemic struck, taking more than 500,000 lives. Finally, the economy went into a depression in 1919 and 1920. Converting from wartime production to peacetime production is never smooth. Readjustment meant some factories slowed down and others shut down completely. This depression was not long, but it affected many people. High unemployment greeted returning soldiers. Strikes, and even riots, broke out in some cities.

Weary from the Wilson crusades, Americans turned away from the Democrats in the election of 1920. They voted to return to "normalcy." This was a phrase that Republican candidate **Warren G. Harding** mistakenly used when he meant "normality." Evidently, normalcy summed up voters' feelings. Harding beat his Democratic opponent in a landslide of better than 2 to 1 in the popular vote.

After all the crusades, Americans wanted a rest, some pleasure, and a better, trouble-free life.

President Harding was popular because he did not challenge America with any great campaigns. He was not a forceful leader. Harding tried to create harmony. He shifted political leadership away from the White House and toward Congress. To get the economy moving again, Congress cut spending and lowered taxes. It also set up the first supervised budget system for the government.

Harding had few programs of his own. He gave his cabinet the responsibility for running the government. He even avoided the controversy over prohibition of alcohol. The President claimed to support the Eighteenth Amendment, but he lacked interest in its enforcement.

Harding allowed public attention to drift away from government. He made it easier for special interest groups to get their way. In the 1920s, corrupt individuals took advantage of the public's lack of concern. Nasty scandals surfaced involving the President's friends. Harding generously gave them jobs and they abused them. The President was shocked as the graft and corruption scandals emerged. On a trip to Alaska in 1923, Harding died from a stroke, and his Vice President, **Calvin Coolidge**, took the nation's helm.

Unaware of the scandals, a sorrowful nation mourned the likeable President Harding. Shortly, the storm of problems swept Washington. The most famous scandal was the **Teapot Dome Affair**. Harding's Secretary of the Interior took bribes from private oil companies to lease government reserves in California and Wyoming. In other scandals, the U.S. Attorney General was tried on conspiracy charges. The chief of the Veterans Bureau was convicted of mishandling funds for hospital supplies. The Custodian of Alien Property was found guilty of fraud.

ISOLATION IN WORLD AFFAIRS

Under Harding, and then Coolidge, there was a retreat from active world involvement. After rejecting the *Treaty of Versailles*, the United States did sign separate treaties with its World War I enemies. Still, the Senate rejected active U.S. participation in the League of Nations and even in the World Court.

Harding (Republican)
Total Electoral Votes = 404
Total Popular Vote = 16,143,000

Cox (Democratic)
Total Electoral Votes = 127
Total Popular Vote = 9,130,000

U.S. 1920 ELECTION MAP

0   500 Miles

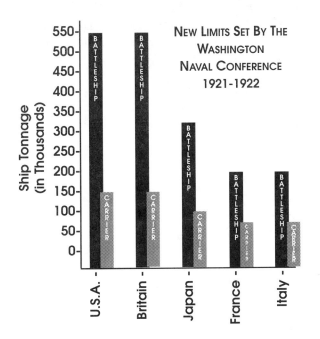

NEW LIMITS SET BY THE WASHINGTON NAVAL CONFERENCE 1921-1922

Ship Tonnage (in Thousands)

The isolationist U.S. did make some efforts to limit the kind of arms buildup that took place before World War I. Harding sponsored the **Washington Conference** of 1921-22. The Conference led to several international agreements reducing naval forces. Under Coolidge, the United States signed the **Kellogg-Briand Pact** (1928). Sixty-two nations joined in this pledge to give up war as a means of settling disputes. However, the Pact had no way of being enforced. It was just a "paper promise."

TURBULENCE, FEAR, AND PREJUDICE

World War I propaganda and fear made Americans suspicious of **subversive activities**. Intolerance spread to any groups that reflected foreign influences (immigrants, Catholics, Jews, African Americans, and radicals). The tension continued into the 1920s. In times of emotional stress, individual rights can be trampled.

One example of this tension was in labor relations. The depression of 1919-1920 caused nearly 3,600 strikes. State and federal courts issued orders arresting strike leaders and breaking the strikes. Workers became frustrated. Some radical labor leaders urged American workers to follow the lead of Russia. Lenin and the Bolsheviks had just taken power there, set up a communist state, and renamed the country the **Union of Soviet Socialist Republics** (U.S.S.R.).

In the spring of 1919, a series of terrorist bombings took place nationwide. Employers played on public fears. They condemned all strikes as revolutionary and communist. The newspapers they controlled blamed radicals for the country's turmoil. During this **"Great Red Scare,"** Wilson's Attorney General launched raids on the headquarters of radical groups

in 33 cities. In the **Palmer Raids**, over 3,000 people were rounded up. Many were held without bail and denied access to lawyers. Over 550 aliens among them were eventually **deported** (sent back to their country of origin).

The fearful mood of the early 1920s allowed a rebirth of the Ku Klux Klan (KKK). The new Klan's racist, anti-foreign teachings attracted thousands. After World War I, waves of immigrants resumed. Anti-immigrant feeling grew. By the mid-1920s, the Klan gained enough strength to pressure Congress into passing new immigration acts. A series of three laws gradually restricted immigration. The final one, the ***National Origins Act*** (1929), set up quotas against Southern and Eastern Europeans and Asians that lasted into the 1960s.

Another example of this tension was in race relations. After the Civil War there was a slow, steady **northern migration** by African Americans out of the South. They tried to escape the poor sharecroppers' life and the Jim Crow segregation system of the South. Because of prejudice, many migrants found only low-paying jobs in industrial cities such as Chicago, St. Louis, Detroit, and New York.

World War I had increased the northern flow of African Americans. The migrants moved into factories producing war goods. They encountered resistance. Northern cities did not have official laws separating the races, but there was still prejudice and unofficial segregation. Offered only the lowest paying jobs, African Americans had to settle into poorest areas of the cities. Ghettoes or ethnic neighborhoods emerged. When the War ended and the postwar depression came, some cities like Chicago experienced race riots.

There were some bright spots in the African American ghettoes. A new cultural consciousness arose

among the migrants. In the South, they had been spread out first on plantations and then on farms. In the Northern cities, they lived closer to each other and they shared their hopes and frustrations through the arts. In the 1920s, Harlem in New York City became a center of African American culture. The novels of **Langston Hughes** and **Jean Toomer**, the poetry of **Claude McKay** and **Countee Cullen**, and the jazz music of **Duke Ellington**, **Louis Armstrong**, and **Bessie Smith** became the core of a cultural movement known as the **Harlem Renaissance**.

CONSUMER ECONOMY

Americans were relieved as the economy revived in 1921. Demand rose, and factories and offices started hiring workers. Incomes rose. With more money to spend, the country's attention turned to having a good time. During the "Roaring Twenties," there seemed to be a new energy. Americans embraced the idea of buying and enjoying a dazzling array of goods and services. They wanted automobiles, suburban homes, and electric appliances. They fell in love with new fashions, dance fads, professional sports, silent pictures, vaudeville, and radio.

Before World War I, **Henry Ford** set up large-scale assembly-lines to produce automobiles. During the War, this and many new ideas sped up production and distribution of goods. After the War, businesses worked at getting more and more goods to the public. Other businesses applied Ford's ideas to produce vacuum cleaners, refrigerators, clothes washers, and radios. They cut production time and energy. Efficient production brought prices down to where average folks could afford these goods.

During the War, power companies increased the supply of electricity for factories. More power for machines and lighting increased production and working hours. After the War, electric companies continued to expand, bringing power to private homes. Besides lighting, electric appliances became more popular. Mass advertising campaigns in newspapers, magazines, radio, and even highway billboards became widespread. People wanted more and more goods, and the factories complied.

In the "Roaring Twenties," industry boomed. Businesses found new ways to get more people to buy. If consumers could not pay cash for goods, stores, and manufacturers offered credit on a large scale. To get customers to buy high-priced goods, producers introduced the **installment plan**. Consumers could "Buy Now, Pay Later." They made a small down payment, received the goods, and then paid the balance in small monthly payments (with interest payments added in, of course).

> ## "The saloon is as dead as slavery!"
> – Prohibitionist leader celebrating the Eighteenth Amendment taking effect, 1920

PROHIBITION

From 1920 to 1933, the **Eighteenth Amendment** to the *Constitution of the United States* banned the making and selling of alcoholic beverages. Long desired by reformers, Prohibition was an experiment aimed at legally regulating moral behavior. It was called the "Noble Experiment." In a quieter, rural America of the 19th century, it might have worked. However, in the rapidly changing, urbanized society of the 1920s, it failed. There was too much diversity in an industrial society. There was no general agreement on proper moral behavior. Alcoholism did decline in the 1920s, but crime increased.

There was a wild, party-like atmosphere in the Roaring Twenties. "Bootleggers" and "rum runners" made millions smuggling illegal liquor into the country. Secret, illegal bars called "speakeasies" made fortunes selling alcohol to customers. If authorities closed them, they paid the fines and reopened somewhere else. They advertised quietly, by word of mouth, the surest way for people to find them.

In the cities, gangsters organized, protected, and supplied the speakeasies. Mob "kingpins" like Chicago's Al Capone even ran their own breweries. Gangs fought over territories. Mobsters bribed police and public officials to leave them alone. Graft and corruption were everywhere. The whole situation was just too much for the government. The 1920s saw a long struggle between the "drys" (prohibitionists) and the "wets" (anti-prohibitionists). By the 1930s, most people felt that the "Noble Experiment" was a failure. The Prohibition Amendment was repealed when three-fourths of the states ratified the **Twenty-first Amendment** in 1933.

CULTURAL VALUES CHANGE

In the Roaring Twenties, technology and science changed the culture. America was no longer a slow-paced, rural society. There was a faster pace to life in an industrial-urban society. Advertising, literature, and films showed a younger generation was rejecting the past. Young people wanted a new life-style. Instead of peace and security, they wanted material pleasure and personal wealth.

Entertainment became an industry. The popularity of ragtime and jazz music, along with dances like the Charleston, showed a changing pace of life. The new music made phonograph recordings and night clubs popular. Professional sports expanded. Americans worshipped sports heroes such as Babe Ruth, Red Grange, Bobby Jones, Bill Tilden, Gertrude Ederle, and Helen Wills Moody. Silent motion pictures attracted millions. The movies created new stars: Rudolph Valentino, Clara Bow, Theda Bara, Harold Lloyd, and Charlie Chaplin.

Considered by many the greatest hitter in baseball, Hall of Famer George Herman "Babe" Ruth (1895-1948) played 22 years, mostly for the Red Soxs and Yankees. The "Babe" had 714 home runs, with 60 in 1927, a record that stood until 1998.

The new culture opened opportunities, especially for women. During the War, women put education to use playing new, vital economic roles. After the War, women stayed in the work force, especially as office workers. The Nineteenth Amendment gave them the vote and a new political status.

A new economic and political freedom emerged for women. A new sense of freedom showed itself in new fashions: shorter skirts, slacks, and shorts. It also showed itself in the break-down of old social restrictions: disappearance of chaperones, increasing participation in sports, co-ed schools, driving automobiles, and traveling alone. This new freedom changed thinking about families and marriage. Divorce rates began to rise in the 1920s.

Writers reflected the unsettled mood of the Roaring Twenties. They questioned old values and helped to popularize the new, youthful spirit of America. Among them were **F. Scott Fitzgerald** (*The Jazz Age, The Beautiful and the Damned, The Great Gatsby*), **Ernest Hemingway** (*The Sun Also Rises, For Whom the Bell Tolls*), and **Sinclair Lewis** (*Main Street, Babbitt*).

PROBLEMS AMID PROSPERITY

A modern industrialized society is very complex. Unlike self-sufficient farmers of the 19th century, people in industrialized societies are interdependent. Millions of transactions have to take place daily to keep an industrial society functioning. It is very hard to explain why an industrialized economy can slow down or even collapse. That is what happened by the end of the 1920s. In 1929, the U.S. and the global economies went into a gigantic tailspin.

In the Roaring Twenties, the economy seemed to be running well and at very high speed. Some people were becoming rich and the country as a whole seemed to be prospering. However, a look at the behavior of corporations, government, stock brokers, workers, and farmers shows that all was not well.

As in the "Gilded Age" (late 19th Century), corporations of the 1920s merged with other corporations. This brought them into conflict with government antitrust laws. In the spirit of harmony and normalcy, Harding's administration returned to the laissez-faire philosophy of the Gilded Age. When mergers led to monopolies, government officials "looked the other way" instead of bringing antitrust suits.

> "The business of America is business ... The man who builds a factory builds a temple. The man who works there, worships there."
> – Calvin Coolidge

Both Harding and Coolidge believed firmly that the leadership and prosperity should be left to the businessman. The Interstate Commerce Commission [ICC], the Federal Reserve Board, and the Federal Trade Commission kept out of the way of business. Even the Supreme Court announced that it would apply the "rule of reason" in antitrust cases. This meant it would be more lenient toward business activities than it had in the Progressive Era.

President Calvin Coolidge, 30th President 1923-1929
(*The Presidents*, White House Historical Association)

Corporations invested in streamlined, efficient factories. Machines and a few unskilled workers did the work formerly done by skilled workers. In the new factories, working conditions and hours were better, but fewer workers were needed. Productivity rose, but so did unemployment. In the 1920s, some skilled workers took pay cuts just to stay on the job. Because of prejudice, African American and immigrant workers often could not find work or were laid off.

Factories produced more, but the average wage did not increase. As the 1920s went on, fewer and fewer people could afford to buy the goods the factories were churning out. Corporations seemed to ignore the decline in demand.

Brokers on Wall Street enjoyed a heyday in the Roaring Twenties. Many stock brokers accepted **margin** purchases. This means the investor would pay only a small part of the stock's value. Some banks allowed customers to borrow money just to buy the stocks on margin. The result was that there were lots of stocks being bought, but very little money backed the purchases. It made the stock market and the economy look more robust than it was. They called it the "**Big Bull Market**," but it was an overinflated market. Real growth and productivity were nowhere near the prices of the stocks of many companies.

Of course, with government ignoring the situation, there were plenty of deceptive stock schemes. Crooked salesmen duped investors into purchasing stock in phony companies that looked good "on paper." Many people invested blindly, and the economy grew more unstable as the decade continued.

There were problems on the farms, too. During World War I, farmers greatly expanded production to feed our allies. After the War, American farmers continued to feed millions through America's international relief programs headed by Herbert Hoover.

By the mid-1920s, however, Europe's farms had rebuilt. Demand for American farm products declined. Farm profits dropped. Many farmers could not pay off the new machinery they had purchased to increase their crops. For farmers, the only way to get more money is to borrow or produce more. However, when the supply increases, prices drop. Many farmers went bankrupt in the 1920s.

THE GREAT CRASH

Like the Gilded Age, the Roaring Twenties was a wild, wonderful time – on the surface. Beneath the care-free mood, problems festered. The economy was like a fragile house of cards. Tariffs were too high and trade suffered. Farm prices were too low to allow farmers to make a living. Factories and farms over-produced, banks made too many bad loans, and investors were swindled in get-rich-quick schemes. Toward the end of the decade, buying slowed down. Companies cut production and wages, and then they laid off workers. As unemployment rose, income levels dropped, and buying slowed down even more. As conditions spiraled downward, companies could not pay loans and their profits declined. When companies make poor showings, investors begin to sell their shares in the companies.

The **Great Crash** came in October of 1929. At the New York Stock Exchange on Wall Street, some big investors began to sell their stocks rapidly. Nervous brokers called for other investors to put up more money. As investors lost confidence, the selling snowballed. Stock prices dropped rapidly as investors dumped stock in a panic. Companies fell apart in the Great Crash of the stock market. People lost fortunes and workers lost their jobs. The economy collapsed into the **Great Depression** – the worst economic downturn in the nation's history.

THE GREAT DEPRESSION

It is natural to have ups and downs in a market economy, especially one as large and varied as that of the United States. Demand for goods and services, savings, investments, and employment can never be perfectly in line for a system that allows freedom of choice. Combinations of hundreds of factors cause the economy to soar at times and decline in others. Economists call the up and down pattern the **cycle of demand**, or the "business cycle."

To chart the economy's condition, economists use a statistic called **GNP** (Gross National Product). GNP is the value of all the goods and services produced by the nation in a given year. When it is properly adjusted, the GNP for one year can be measured against other years. (Note: Statistics before the 1980s are usually given in GNP figures. In the 1980s, the government's economists started using another, more accurate statistic, **Gross Domestic Product** or GDP.)

KEY CAUSES OF THE GREAT DEPRESSION
Overproduction
Low Wages
Problems in the banking system
Risky speculation in stocks
Wealth concentrated in too few hands
High tariffs
Farm problems
Lax government regulation
Weaknesses of European economies after WW I

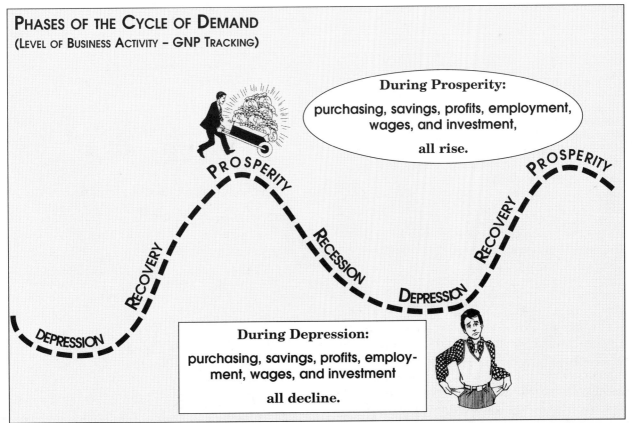

PHASES OF THE CYCLE OF DEMAND
(LEVEL OF BUSINESS ACTIVITY – GNP TRACKING)

PROSPERITY

RECOVERY

RECESSION

DEPRESSION

PROSPERITY

RECOVERY

DEPRESSION

During Prosperity:
purchasing, savings, profits, employment, wages, and investment, **all rise.**

During Depression:
purchasing, savings, profits, employment, wages, and investment **all decline.**

President Herbert Hoover, 31st President 1929-1933
(*The Presidents*, White House Historical Association)

RESPONSES TO ECONOMIC WOE

In the election of 1928, the people elected Herbert Hoover as President. He was a businessman and one of the most talented public administrators ever to be elected to the White House. After just six months, his administration had to struggle with the worst economic catastrophe in history.

HOOVER'S RESPONSES TO THE DEPRESSION

- Authorized some government spending to relieve suffering.
- Increased federal building projects to push some money into the economy.
- Suspended World War I debt payments to the U.S. by European nations.
- Set up the Reconstruction Finance Corporation (RFC) to give low-interest federal loans to save businesses from bankruptcy.
- Created the Federal Home Loan Bank to give low-interest federal loans to boost construction and decrease foreclosures.

Like Presidents Harding and Coolidge, Hoover believed in laissez-faire. He and his advisors felt the economy could repair itself. They did not want to start federal programs that took power from state and local governments. They thought that federal government interference destroyed individual freedom. At first, he did little. He held White House conferences with busi-

ness leaders. He encouraged them to increase production and raise wages, but little came of these meetings.

However, Hoover's efforts were not enough. The economy spiraled downward. In 1932, the GNP was half of what it was in 1920. More than 5,000 banks had closed. Wages and prices continued to fall, and by 1932, unemployment rose by nearly 20 percent.

Other groups took actions. States and cities set up soup kitchens to feed the growing numbers of poor. However, with people out of work, the taxes paid to states and local governments shrank. They had little money for welfare programs. They looked to the federal government for assistance, but little came.

In 1932, Congress passed a law letting the Federal Reserve Bank expand business credit. The problem was **incentive** (expectation of reward). Business sees reward in rising consumer demand. With consumers out of work or earning less, they were unable to demand goods. People made do with less and demand continued to shrink in the sagging market. Businesses saw no incentive to borrow to expand their production, even if the government made the loans very reasonable.

While many were unemployed, most people managed to hold onto their jobs. However, with demand for goods and services shrinking, employers did cut hours and wages. Many people had to take second jobs, if they could find the additional work. Some people could not pay their rents and mortgages. Some became homeless. Some moved into shantytowns and got food from churches. There was shame in all of this. People take pride in being able to support their families. Sadly many unemployed fathers abandoned their families.

LABOR FORCE AND UNEMPLOYMENT: 1929-1941 (NUMBERS IN MILLIONS)

YEAR	LABOR FORCE	NUMBER UNEMPLOYED	PERCENT UNEMPLOYED
1929	49.2	1.6	3.2
1930	49.8	4.3	8.7
1931	50.4	8.0	15.9
1932	51.0	12.1	23.6
1933	51.6	12.8	24.9
1934	52.2	11.3	21.7
1935	52.9	10.6	20.1
1936	53.4	9.0	16.9
1937	54.0	7.7	14.3
1938	54.6	10.4	19.0
1939	55.2	9.5	17.2
1940	55.6	8.1	14.6
1941	55.9	5.6	9.9

Dynamic Response: The New Deal

In the election of 1932, the people expressed their dismay with Hoover's restrained leadership. Democrat **Franklin Delano Roosevelt** (FDR) promised a **"New Deal"** – aggressive action by the government to fight the Great Depression. FDR won a landslide victory and pulled many Democratic candidates for Congress into office with him. Roosevelt won 59% of the popular votes (23 million to Hoover's 16 million), and he won 88% of the electoral vote (472-87).

Once in the White House, President Franklin D. Roosevelt and his advisors took a more aggressive approach to the problems of the Great Depression than had Hoover's administration. Instead of focusing on stimulating business, FDR's administration took actions to restore the public's confidence. The New Deal tried government programs to increase consumer spending. The media nicknamed the process "pump priming." When the government put a little money into the system, it would get the main buying and selling mechanism operating again. His "Three Rs" were edging away from laissez-faire as government launched more economic programs.

Roosevelt quickly took dramatic action to boost the country's confidence. Banks were closing at the rate of 5,000 per year in 1932 and 1933. People were frightened and withdrawing money. Without depositors' money, banks could not make new loans for business and purchasing. Right after his inauguration, FDR closed all banks, had them examined for soundness, and reopened the ones in good condition. The President went on nationwide radio and talked to the people directly in his first **"fireside chat."** He told them that their money would be safer in the banks than "under the mattress." In the weeks that followed, the bank crisis subsided, and people began depositing their money again. Throughout the Depression and World War II, Roosevelt used the fireside chats to rebuild public confidence that the country could survive its problems.

In the first four months after taking office, FDR and his advisors pushed a whirlwind of bills through Congress. Among the laws of this **"Hundred Days"** period were a number of programs designed to attack economic problems and get the economy moving. The New Deal was not a plan; it was an experiment. Some of the ideas worked and some did not. The main thing was that government was trying to lead in a dynamic way. FDR continued to push new programs to rebuild the people's faith in government, and he was overwhelmingly re-elected in 1936.

FDR's Responses: Key New Deal Actions

Action	Reason
Federal Emergency Relief Administration (1933)	Federal money was given to states to help unemployed and poor.
Civil Works Administration (1933)	Gave the unemployed work on federal, state, and municipal road and clean-up projects.
Agricultural Adjustment Administration (1933)	Restored farmers purchasing power; paid farmers to reduce surplus production to raise prices.
National Industrial Recovery Administration (1933)	Set up plans for businesses on wages, prices, and working hours.
Civilian Conservation Corps (1933)	Environmental projects to give work to 16-30 year-olds.
Federal Deposit Insurance Corporation (1933)	Provided deposit insurance to make people confident in banks.
Securities and Exchange Commission (1934)	Regulated the trading of stocks and bonds.
Social Security Administration (1935)	Provided government pensions for older people.
National Labor Relations Act (1935)	Guaranteed workers collective bargaining process (*Wagner Act*).
Fair Labor Standards Act (1938)	Set up a minimum wage of 44 cents/hour and controlled child labor.

I've lost my brakes!

I thought you had some control!

ROOSEVELT LEADERSHIP

HOUSE

SENATE

CONGRESS

PUBLIC

FDR's spirit of reform was very popular, but not everyone appreciated all the New Deal activity. For one thing, he unbalanced the government's budget. He spent more than the government took in revenue from taxes and tariffs. Economists call this **deficit spending**. It put the government in debt, and critics were uncomfortable about the unbalanced budget.

Most state and local governments responded well to the offers of New Deal aid. However, some conservatives opposed federal interference, and a number of rural communities refused to participate. Critics said government was getting too big. They labeled the government programs "FDR's creeping socialism."

No one liked the idea of government interfering with the economy. However, New Deal supporters hoped that government programs like the Civil Works Administration and Civilian Conservation Corps would generate buyers' demand. They hoped the boost in income would "jump start" business activity and economic growth. Defenders of the New Deal said government was the only part of society that had the power to repair the economy.

Critics of the New Deal pointed out that with each step the government takes into the economy, some individual economic freedom is lost. Each program had a cost, government debt grew, and the taxpayer had to pay that debt. Critics were angry as government grew and the old idea of laissez-faire declined.

CRITICISMS OF THE NEW DEAL

- The growth in federal spending to finance the New Deal
- The growth in federal debt to finance the New Deal unbalanced the budget
- The growth of the federal agencies and their staffs
- The stretching of legislative and executive power

In 1936, some businessmen formed the American Liberty League. It raised funds for conservative candidates to oppose the New Deal. The League backed Kansas Governor **Alf Landon**, the Republican Party's Presidential candidate in 1936. In another landslide, FDR received 28 million popular votes to Landon's 17 million. (FDR won 523 of the 531 electoral votes.)

Opponents of some New Deal laws began to challenge them in the Supreme Court. By 1935, the Court found several of FDR's programs unconstitutional (e.g., the *National Industrial Recovery Act* in *Schechter Poultry Corp. v. U.S.* and the *Agricultural Adjustment Act* in *U.S. v. Butler*). In 1937, FDR tried to get Congress to change the Court to make it friendlier to the New Deal. He proposed legislation that would let him name additional federal judges. The newspapers thought the President was going too far. They called his proposal the "**Court Packing Plan**." The plan received nationwide criticism. Congress checked the President by refusing to pass the judicial law he wanted.

Critics were outraged when President Roosevelt decided to run for a third term in 1940. At the time, it was legal (there was no constitutional limit on the number of presidential terms). However, it broke a long tradition. The two-term precedent went back 150 years to George Washington. Critics felt that a third term for FDR undermined the constitutional principle of limited power. FDR won the third term by a popular vote of 55 %to 45% (electoral vote = 449-82). Later, he won a fourth time by the same margin in 1944. (In 1951, the **Twenty-second Amendment** to the Constitution was adopted to limit Presidents to two terms.)

There were also critics that said the government did not do enough for the people. They included California's Doctor **Francis Townsend**, Louisiana's Senator **Huey Long** who wanted assistance for the poor and the farmer, and Michigan's "Radio Priest," Father **Charles Coughlin**.

Doctor Townsend led an old folks crusade for larger pensions and health care for the elderly. Senator Long wanted more social programs and welfare aid. Father Coughlin called for more socialist programs. He wanted the government to print and distribute more money (inflation). He wanted government to run the banks as governments were doing in Europe.

The New Deal did not help minority groups very much. African Americans always suffered from discrimination in housing and jobs. However, in the Great Depression, they saw increased layoffs, foreclosures, and evictions. In 1932, African Americans made up nearly 20% of the unemployed. By 1935, three times as many African Americans were on relief as whites. FDR did have some African Americans as advisors including **A. Philip Randolph**, **Ralph Bunche**, **Robert Weaver**, and **Mary McLeod Bethune**, a director of the National Youth Administration.

Native Americans did little better than African Americans. However, the ***Indian Reorganization Act*** (Wheeler Act, 1934) gave them greater control over their lands. It improved educational opportunities for Native American youth. A special bureau was also created for reservation work under the CCC (Civilian Conservation Corps).

Dorothea Lange Photo – *Depression Mother*
Library of Congress

THE CULTURE OF THE THIRTIES

History shows that art and literature reflect what is happening in a society. In the Great Depression, there were two themes: change and escape. The New Deal had programs to help creative artists. The Works Projects Administration paid artists to decorate buildings, and it set up oral history, regional folklore, and photographic projects. The WPA helped photojournalists, such as **Dorothea Lange**, produce dramatic records of rural life and poverty in the Great Depression. Playwrights and choreographers created new works under the **Federal Theater Project**. Many of these plays criticized society for causing the problems of the 1930s and called for radical change.

In the entertainment field, writers, movies, and radio catered to the public's desire to escape the problems of the Depression. Americans loved to watch films with Fred Astair and Ginger Rogers or Shirley Temple dancing their cares away. They wanted to laugh with the Marx Brothers or the "Little Rascals." They wanted to escape to other times and places with films like *King Kong*, the *Wizard of Oz*, or *Tarzan*. In their homes, it was the same. Popular radio helped them enjoy the comedy of Jack Benny, the music of Bing Crosby, or the adventure programs such as *Suspense* and *Mercury Theater*.

INTERNATIONAL EFFECTS OF THE DEPRESSION

The European and American economies were interdependent. European nations and their colonial empires in Africa, Asia, and the Pacific endured the Great Depression, too. Trade and loans tied the industrial economies together. Just as in the United States, Europe's credit and the money supply contracted, and demand declined causing businesses to fail and unemployment to rise. Also as in the United States, governments were not geared to meet such a financial collapse. In almost every major industrial nation, governments lost popular support. Several new democracies were formed in Central Europe as a result of the *Treaty of Versailles* after World War I. They were very fragile and the wrecked economy hurt them. Countries such as Hungary, Czechoslovakia, and Latvia were still struggling to rebuild after the War. The Depression stopped their development.

Italian Fascist leader Benito Mussolini and German Fuehrer Adolf Hitler parade together in Munich, 18 June 1940. Photo credit: U.S. National Archives

Older countries struggled in the 1920s also. Britain's national wealth had been drained by the War. France saw great damage during the War. It was still rebuilding when the Great Depression struck. In Russia, the communists reorganized the country and called it the U.S.S.R. (Union of Soviet Socialist Republics). **Josef Stalin** made it a **totalitarian** state (government exercises absolute control over all aspects of life). In Japan, the military leaders took over and ran the country behind the scenes.

In Italy, **Benito Mussolini** took over the government in 1922. Through terror tactics and propaganda, his Fascist Party ruled Italy tightly. Italy became a totalitarian state. The Fascists Party began public works projects and built up the military. When the Great Depression hit, Mussolini began to use the military. He set out to spread Italy's power in the Mediterranean. In the 1930s, Italy launched attacks on Ethiopia and Albania to keep military spending stimulating the economy.

Germany had a weak democratic government after the Kaiser abdicated. Germany not only had to rebuild, but the *Treaty of Versailles* required it to make **reparation** payments to help repair the Allied countries. In the 1920s, there were strikes and terrible inflation wracking the country. No one party could control the government and there was chaos. When the Great Depression came, Germany's government was too weak to solve the economic problems.

Germans resented being punished for losing World War I, and **Adolf Hitler** used their resentment to take power. His Nazi Party rallied angry Germans by denouncing the *Treaty of Versailles* and the reparations. The Nazis blamed communists, Jews, and surrounding nations for conditions in Germany.

In 1933, Hitler became chancellor. He put his fellow Nazi Party members in powerful positions. Germany became a totalitarian state. The government controlled the mass media, education, and religion. Criticism of the government was forbidden.

Hitler launched a drive to rebuild Germany's military power. This action violated the *Treaty of Versailles*. The League of Nations condemned Hitler, but did nothing to stop him. Unconcerned, Hitler pushed large amounts of money into armaments. This government demand for weapons stimulated the economy. Spending by arms manufacturers and their workers for goods and raw materials spurred the rest of the economy.

In the United States, there was some concern with what was going on in Europe, but Congress and the President were still focused on the New Deal. Americans of the 1930s still had bad feelings at the way World War I had ended. Most Americans showed little concern for Europe or any place else in the world. The U.S. was one of the most powerful and wealthy nations on Earth. Yet, among a majority of the people, there was a quiet, wishful pretense that America could remain isolated from what was happening across the Atlantic.

REMINDER: For help in handling questions, see ADVICE CHART on page 184.

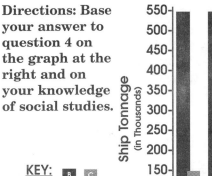

UNIT 9
MULTIPLE CHOICE

1 President Warren Harding was popular with the American people because he
   1 tried to create harmony and a return to "normalcy"
   2 began a series of programs offering equal opportunity to all regardless of race
   3 took strong steps to enforce the prohibition of alcohol
   4 moved to have the U.S. join the League of Nations

Directions: Base your answer to question 2 on the graph below and on your knowledge of social studies.

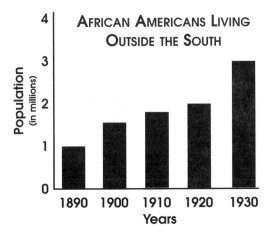

AFRICAN AMERICANS LIVING OUTSIDE THE SOUTH

2 Which is a statement of fact about African Americans living outside of the South?
   1 African American mitration to the North slowed after World War I.
   2 The fewest African Americans lived outside the South from 1910-1920.
   3 The graph shows that most African American migrants ended up in Northern slums.
   4 The largest number of African Americans lived outside the South from 1920-1930.

3 A major factor helping to provide more consumer goods for Americans in the 1920s was the
   1 development of sophisticated robots
   2 institution of large-scale assembly line production
   3 tremendous increase in imports of automobiles from the U.S.S.R.
   4 use of computers to improve the speed of production

Directions: Base your answer to question 4 on the graph at the right and on your knowledge of social studies.

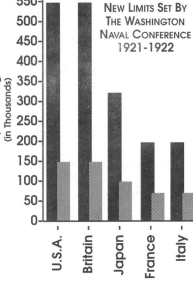

KEY: BATTLESHIP CARRIER

NEW LIMITS SET BY THE WASHINGTON NAVAL CONFERENCE 1921-1922

4 The Washington Naval Conference (1921-1922) allowed the
   1 largest aircraft carrier tonnage to France and Italy
   2 Japanese to have double the battleship tonnage of the U.S.
   3 U.S. and Britain to have the greatest battleship tonnage
   4 Italians to equal Japan in aircraft carrier tonnage

Directions: Base your answer to question 5 on the poem, "I Too," below and on your knowledge of social studies.

> I, too sing America.
> I am the darker brother
> They send me to eat in the kitchen
> When company comes,
> But I laugh
> And eat well
> And grow strong
> Tomorrow,
> I'll be at the table
> When company comes
> Nobody'll dare
> Say to me,
> "Eat in the kitchen,"
> Then.
>
> – Langston Hughes, 1926

5 In this poem, African American poet Langston Hughes is expressing
   1 optimism that conditions will improve for African Americans
   2 concern that African Americans will always be household workers
   3 a desire to see an improvement in the diet of African Americans
   4 support for the way African Americans were treated in the U.S. in the 1920s

6　During the 1920s the Harding and Coolidge administrations adopted a policy of
1　joining international trade groups
2　quickly persecuting anti-trust violations
3　removing all trade barriers
4　laissez-faire toward businesses

7　During the late 1920s, the signs of economic distress that began to appear in the American economy included
1　a decline in demand for American farm products
2　little interest in investment in stocks
3　a sizable increase in the hourly wage for factory workers
4　a decline in overall factory production

Directions: Base your answer to question 8 on the photograph below.

White Angel Bread Line, San Francisco, 1933.
(Photograph by Dorothea Lange.)

8　This 1930s Dorothea Lange photograph represents the
1　escape from everyday life offered by motion pictures
2　mood of "normalcy" after World War I
3　atmosphere of the Jazz Age
4　despair of many during the Great Depression

9　In a number of European countries, an effect of the Great Depression was
1　an increase in control by local governments
2　the establishment of economic organizations to increase unity
3　a rise in totalitarian governments
4　the beginning of free trade among nations

Directions: Base your answer to question 10 on the diagram below and on your knowledge of social studies.

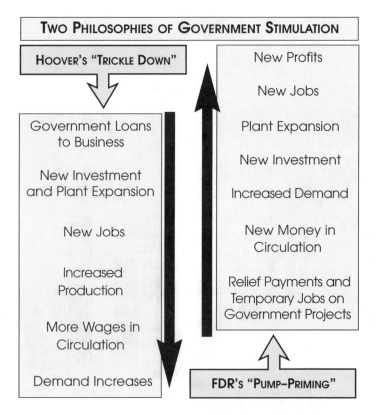

TWO PHILOSOPHIES OF GOVERNMENT STIMULATION

HOOVER'S "TRICKLE DOWN"

Government Loans to Business

New Investment and Plant Expansion

New Jobs

Increased Production

More Wages in Circulation

Demand Increases

New Profits

New Jobs

Plant Expansion

New Investment

Increased Demand

New Money in Circulation

Relief Payments and Temporary Jobs on Government Projects

FDR'S "PUMP-PRIMING"

10　A major difference between Hoover and Roosevelt in solving the problems of the Great Depression was that
1　Roosevelt placed businesses first and Hoover ignored them
2　Hoover's approach to the problems was more aggressive than Roosevelt's
3　Roosevelt wanted to help the people first and Hoover placed businesses first
4　Hoover worked from the bottom up and Roosevelt from the top down

Constructed Response

Set 1

Directions: Base your answers to questions 1 and 2 on the illustration at the right and on your knowledge of social studies.

1 Identify TWO (2) of the items in the drawing that symbolized life in "The Roaring Twenties."

_____

_____

2 For ONE (1) of the items identified, explain the effect it had on life in the 1920s.

_____

_____

Set 2

Directions: Base your answers to questions 3 through 5 on the cartoon and on your knowledge of social studies.

3 Identify TWO (2) reasons that African Americans moved North in the 1920s.

_____

_____

_____

4 What type of work were the African Americans leaving behind in the South?

_____

_____

5 Briefly describe the conditions many African Americans faced in the North after they moved.

_____

_____

_____

Practice Skills for DBQ

Directions: The following task is based on the accompanying documents. The documents may have been edited for the purposes of this exercise. The task is designed to test your ability to work with historical documents. As you analyze the documents, take into account both the source of the document and the author's point of view where relevant.

Historical Context: Beginning in 1929, the United States entered the Great Depression. It was a time when the country faced many economic, social, and political problems. When President Franklin Delano Roosevelt took office in 1933, he offered a plan, "The New Deal," to deal with these problems and ease the difficulties people were facing.

Part A - Short Answer

Document 1

1 According to President Roosevelt, what were TWO (2) problems that Americans faced in 1933?

_____

_____

_____

> "This great nation will continue as it has and will prosper. So, first of all. Let me state my firm belief that the only thing we have to fear is fear itself - nameless, unreasoning, unjustified terror which paralyzes needed efforts to bring about change.
>
> "Values have shrunken to fantastic levels; taxes have risen; our ability to pay has fallen; government of all kinds is faced by serious need of funds; industries lie wounded; farmers find no markets for their produce; the savings of many years in thousands of families are gone.
>
> "More important, a host of unemployed citizens face the grim problem of surviving, and an equally great number work for little wages."
>
> – President Franklin Delano Roosevelt, First Inaugural Address, 1933

Document 2

KEY NEW DEAL ACTIONS	
Action	**Reason**
Civil Works Administration (1933)	Gave the unemployed work on federal, state, and municipal road and clean-up projects.
Agricultural Adjustment Administration (1933)	Restored farmers purchasing power; paid farmers to reduce surplus production to raise prices.
Civilian Conservation Corps (1933)	Setup environmental projects to give work to 16-30 year-olds.
Federal Deposit Insurance Corporation (1933)	Provided deposit insurance to make people confident in banks.
Securities and Exchange Commission (1934)	Regulated the trading of stocks and bonds.
Social Security Administration (1935)	Provided government pensions for older people.

2 Select TWO (2) of the programs started under the New Deal and for each one selected, explain what it did to ease a problem identified in Roosevelt's speech.

_____

_____

_____

_____

Part B - Essay Response

Task: Identify at least TWO (2) problems the U.S. faced during the Great Depression and discuss ONE (1) action that the FDR administration took to try to solve each problem identified. (State your thesis in the introduction.)

ADDITIONAL SUGGESTED TASK

From your knowledge of social studies, make a list of additional problems the U.S. faced during the Great Depression and along side each problem, list an action taken by the FDR Administration to try to solve it.

THE UNITED STATES ASSUMES WORLDWIDE RESPONSIBILITIES

WORLD WAR II:
ORIGINS OF THE WAR

The resentment of Germans for the way they were treated after World War I was a powerful force. They hated the *Treaty of Versailles* and the reparations they had to pay. A strong leader channeled their hatred into a desire for revenge. In this emotional state, they let Hitler assume control of the nation. Like Mussolini in Italy and militarists in Japan, Hitler staged a military buildup and behaved aggressively in the 1930s.

The rest of the world stayed out of the aggressors' way. Afraid of starting another World War, the League of Nations warned the dictators, but did nothing to stop them. There was no response when Hitler moved to unify Austria with Germany in 1938. Later that same year, he moved to annex a German-speaking area of Czechoslovakia. France and Britain protested and called for a conference on the matter. At the **Munich Conference**, they tried to **appease** Hitler.

They agreed to let him take the area if he agreed to stop the aggression. Once he had what he wanted, Hitler ignored his pledge and invaded Poland the following year, beginning World War II.

PRELUDE TO WORLD WAR II		
ACTION	**RESPONSE**	**RESULT**
1931 Japan Invades North Manchuria	League of Nations reprimand; U.S. issues Stimson Doctrine, refuses to recognize Japanese claim to territory.	Japan quits League of Nations, annexes Chinese conquests.
1935 Italy Invades Ethiopia	U.S. passes *Neutrality Act*, no arms sales to belligerents. League of Nations reprimand.	Italy conquers and annexes part of Ethiopia.
1936 Germany Invades Rhineland Region	No response made.	Germans build fortifications along Rhine River borders in violation of Versailles Treaty.
1936 Germany & Italy back Franco in Spanish Civil War	U.S. broadens *Neutrality Acts* to include arms trade ban for civil war belligerents	Franco is victorious, becomes "silent partner" for Axis alliance.
1937 Japan Invades China	FDR calls for "quarantine" of aggressor nations. League of Nations fails with trade embargo against Japan.	Japan conquers and occupies most of N.E. China.
1938 Germany Invades Austria	No response made.	Germany proclaims "Anschluss" – unification of Germany and Austria.
1938 Germany Claims Czech Territory	Britain and France appease Hitler, allow Germans to take over the area at Munich Conference.	Germany annexes Sudetenland region.
1939 Italy Invades Albania	No response made.	Italy conquers and occupies Albania.
1939 Germany & U.S.S.R. Invade Poland	Britain and France declare war; U.S. modifies *Neutrality Acts* to allow "cash and carry."	World War II begins.

ACT	PROVISION
Neutrality Act of 1935	When the President proclaimed that a foreign war existed, no arms could be sold or transported on American ships to the nations involved. No Americans could travel on the ships of warring nations.
Neutrality Act of 1936	When the President proclaimed that a foreign war existed, no loans could be made to the warring nations.
Neutrality Act of 1937	No Americans could travel on ships of warring nations. All provisions of the above *Neutrality Acts* applied to civil wars.
Neutrality Act of 1939	Nations fighting aggression were allowed to buy war material from U.S. manufacturers on a "cash and carry" basis. President could proclaim "danger zones" and forbid U.S. ships to enter the danger zone.

As the winds of war whipped through Europe again, the U.S. played an isolation game. Congress passed *Neutrality Acts* to avoid the problems that had drawn the country into World War I. The Acts kept President Roosevelt from taking any serious diplomatic actions. Historians called it "Storm Cellar Diplomacy" because the country tried to hide from the violence brewing in Europe.

Hitler's rapid conquest of Poland jolted the United States. From 1939 to 1941, the government of the U.S. remained neutral, but began preparing for war. President Roosevelt worked with Canada and Latin American countries on a defense plan. Congress raised taxes and arranged for more military purchasing. National Guard units were placed under U.S. armed forces command. In 1940, Congress set up the nation's first peacetime draft. The *Smith Act* was also passed to keep aliens under surveillance.

After France fell in 1940, only the British stood against Hitler and Mussolini's Axis forces. In the fall of 1940, Britain was being bombed daily by the German air force. The *Neutrality Acts* of the late 1930s blocked President Roosevelt from helping the British. However, as commander-in-chief, FDR made an executive agreement with the British. In the **Destroyers-for-Bases Deal**, the President gave 50 old destroyers to Britain. In return, the British allowed the United States to set up bases in Canada and Bermuda.

At the President's urging, Congress passed a *Lend-Lease Act* in early 1941. It allowed the President to lend and transfer arms and war supplies to Britain and other "victims of aggression." After Hitler attacked the U.S.S.R. in June 1941, Roosevelt extended *Lend-Lease* to the Soviets.

In the summer of 1941, President Roosevelt and Prime Minister **Winston Churchill** drew up an informal set of war aims known as the *Atlantic Charter*. Later the Charter became the basis for the *United Nations Charter*.

London in ruins after Hitler's blitz – the relentless series of air attacks and civilian bombing.
(U.S. National Archives)

Children – orphaned, hungry, and homeless – following the German Blitz on London 1940.
(U.S. National Archives)

Problems also arose in Asia and the Pacific. In the fall of 1940, when Japan joined Germany and Italy in the Axis Alliance, FDR decided to stop shipments of U.S. steel outside the Western Hemisphere (except Britain). The U.S. warned Japan that it disapproved of Japan's aggressions in China and its conquest of French colonies in Southeast Asia. Finally, when Japan attacked Thailand and the nearby French colonies in July 1941, FDR halted nearly all trade with Japan.

American assault troops of the 16th Infantry Regiment, wait by the Chalk Cliffs for evacuation to a field hospital. During the Invasion, thousands were killed or injured while storming Omaha Beach at Collville-sur-Mer, Normandy, 6 June 1944, "D-day." (U.S. National Archives)

U.S.S. Arizona on fire, following the Japanese attack on Pearl Harbor on 7 December 1941.
(Official U.S. Navy photograph)

Japan's ruling military group planned a secret attack against U.S. naval bases. America's main concern was for the forces in the Philippines, which was still a U.S. possession. The Japanese struck **Pearl Harbor** on 7 December 1941 in a surprise attack that wrecked the American fleet. The U.S. lost 18 ships and 200 planes with over 5,000 dead and wounded. The next day, Congress declared war on Japan. A few days later, Japan's Axis allies, Germany and Italy, declared war on the United States.

U.S. WAR STRATEGY

The United States faced a two-front war. FDR and his advisors determined that Germany presented a greater threat than Japan. From bases in England, General Eisenhower launched a steady stream of bombing raids on German production centers. The Allies announced they would seek "unconditional surrender." This meant there would be no peace negotiations or treaty to end the War. In 1943, Allied armies forced the Germans out of North Africa. Also in 1943, the Allies attacked Italy and slowly advanced northward, while the Soviets managed to force the Germans to retreat from Russia.

Finally, with enough men and equipment, General Eisenhower launched "Operation Overlord" in June, 1944. In one month, one million American, British,

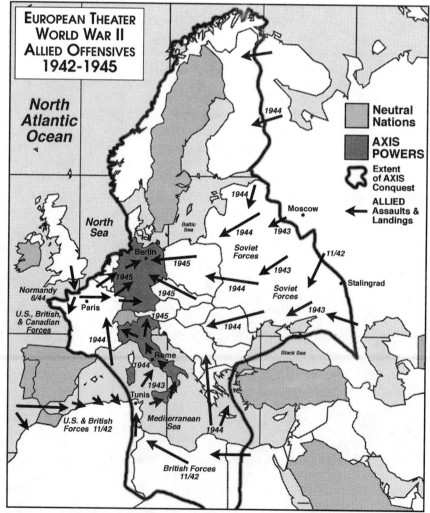

EUROPEAN THEATER WORLD WAR II ALLIED OFFENSIVES 1942-1945

North Atlantic Ocean

Neutral Nations

AXIS POWERS

Extent of AXIS Conquest

ALLIED Assaults & Landings

North Sea

Normandy 6/44

U.S., British, & Canadian Forces

Paris

Berlin

Baltic Sea

Moscow

Soviet Forces

Stalingrad

Soviet Forces

Black Sea

Rome

Tunis

U.S. & British Forces 11/42

Mediterranean Sea

British Forces 11/42

Canadian, and French soldiers invaded France in history's largest amphibious operation. The **D-Day Invasion** used more than 5,000 ships of all kinds and about 11,000 Allied aircraft. In the next year of brutal fighting, the Germans slowly retreated back across France. Early in May 1945, Hitler committed suicide and the Germans surrendered a few days later.

In the Pacific, FDR ordered commanders such as General Douglas MacArthur and Admiral Chester Nimitz to "hold the line" and fight a defensive war against Imperial Japan. In 1942, the Japanese overran the Philippines and threatened Australia. America's few remaining carriers and destroyers raced back and forth blocking the Japanese at Midway and in the Coral Sea. Not until war plants began replacing the ships lost at Pearl Harbor could the Americans throw any weight against Japan. In a brutal six-month battle for the island of Guadalcanal, U.S. Marines handed the Japanese their first major land defeat. Guadalcanal began the Allies' "**island-hopping**" strategy. The Allied forces moved northward toward Tokyo skipping some islands and isolating Japanese forces. The commanders targeted key Japanese bases and launched invasion forces on the most strategic islands with good harbors and airfields to launch new invasions.

NEW KINDS OF WARFARE

World War II was a highly mobile war. Use of fast-moving tanks made battle lines fluid. Hitler's Panzer tanks spearheaded rapid drives into Poland, France, and the U.S.S.R. Supported by waves of fighter planes, these *blitzkriegs* (lightening attacks) threw opponents into retreat.

Continual strategic bombing raids with incendiary bombs interrupted industrial production. They destroyed bridges, railroads, and roads. These behind-the-lines attacks did great damage. In the summer of 1943, for example, three-quarters of Hamburg was destroyed in combined raids. Round-the-clock bombing mounted steadily until all of Germany was subjected to massive air raids.

Air power even altered the War at sea. In several Pacific battles, fighter planes launched from aircraft carriers determined the outcome. At the Battle of the Coral Sea, the ships of the two sides never faced each other. Even un-manned missiles were used. Toward the end of the War, the Germans launched about 1,000 V-2 rocket bombs on Britain, killing and injuring nearly 25,000 people and destroying several cities.

Many civilian lives were lost in World War II from the bombing raids. However, more lives were lost

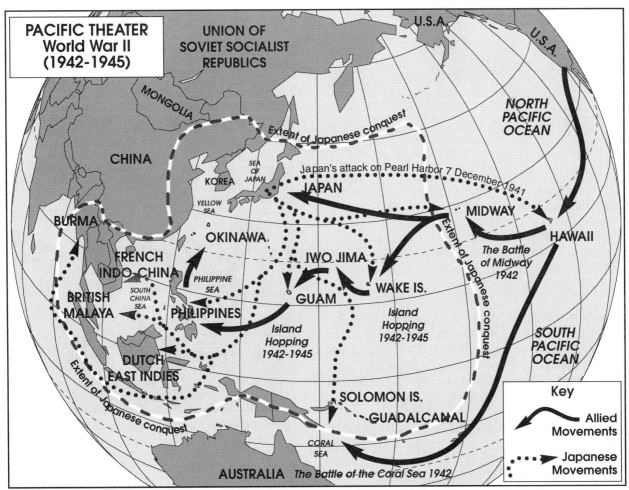

because of the Nazis' program of genocide. Their hatred for gypsies, Christian fundamentalists, and especially Jews led to mass imprisonment and executions before and during the War. The world was shocked beyond belief by the documentation of the systematic exterminations of six million Jews in the Nazi death camps such as Auschwitz, Belzec, and Treblinka. The **Holocaust** could not be brushed aside in dealing with the captured enemy leaders. Later, it was determined that an additional six million gypsies, homosexuals, and Christian fundamentalists were also exterminated by the Nazis.

In the Nazi Concentration Camp at Dachau, prisoners were forced to stand without moving for endless hours as a punishment. (U.S. National Archives)

More inhuman Nazi practices were revealed at the **Nuremberg Trials** conducted by the Allies in 1946. Twenty-two major Nazi leaders were placed on trial for violations of the basic rules of war and inhumane treatment of political prisoners. Half of the accused were sentenced to death, half received prison terms.

Of course, the most devastating weapon was the atomic bomb. Increased Allied bombing of Japan in 1945 did not force a surrender. The Japanese denounced the idea of unconditional surrender and said they would fight to the last. Truman felt that the loss of life in an invasion would be very high.

Scientists working on the **Manhattan Project** in the New Mexico sent word that an atomic weapon had been successfully developed. No none knew how destructive it was, but Truman decided it could end the

War quickly. On 6 August 1945, an American B-29 dropped the first atomic bomb on **Hiroshima**, killing 75,000 people in seconds. There was no reply from the Japanese. On 9 August a second bomb was dropped on the naval base of **Nagasaki**, killing another 75,000.

On 9 August 1945, the United States dropped the 2nd Atomic Bomb of the War, "Fat Man." The photo is of the mushroom cloud as it rose over Nagasaki where 75,000 died from the bomb. (U.S Air Force Photo)

The following day, Japanese Premier **Suzuki** offered to surrender if the Emperor **Hirohito** was allowed to keep his throne. The Allies accepted the Japanese surrender on 14 August 1945. America suffered over a million casualties in World War II (407,000 dead and 700,000 wounded).

The Japanese envoy signs the document of surrender on board the USS Missouri in Tokyo Bay, 2 September 1945. (U.S. National Archives)

ECONOMIC WAR AGENCIES

Agency	Purpose
War Production Board	Supervised military production; it forbade production of "nonessential items" such as autos, kitchen appliances, and toys).
War Manpower Commission	Kept trained workers moving into the nation's factories; in 1939, unemployment was 17.2 percent, by 1945, it was 1.9 percent; weekly wages jumped from $25.25 in 1939 to $47.08 in 1945.
War Labor Board	Kept the country relatively strike-free; the government helped with temporary housing units for factories.
Office of Price Administration (OPA)	Controlled scarce consumer goods; it supervised this rationing program so that people would be able to get a fair share of goods in short supply (shoes, sugar, coffee, tires, gasoline).

Cartoon illustrating humorous side of OPA restrictions (1943).
(O.Soglow – National Archives)

THE HOME FRONT

World War II brought many social and economic changes at home. It moved the country out of the Great Depression. Total resource mobilization meant President Roosevelt had to convert the country's economic capacity to war production. This created scarcity and government had to regulate supplies through **rationing** (see charts). Congress created agencies to manage the home front. Federal spending jumped from 20 billion dollars in 1941 to almost 98.4 billion dollars in 1945. FDR persuaded industry to donate the services of their top managers such as Sears-Roebuck's Donald M. Nelson, who ran the War Production Board.

World War II cost the American people more than $300 billion. To finance it, Congress raised income taxes. Also, Congress made employers withhold taxes from workers' paychecks. War bond purchases accounted for nearly two-thirds of government war revenues. The government made it patriotic to buy war bonds. Americans heard and saw daily appeals to buy bonds in newspapers, on the radio, and at the movies. Famous entertainers such as Kate Smith, Jane Froman, Al Jolson, Frank Sinatra, Bob Hope, and Bing Crosby staged bond rallies around the country.

World War II expanded the role of women in the economy. As men were drafted for military service, seventeen million women entered the work force. Many women took non-traditional jobs. Patriotic posters, animated film shorts, and even a pop song glorified a new American heroine, *"Rosie the Riveter."*

RATIONING REGULATIONS

"Each person, regardless of age, will be allowed sixteen points a week for the whole group of new items to be rationed. There will be no exact meat ration, although the amount of meat available will average two pounds per person per week ...

"Blue stamps in War Ration Book No. 2 are used for most canned goods and for dried peas, beans, lentils and frozen commodities like fruit juice.

"The Red stamps are used for meats, canned fish, butter, hard cheese, edible fats, and canned milk.

"You have to give up more points when buying scarce food than when buying the same quantity of a plentiful one ..."

– Office of Price Administration, *Directives*, Washington, DC, March 1943.

"Rosie the Riveter" – Women welders in Connecticut war production plant, 1943.   (Library of Congress)

Factories set up day care and nursery schools near their defense plants. More than a quarter of a million women joined newly created corps of the Army (WACs), Navy (Waves), Marines, and Coast Guard to relieve men of non-combatant duties. However, after the War, women were dismissed from jobs in favor of returning servicemen. Very little of the workplace equality and status women achieved during the War lasted into the postwar era.

On the home front, there was fear of an invasion by the enemy, especially when German submarines were spotted off the Atlantic Coast. There was greater fear that spies and saboteurs were at large in the country.

The War created many problems for minority groups. After Pearl Harbor, people on the West Coast were in a near-panic. Japanese-Americans were most densely settled in California. Anti-Japanese prejudice became strong. In the emotional atmosphere, people made allegations of disloyalty against Japanese aliens and **Nisei** (U.S. citizens of Japanese ancestry).

The government feared sabotage and espionage. In the early spring of 1942, the Western Defense Commander advised the President to set up the War Relocation Authority. Soldiers rounded up 100,000 Japanese-Americans, most of them citizens. The WRA sent them to ten relocation centers in Arkansas, Arizona, Utah and several other western states. Many remained in these **internment camps** for the duration of the War. (Citizens of German and Italian descent were not treated in this way.)

Opponents protested that the relocation was race discrimination. It was challenged in the Supreme Court as a denial of constitutional due process rights. In *Korematsu v. U.S.* (1944), the Court said the War fit the "clear and present danger" rule based on the World War I era *Schenck* decision (1919). The Court upheld the government's relocation.

Even after the *Korematsu Decision*, Japanese-Americans campaigned against this great injustice. In the 1950s and 1960s, the Nisei won appeals. Partial compensation was made by the government for their suffering. Finally, in 1988, President Reagan signed a bill that publicly apologized to the Japanese American internees and granted to each of the survivors a tax-free payment of $20,000.

THE IMPACT OF THE WAR

The surrender of the Axis powers ended fighting that engulfed the world for six years. Entire countries were physically and demographically devastated. In loss of lives, World War II was the costliest war in history. Rough figures can only approximate the loss of lives at between 15 and 20 million military personnel killed. Civilian dead numbered approximately 25 million. Expenditures for war materials and armaments totaled at least $1.154 trillion. It is impossible to estimate the cost of the physical damage inflicted. Britain, France, Germany, and Japan were physically and financially destroyed by the War.

OF JAPANESE ANCESTRY ...

"We were the last group of Japanese-Americans to leave Los Angeles. I was full of deep emotion when I thought that from tomorrow there would be not even one Japanese walking the greater Los Angeles area...
"Roll call started at 6:00 A.M. We all got instructions and boarded the train ... In each coach there were two soldiers with rifles and bayonets ... At 5:45 P.M., the train crossed the Colorado River and arrived at the station... Buses came ... Finally we arrived at the camp... My family registered and got Block 45-1-C. It was no better than a beggar's hut. We had to make our own mattresses by filling bags with hay... I felt like crying..."
– Kasen Noda in *War Relocation Memoirs and Diaries*, 29 May 1942

These young evacuees of Japanese ancestry await their turn for baggage inspection upon arrival at the Assembly Center in Turlock, CA, 2 May 1942.
(photo Dorothea Lange, U.S. National Archives)

ESTIMATED WORLD WAR II LOSSES		
Nation	**Battle Deaths***	**Civilian Deaths**
U.S.S.R.	7,500,000	10,000,000
Germany	3,500,000	500,000
China	2,200,000	6,000,000
Japan	1,500,000	600,000
Britain	300,000	65,000
France	210,000	400,000
Italy	200,000	145,000
United States	292,000	115,000

* Combat Soldiers

THE POSTWAR WORLD
PEACE EFFORTS

At the Teheran and Yalta **summit meetings**, Franklin Roosevelt and British Prime Minister Winston Churchill bargained intensely with Stalin to create effective world peace organization, the **United Nations**. He knew the organization could survive only with the cooperation of the United States and the Soviet Union.

British Prime Minister Winston Churchill, along with U.S. President Franklin Roosevelt and Soviet Premier Josef Stalin, attend the conference at Yalta. (Library of Congress)

On 25 April 1945, less than two weeks after FDR's death, 50 nations met in San Francisco to sign the United Nations charter. It created a **General Assembly** to be the great debating body of all member nations. The charter set up the **Security Council** to negotiate disputes among nations or use force to stop acts of aggression. The Security Council is dominated by the great powers. Each of the five permanent members of the Security Council (Britain, China, France, U.S.A., and U.S.S.R.) have a **veto**. Sometimes the U.N. has failed to stop aggression because of disagreements among the great powers. However, the U.N. has brought world problems to public attention, coordinated humanitarian actions to save lives, and assisted former colonies to become independent nations.

POLITICAL RESULTS OF WORLD WAR II

The Allies divided Germany and its capital, Berlin into four occupation zones, but could not set up a central administration for the zones; the Allies failed to negotiate a peace treaty.

The Allies divided Austria and its capital, Vienna into four zones, but could not formulate a peace treaty.

In 1946, the four Allies worked out peace treaties with lesser countries of the Axis alliance (Italy, Romania, Bulgaria, Hungary, and Finland).

50 nations signed the charter creating the United Nations at the San Francisco Conference in 1945.

U.S.S.R. created puppet or "satellite" governments in Eastern Europe (East Germany, Poland, Hungary, Czechoslovakia, Romania, and Bulgaria).

U.S. military occupied Japan; Gen. MacArthur set up a democratic constitution and made the emperor a constitutional monarch; U.S. rebuilt the economy, but it broke up industrial and banking monopolies; peace treaty signed in 1951.

In 1948, the United Nations adopted the ***Universal Declaration of Human Rights***. It sums up the ideals to which all freedom-loving people have long aspired. It states that all individuals should be able to live their lives in peace and dignity, free from the oppression of political forces and discrimination. The Declaration became a set of goals for justice and human dignity throughout the world.

COLD WAR

The spirit of cooperation that allowed the Allies to defeat Hitler did not last very long. The United States and the Soviet Union emerged as the two **superpowers**. Most other major nations were falling apart after the War. The U.S. was not damaged physically, and its productive capacity was greatly enlarged. The U.S.S.R. lost more military and civilian lives than any country involved in World War II. The fighting in the U.S.S.R. left great damage. However, Soviet dictator Josef Stalin pushed the government-owned factories hard during the War and greatly increased the country's production.

Throughout its history, Russia had been invaded from the west. Stalin mistrusted western nations that opposed the communist system. He wanted a **buffer** (protection area) between his country and Western Europe. Stalin decided that the U.S.S.R. would control the small countries of Eastern Europe. Soviet troops already occupied Eastern Europe from the great drive on Germany at the end of the War. The other Allies wanted the countries free and independent, but the Soviets remained. The Soviets set up puppet or "satellite" communist governments under their control.

POST WORLD WAR II ALLIANCES

NATO Countries (NATO nations not shown include Canada and U.S.) 1949 to present

Warsaw Pact Countries 1955-1991

Non-aligned Countries

Strong economies can resist economic rebellion and violence and keep democratic governments stable. Truman and his advisors realized that all of Western Europe needed financial help to rebuild after World War II. In 1947, they convinced Congress to create an aid program called the **Marshall Plan**. Sixteen countries received $13.15 billion in U.S. aid from 1948 to 1952. The Marshall Plan revived, stabilized, and strengthened the economy of Western Europe.

In 1948, the United States, Britain, and France decided to unify their occupation zones in Germany. The Soviets refused to unify their zone. The city of Berlin was inside the Soviet Zone, but it was divided into four occupation zones also. The Soviets blocked land access from the unified zone into the city. For more than a year, Britain and the U.S. kept the Western part of the city alive. The **Berlin Airlift** flew more than 2 million tons of supplies to Berlin. The Soviets finally lifted the blockade in September of 1949.

The world became divided into two camps: the United States and its Western European allies, and the U.S.S.R. and communist countries. This bipolar struggle became known as the **Cold War**. For the next generation, the two camps opposed each other in many ways. Each side tried to restrain the influence of the other. The U.S. even used the term "**containment**" to describe its policy. Every action seems to have been met with a counter balancing action. For example, in 1949, western nations set up a military alliance called **NATO** (North Atlantic Treaty Organization) for **collective security**. The U.S.S.R. set up an opposing military alliance with Eastern European countries – the **Warsaw Pact**.

CONTAINMENT

CONTAINMENT IN EUROPE

During the postwar era, whenever the U.S. sensed that the Soviet camp was trying to spread its influence, it took action to counter balance the Soviets. In 1947, President Truman saw the Soviets helping communist groups take over Greece and Turkey. He asked Congress for financial aid. This part of the containment became known as the **Truman Doctrine**.

"The free people of the world look to us for support in maintaining their freedom. If we falter in our leadership we may endanger the peace of the world – and we shall surely endanger the welfare of our own nation."
– Pres. Truman to Congress asking for aid to Greece and Turkey, 1947

CONTAINMENT IN ASIA

The struggle to contain communist expansion went beyond Europe. When Japan surrendered in World War II, its troops left the Asian mainland. In China, communists and nationalists resumed an earlier civil war. The Soviets sent supplies and advisors to **Mao Zedong**'s communist forces, the U.S. aided **Jiang Jeshi**'s (Chaing Kai Shek) nationalists. U.S. diplomats failed at negotiat-

Germany Post World War II

ing a truce and general elections. The communists forced the nationalists into exile on Taiwan in 1949.

On the Korean Peninsula, another long Cold War struggle unfolded. After World War II, Japan gave up Korea as a colony. The U.S.S.R. moved troops to occupy the northern half of Korea. The U.S. occupied the southern half. The U.N. was supposed to organize democratic elections and unify the country. The elections were held in the south in 1947. The Republic of Korea was set up in 1948, and the U.S. withdrew. In the north, the Soviets refused to unify. They set up a separate country with a communist government.

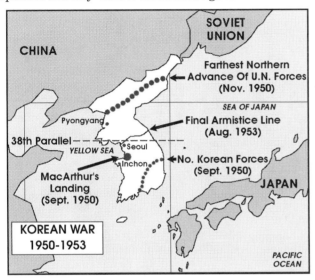

In June 1950, the **Korean War** began. North Korean forces invaded South Korea and pushed its forces southward. The U.S. asked the U.N. Security Council to send assistance to the South Koreans. The Soviets were not present at the Security Council and could not veto the U.S. request. A 17-nation coalition force, spearheaded by the U.S., pushed the North Koreans back in a few months. Continued fighting brought China into the War to help North Korea. The War stalemated until a truce ended the fighting in June 1953. There were nearly 1.8 million military casualties in the Korean War.

U.S. & WORLD TURMOIL
END OF COLONIAL EMPIRES

The post World War II era saw a breakdown of the European colonial empires in Asia and Africa. Devastated by the War, Britain, France, and other European countries were too weak to keep up their overseas colonies. In some areas, nationalists campaigned for independence even before World War II. Colonial powers did not always prepare their colonies for independence. They did improve transportation, city facilities, and education. However, these things were done so that it was easier to run the colonial industries that extracted raw materials.

After World War II, colonial independence movements became stronger. Some even became violent. There are many examples of the struggle for colonial independence becoming Cold War battlegrounds. The superpowers tried to influence the new countries. Soviet-supported communist groups fought for power against those who wanted democracy.

Often, the United States sent aid to help the emerging nations maintain freedom. The U.S. granted independence to the Philippines in 1946. The U.S. found itself supporting democratic governments against communist rebels in many places. After Britain granted independence to India in 1947, the U.S. and Soviets tried to influence the Indian government. India chose neutrality. However, Pakistan became an American ally. In Vietnam, communist rebels forced France to grant independence in 1954. As with Korea, Vietnam was split into a communist north and a democratic south.

The former colonies that became nations between 1945 and the 1970s were poor and not economically balanced. They could sell raw materials and cash crops, but they had no way of supplying finished goods to their people. These **LDCs** (Less Developed Countries) made up a new global political force – the **Third World**. Supposedly, Third World countries were aligned with neither the communists nor the democratic countries. In reality, most found neutrality brought them nothing. Some had strong economic ties to their former colonial masters. Some wanted to be

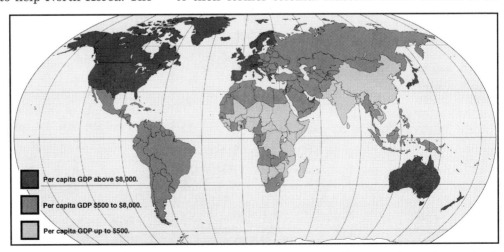

The "Have" and "Have Not" Countries (based on per capita gross domestic product) In general, the lower the per capita GDP, the lower the standard of living and the poorer the country. In most cases, the low GDP countries are the "have nots" or LDCs.

free of those ties. Some favored whichever side would give it the most assistance. Behind the scenes, the superpowers competed for their favor.

COLD WAR FLASH POINTS

The Cold War went on for more than two generations (1940s-1990s). From 1945 to 1949, only the U.S. had nuclear bombs. In 1949, the U.S.S.R. exploded its first nuclear device, followed by Britain and France. In the early 1950s, both superpowers exploded **hydrogen bombs**, which were hundreds of times more powerful than those dropped in 1945. The world realized that nuclear confrontation between the superpowers could destroy human civilization.

The superpowers often exchanged angry words and threats. More often, they confronted each other indirectly through smaller allies as they did in Korea. Key flash points appeared: the Middle East, Cuba, and Southeast Asia.

The great supplies of petroleum made the Middle East an important area. The conflicts over creating a Jewish country (Israel) in the midst of the Muslim World made affairs complex. The U.S. supported nationhood for Israel. The U.S.S.R. took the Muslim side and aided neighboring countries such as Egypt and Syria. In the 1950s, President Eisenhower applied the idea of the *Truman Doctrine* to the Middle East. He asked Congress for funds to contain communist aggression. When the Soviets backed a revolution in Lebanon in 1958, Eisenhower sent a force of U.S. Marines. The Soviets protested, but the situation was brought under control.

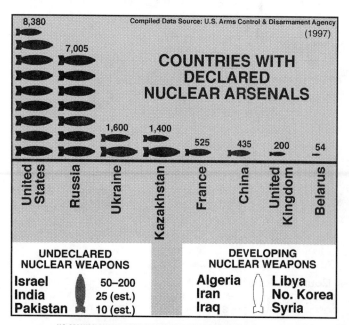

Keeping Middle East oil flowing was the basis of the **Suez Crisis**. The British government owned nearly half the shares in the Suez Canal Company. Egypt was angry that the U.S. and Britain would not fund a Nile River dam project. Egypt took over the Suez Canal in 1956. Great Britain, France, and Israel attacked Egypt. The U.S.S.R. pledged aid to the Egyptians. The U.S. got the U.N. to work out a cease-fire, and the U.N. sent in a peace-keeping force to keep the Canal open.

Cuba became a flash point in the Cold War in the 1960s. Rebels led by **Fidel Castro** took control of Cuba in 1958. Castro announced that Cuba would be a communist state, allied with the Soviet Union. The U.S. Central Intelligence Agency trained Cuban refugees for a counterrevolution. In April 1961, the CIA helped two thousand refugees land at the **Bay of Pigs** in Cuba. The invaders were captured on the beach. Castro and Soviet Premier Khrushchev openly denounced the United States.

Another flash point was the 1962 **Cuban Missile Crisis**. The Soviets began building missile bases in Cuba. President John F. Kennedy demanded that Khrushchev remove the missiles. The President ordered a naval blockade to stop Soviet ships from delivering any additional nuclear missiles. Khrushchev

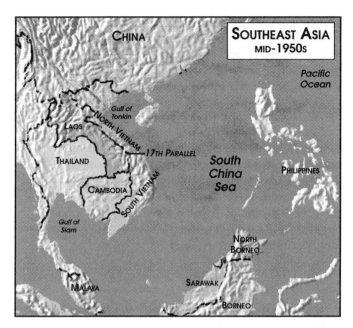

SOUTHEAST ASIA
MID-1950s

At the 1954 Geneva Conference, the U.S. agreed to supervise elections to unite Vietnam in 1956. Because of continued attacks by communist **Viet Cong** guerrillas, the elections did not take place. From communist North Vietnam, Ho Chi Minh distributed Soviet supplies to the Viet Cong rebels. The U.S. supported unpopular, but anti-communist leaders in South Vietnam. President Eisenhower gave military supplies, advisors, and financial support to South Vietnam.

With aid from the Soviets and North Vietnam, the Viet Cong grew stronger in the early 1960s. The U.S. became more and more involved. President Kennedy increased the U.S. commitment by sending 15,000 military personnel as advisors. South Vietnamese military officers overthrew the government in 1963. The fighting against the Viet Cong continued.

The Vietnam War became the longest armed conflict in American history. In 1964, North Vietnamese gunboats fired on U.S. ships in the Gulf of Tonkin. In the **Tonkin Gulf Resolution**, Congress authorized the President to *"take all necessary action to protect American interests."* President Lyndon B. Johnson ordered bombing of North Vietnamese harbors, but the Viet Cong appeared to be gaining strength. Johnson ordered U.S. combat units into South Vietnam in 1964.

The American troops were not trained for a guerrilla war. Viet Cong guerrillas attacked towns and villages with no logical pattern, then retreated into the rain forests. Even the use of toxic chemicals such as **Agent Orange** by the U.S. forces had little military effect. The Viet Cong received an endless stream of troops and supplies from the communist North. Supply lines flowed through Laos and Cambodia. The Vietnam War stalemated.

As it dragged on through the 1960s, the War became unpopular in the United States Anti-war protests and demonstrations became violent. They tore the country apart. Because of the War, **President Lyndon Johnson** decided not to run again in 1968. **President Richard Nixon** promised to end the War. The United States began peace talks in Paris, but Nixon also ordered new bombing raids on Vietnam and Cambodia. Protests intensified. At one demonstration in 1970, four students were killed by National Guardsmen at the **Kent State** campus of the University of Ohio. Nixon shifted more and more responsibility for fighting to the South Vietnamese themselves. He began a reduction of U.S. ground forces.

The peace talks in Paris dragged on for nearly four years, and so did the killing in Vietnam. Finally, both sides agreed to a cease fire in 1973. America

backed down and removed the missiles. Afterwards, Kennedy set up the **Alliance for Progress**. He wished to strengthen Latin America's ability to contain communism. The program gave 20 billion dollars for housing, schools, hospitals, and factories.

Southeast Asia became another flash point in the Cold War in the 1960s. After World War II, a nationalist revolution headed by communist leader **Ho Chi Minh** began in France's colonies in Southeast Asia (French Indochina). The guerrilla war lasted eight years until the French suffered a final defeat at **Dien Bien Phu**.

In 1954, a peace conference in Geneva worked out a cease-fire agreement. The agreement divided Vietnam at the 17th Parallel. It gave Ho and the communists control of the north and an anti-communist government control of the south. U.S. leaders feared that if one area in Southeast Asia fell to communism, the other areas would fall, too. With this **"Domino Theory"** in mind, U.S. leaders knew they would have to take action if communism was to be contained.

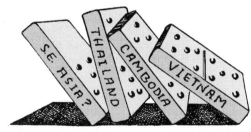

To avoid a chain reaction of communist takeovers in Southeast Asia, the United States formed a NATO-like organization in 1954 called **SEATO** (Southeast Asia Treaty Organization). This defense alliance included Australia, France, Great Britain, New Zealand, Pakistan, the Philippines, Thailand, and the United States. SEATO lacked the unity and power of NATO and was unsuccessful. It was disbanded in 1977.

withdrew its troops. Communists overran South Vietnam and Cambodia within two years. After nine years of fighting and more than 50,000 lives sacrificed, the Vietnam War ended. America came away unsure about containment and its role in the world.

GLOBAL INTERDEPENDENCE

The Cold War came to an end when the U.S.S.R. collapsed in 1991. Except in China, Cuba, and a few small Asian and African countries, communism lost its influence in global politics. In the late 20th century, countries of the world tried to be more cooperative. They found that the scarcity of resources and environmental problems made them more dependent on each other. Countries realized their need for information made them interdependent. Economic survival in a fast-changing world made bridging cultural differences necessary. Cultures differed, but the worldwide web, communication satellites, and air travel made societies realize their similar economic needs.

COOPERATION IN THE WESTERN HEMISPHERE

The economic and social forces that make modern nations interdependent led to cooperative ventures in the Western Hemisphere. The **Organization of American States** is an example. All the nations of North, Central, and South America belong to this regional body which settles disputes among the nations. The OAS now focuses much of its work on economic affairs for its members.

Several groups promote economic cooperation to reduce **tariffs** (entry taxes on goods from other countries). Their idea is to allow the free movement of goods. In 1980, **LAFTA** (Latin American Free Trade Association) formed the **Latin American Integration Association**. Argentina, Bolivia, Brazil, Chile, Colombia, Ecuador, Mexico, Paraguay, Peru, Uruguay, and Venezuela began eliminating tariff barriers among all members.

In 1984, the **CBI** (Caribbean Basin Initiative) was created to boost economic development in Caribbean and Central American countries. CBI tries to combine government aid and private investment. CBI makes it easier for U.S. manufacturers to locate new plants in the Caribbean.

In 1994, Canada, Mexico, and the United States began working together in **NAFTA** (North American Free Trade Agreement). Its goal is to gradually cut out all trade barriers among the three countries over a period of 15 years.

REMINDER: For help in handling questions, see ADVICE CHART on page 184.

UNIT 10
MULTIPLE CHOICE

1   A major factor in Hitler's rise to power in Germany was the
    1   establishment of NATO
    2   German resentment toward the *Versailles Treaty*
    3   U.S. neutrality legislation
    4   conquest of Poland

2   Which is an example of appeasement?
    1   instituting a peacetime draft
    2   beginning the Lend-Lease program
    3   permitting Hitler to seize Czechoslovakia
    4   coming to the aid of Poland when it was attacked

3   When Japan expanded in Asia in 1940, the U.S.
    1   took no action
    2   sent military aid to China
    3   increased the sale of steel in Asia
    4   halted most trade with Japan

Directions: Base your answer to question 4 on the chart below.

JEWISH LOSSES IN WORLD WAR II			
Nation	Jewish Population Sept. 1939	Jewish Losses	Percentage of Jewish Losses
Poland	3,300,000	2,800,000	85.0
U.S.S.R. (Nazi occupied)	2,100,000	1,500,000	71.4
Czechoslovakia	315,000	260,000	82.5
France	300,000	90,000	30.0
Austria	60,000	40,000	66.6
Italy	57,000	15,000	26.3

Source: Holocaust Museum, Washington, D.C.

4   These Holocaust statistics indicate that
    1   Austria had the smallest pre-War Jewish population
    2   Poland had the largest percentage of Jewish losses
    3   France lost more Jews then were lost in Nazi occupied U.S.S.R.
    4   Italy, Austria, and France lost less that 50% of their Jewish population

Directions: Base your answer to question 5 on the map below and on your knowledge of social studies.

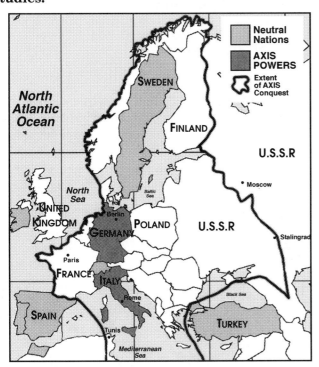

5   This map indicates that the Axis Powers
1   seized control of the United Kingdom
2   occupied Eastern European countries
3   included Germany, Italy, and Spain
4   did not allow European nations to be neutral

6   Which event was crucial to the defeat of Germany in World War II?
1   invading France on D-Day
2   island-hopping through the Caribbean
3   dropping the atomic bomb on Nagasaki
4   signing the Warsaw Pact

7   Which statement best describes the role played by the League of Nations during the 1930s?
1   It solved most threats to international peace.
2   It supported German expansion, but opposed Japanese imperialism.
3   It concentrated its efforts on increasing world armaments.
4   It often failed to act when a powerful nation was involved.

Directions: Base your answer to question 8 on the chart below and on your knowledge of social studies.

8   Which of the following is a correct conclusion about the Cold War?
1   Each action taken by one side was met by a counter action by the other.
2   The U.S. and the U.S.S.R. fought numerous military battles during the Cold War.
3   The Marshall Plan was the U.S. answer to the U.S.S.R.'s Warsaw Pact.
4   Neither side was willing to give economic aid to war damaged nations.

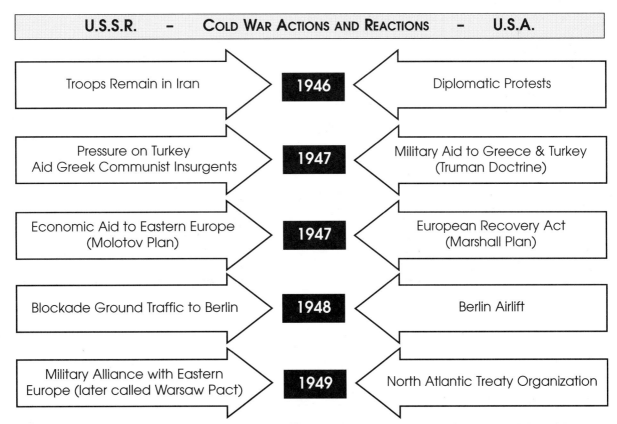

9 Which statement is most accurate about the U.S. home front during World War II?
1 The federal government saw its power severely decreased.
2 Few effects of the War were felt by the civilian population.
3 Sacrifices were demanded of all classes and age groups.
4 Unemployment was high and many strikes occurred.

Directions: Base your answer to question 10 on the quotation below and on your knowledge of social studies.

"After Pearl Harbor we [Japanese Americans] started to get worried because the newspapers were agitating and printing all those stories all the time. And people were getting angrier. ...You heard that people were getting their houses burned down and we were afraid that those things might happen to us. ...When the evacuation order finally came I was relieved...

"You could only take one suitcase apiece, but people who had gone to camp before us were able to tell us what to bring ..."

– Margaret Takahashi, 1942

10 The event described in this quotation is the
1 dropping of the first atomic bomb
2 Holocaust
3 island hopping in the Pacific
4 internment of Japanese-Americans

11 During the Cold War, the newly independent former colonies were
1 denied economic and military aid by the U.S.
2 able to play one superpower off against the other for assistance
3 economically strong and independent of foreign influence
4 members of the Warsaw Pact

12 The Middle East was a major U.S. concern during the Cold War because it
1 had great supplies of petroleum
2 was a major producer of atomic weapons
3 had vast supplies of drinking water
4 was a highly industrialized area

13 The U.S. Central Intelligence Agency encouraged the overthrow of Fidel Castro in Cuba during the
1 Cuban Missile Crisis
2 Alliance for Progress
3 Bay of Pigs invasion
4 Good Neighbor Policy

Directions: Base your answer to question 14 on the map below and on your knowledge of social studies.

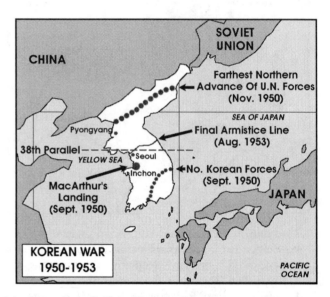

14 According to this Korean Conflict map, the
1 North Koreans never crossed the 38th parallel
2 MacArthur's Inchon landing occurred in North Korea
3 final armistice line was far south of the 38th parallel
4 U.N. Army came close to the Chinese/U.S.S.R. borders

15 The Organization of American States, the Caribbean Basin Initiative, and the North American Free Trade Agreement are similar because they
1 were established to fight communist expansion
2 are examples of Western Hemisphere cooperation
3 are agencies of the United Nations
4 were designed to promote the growth of democracy

CONSTRUCTED RESPONSE

SET 1

Directions: Base your answers to questions 1 and 2 on the chart below and on your knowledge of social studies.

WORLD PEACE ORGANIZATIONS	
United Nations	**League of Nations**
• All major nations joined • Security Council requires a majority vote to take actions (including the 5 permanent members) • It was established by the *U.N. Charter* and not a part of any World War II peace treaties • It has raised volunteer armies and peacekeepers from member nations to combat aggression and keep warring groups apart	• The U.S. never joined. Other major powers joined late and/or were expelled or left before World War II • The Security required a unanimous vote of all members to act • It was established by the Treaty of Versailles and linked to opposition to the Treaty in many countries • It included no provision for an international force to preserve peace and prevent aggression

1   Why was there less opposition to establishment of the United Nations than there was to the League of Nations?

_____

_____

_____

_____

2   What are TWO (2) reasons why the United Nations has been more successful than the League of Nations in acting to keep the peace and prevent aggression?

_____

_____

_____

_____

SET 2

Directions: Base your answers to questions 3 through 5 (found on the next page) on the quotation below and on your knowledge of social studies.

> "An iron curtain has descended across the continent of Europe. Behind that line lie all the countries of Central and Eastern Europe. All these countries lie in the Soviet area of influence and all are subject to a very high and increasing degree of control from Moscow. I do not believe that the Soviet Union desires war. What it desires is the fruits of war and the indefinite expansion of its power and doctrine."
>
> – Prime Minister Winston Churchill of the United Kingdom, *Congressional Record*, March 5, 1946

3 What TWO (2) areas of Europe came under Soviet control?

_____

_____

_____

4 What does Churchill think the goals of the Soviet Union were?

_____

_____

_____

5 What policy did the U.S. begin to keep the Soviet Union from achieving its goals?

_____

_____

_____

PRACTICE SKILLS FOR DBQ

Directions: The following task is based on the accompanying documents. The documents may have been edited for the purposes of this exercise. The task is designed to test your ability to work with historical documents. As you analyze the documents, take into account both the source of the document and the author's point of view where relevant.

Historical Context: During World War II, American people of all ages and from all walks of life contributed to the war effort. From the youngest to the oldest; males and females: African Americans, Whites, Native Americans, and other minorities all worked to achieve victory.

Part A - Short Answer

Document 1

1 What are THREE (3) ways in which World War II affected the life of this young child and many more like her?

_____

_____

_____

"I remember:
- finding sugar in the grocery store and running home to tell my mother to bring the ration books to buy this precious commodity
- collecting milk weed pods and bringing them to school so that their wispy fibers could be used to make life vests for sailors and pilots
- getting the same doll every Christmas clothed in a new home made dress because toys were not in plentiful supply
- saving my pennies all week long in order to bring 25 cents to school to buy a war bond stamp
- helping to weed the Victory Garden and harvest the vegetables
- crying when the practice air raid siren sounded and the lights went out
- getting spanked when a friend and I consumed the scarce chewing gum my mother was accumulating to send to my cousin on a destroyer in the Pacific
I remember all this and much more."

– Sue McCarthy, (age six in 1945)

_____

_____

Document 2 (includes 3 posters)

Women of America, Uncle Sam needs you, too!
Women's Army Corps

Preserving Food Helps Preserve Your Democracy!

2   What are TWO (2) ways in which women aided in the war effort?

_____

_____

_____

_____

_____

_____

_____

_____

_____

A Factory Line Is Needed As Much As The Front Line!

Part B - Essay Response

   Task: Discuss the role that at least two groups played in helping the American war effort. (State your thesis in the introduction.)

ADDITIONAL SUGGESTED TASK

   From your knowledge of social studies, identify another group(s) that played a role in the American war effort and indicate what that role was.

1944	G.I. BILL OF RIGHTS
1947	BABY BOOM BEGINS
1952	TV IN 15 MILLION HOMES
1954	*BROWN V. BD. OF ED. OF TOPEKA* DECISION
1956	*INTERSTATE HIGHWAY ACT*
1964	*CIVIL RIGHTS ACT*
1965	MEDICARE
1969	MOON LANDING
1979	ARAB OIL CRISIS
1981	REGANOMICS
1989	SAVINGS AND LOAN BANKING COLLAPSE
1994	NAFTA
1998	IMPEACHMENT OF PRESIDENT CLINTON
1999	PRESIDENT CLINTON ACQUITTED
2000	MICROSOFT ANTITRUST SUIT
	HILLARY CLINTON ELECTED TO U.S. SENATE

UNIT 11

THE CHANGING NATURE OF THE AMERICAN PEOPLE FROM WW II TO THE PRESENT

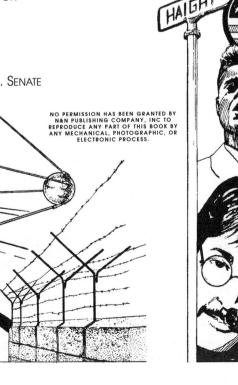

AGE OF PROSPERITY (1945-1965)

EXPANSION CHANGED PATTERNS OF PRODUCTION AND CONSUMPTION

After World War II, the economy dipped into a short recession as the country converted to peacetime production. However, conversion was fast and the economy was booming by 1947. This short conversion and rapid expansion had a number of causes.

The post World War II economic boom continued into the 1950s. Even the Korean War spurred production in the early 1950s. Korea was not an all-out war like World War II, but government demand for military goods boosted production.

As production soared, the **Gross Domestic Product** (GDP) showed that economic performance improved greatly. GDP is the value of all the goods and services produced within the nation in a given year. When GDP is properly adjusted, the calculation for one year can be measured against other years.

(Note: In the 1980s, the government's economists changed from using Gross National Product -GNP- as a statistic to GDP.)

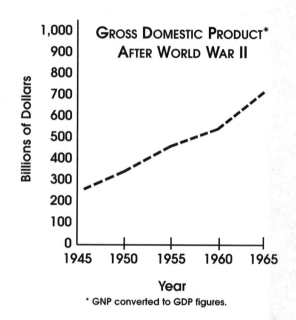

GROSS DOMESTIC PRODUCT* AFTER WORLD WAR II

Billions of Dollars (y-axis: 0 to 1,000)
Year (x-axis: 1945 to 1965)

* GNP converted to GDP figures.

REASONS FOR THE POSTWAR BOOM

• **Managed conversion**: As the War came to a close, Presidents Roosevelt and Truman allowed some factories to start producing more consumer goods. For example, the government cut quotas on tanks and military vehicles. Auto makers started building cars. Clothing manufacturers slowed uniform production and cranked up civilian fashions.

• **The G.I. Bill**: In 1944, Congress passed the *Servicemen's Readjustment Act*. Known as the "**G.I. Bill of Rights**," it awarded servicemen and women government aid to: go to colleges or technical schools, get loans to buy houses, and start businesses. This greatly stimulated the economy. Colleges had to expand programs, hire staff, and build new facilities for the flood of enrollees, and home building soared. (It also kept unemployment down. So many returning military personnel went to school instead of jumping back into the job market.)

• **Pent-up savings**: The economy expanded because workers cashed in the war bonds they had bought regularly during the War. They started buying the cars, refrigerators, and radios that were in short supply during the War. The government also lifted its rationing and price controls gradually. Prices did not inflate rapidly while suppliers caught up with consumer demand.

• **Continued military and recovery spending**: The government kept occupation troops in various countries, so it still needed military goods. Also, because of the hostile behavior of the U.S.S.R. the government did not cut the armed forces as much as it had expected. Later, under the Marshall Plan, the government sent billions of dollars of goods and machinery to other countries to help them rebuild. This kept the government demanding goods and services after the War ended.

• **Technological advancement**: During the War, technological advances made production more efficient. Wartime development of new materials, energy sources, and substitute products, had a lasting impact on industry. Aluminum became a lighter, less corrosive replacement for steel; it was also substituted for electrical wire. Plastics replaced rubber and fabrics. Nylon replaced textiles. Rayon, used in the War as a substitute for silk in parachutes, became a base for synthetic fabric. After the War, old and new industries adapted these substances to improve goods and production facilities.

1950s: TV becomes the center of home entertainment. ©PhotoDisc

Television changed the economy, too. Advertising blossomed. Radio could only talk about a product. At the rate of 20 commercials per hour, television could show the product and show people using it, while bouncing the brand name off and on the screen. Television started fads in dressing (capri pants, poodle skirts, white buck shoes) and toys (hula hoops, the Slinky, Davy Crockett caps, and Barbie dolls), and even food (TV Dinners). Consumers no longer had to shop in stores to find out what was available. Every day, television brought a raft of animated and real-life images of new appliances, homes, and cars into the living room.

UNEMPLOYMENT DROPS

Increased production and a higher standard of living meant more jobs. Unemployment in the Great Depression exceeded 25%; one in four people were without jobs. In the 1950s and 1960s, unemployment dwindled to between 4 and 8 percent.

At first glance, it seems that *any* unemployment is undesirable. However, economists say a 4 to 8% average is an acceptable level in a free market economy. If there is true economic freedom, there will always be people moving in and out of the job market. Workers want the freedom to change jobs, careers, or professions. Some workers take time off to go back to college or get training in a more attractive field. Some quit jobs with companies to go into business for themselves. Technical advances make some jobs obsolete and workers have to retrain for other jobs. In other cases, employers are also free to fire an undesirable or unproductive worker. Therefore, a low level of unemployment is acceptable.

ENVIRONMENTAL IMPACT

Any intense human activity modifies the environment. Significant industrial growth usually comes with an environmental price: air pollution, water pollution, strip mining, and acid rain to name a few. In the 1950s, there were few environmental laws in place, and the economic expansion took a toll on the environment. Not until the late 1960s were there movements to control the damage done to the environment.

ENVIRONMENTAL POLLUTION		
Type	**Cause**	**Solution**
Air	Factories and automobiles	Burn cleaner fuels; Install pollution control equipment
Water	Factory discharges, municipal sewage waste plants	Conservation of water sources; treatment and filtration of water
Land	Garbage dumps buried toxic waste	Recycling paper, metals, and glass; clean up landfills and toxic waste dumps; seek safer storage areas

Even positive uses for the land, such as the great interstate highway system begun in the mid-1950s, destroyed natural habitats and led to more auto emissions. Building bridges, tunnels, dams, pipelines, and power grids have environmental consequences. However, in the hustle and bustle of the 1950s, American society showed little concern for these matters. Later generations would pay the price for the economic boom.

POVERTY AMIDST PLENTY

Amid all the economic expansion, there was still poverty in America. Worker retraining became difficult for manual laborers when technology replaced them. Many areas of the country did not have the money to upgrade educational facilities, and some children fell behind. Inner city and rural schools received less money than suburban ones. Socialist writer Michael Harrington's 1962 book, *The Other America*, showed that nearly 18% of Americans earned less than a living wage.

The Other America triggered a national dialog on poverty. In 1964, President Johnson launched a **War on Poverty**. The goal, he said, was to help the "many Americans that live on the outskirts of hope." Johnson pushed legislation through Congress that authorized nearly $950 million in aid to the poor. The program created the **Office of Economic Opportunity**. The OEO launched the **Job Corps** for work training for youth, **VISTA**, a volunteer corps to aid education in inner cities, and a **Community Action Program** to help the poor change their own communities. (See Great Society chart on page 157.)

THE CHANGING NATURE OF WORK

Since World War II, many older industries such as steel and textiles closed due to the expense of updating equipment and competition from overseas. Some companies became large international operations. Many of these companies moved operations to other countries with lower employment costs. Today, the labels of the clothing Americans wear and the appliances in their homes show that many products are manufactured outside the U.S.A.

Work changed as manufacturing declined and service industries grew. "**Blue collar jobs**" (manufacturing, mining) began to decline after World War II. With better education and more demand by employers, many Americans began working in "**white collar jobs**" – clerical office jobs, managerial work, or professional positions.

Gradually, the U.S. economy converted from manufacturing to **service industries**. These are industries where work is done for other people. Service industries include health care, retailing, education, finance, food service, and recreation. For the American worker, this meant more frequent occupation changes during their work lives as changes sweep the society. For example, in 1950 or even 1960, very few high school or college seniors were thinking about jobs involving computers. Think how that situation has changed. Rapid change in the economy also meant less job security and more education.

EQUAL RIGHTS FOR WOMEN

The economic role of women changed greatly in the generation after World War II. Right after the War, many women left their jobs in war production plants. Many more were dismissed in favor of returning servicemen. There were no legal protections, and no one talked about gender discrimination. They were just fired if they would not resign.

In the generation after the War, more and more women enrolled in colleges. Economic demand opened some new employment opportunities, but the real progress came with the Civil Rights Movement in the late 1950s and 1960s. Demonstrations and marches opened the people's eyes to the unfairness of racial segregation. At the same time, the nation became more aware of the social and economic inequality of women.

The Civil Rights Movement opened a door for women. In the 1960s, the Womens' Liberation Movement campaigned for equal opportunity. In 1963, Congress passed the *Equal Pay Act*. It provided that men and women doing the same job be paid equally. **Title VII** of the *Civil Rights Act of 1964* banned discrimination against women in employment and job promotions. The **National Organization for Women** (**NOW**) was founded in 1966. NOW sought change through legislation and court challenges. NOW became a political force. It supported certain candidates and spearheaded campaigns for legal rights for women.

CHANGING COMMUNITY PATTERNS

Very few new homes were built during the Great Depression and World War II, despite a growth in population. After the War, returning servicemen wanted to start building the lives the War interrupted. Demand for homes skyrocketed. City housing was expensive. The *G.I. Bill* helped veterans get mortgage loans. Roads were built to the areas outside the cities.

POST WORLD WAR II SUBURBS
©PhotoDisc

The next decade saw millions of new, affordable homes springing up in suburbs. Commuting from the affordable suburban areas to city jobs became common. Arthur Levit made millions building the **Levittown** developments in New York and Pennsylvania. Thousands of mass-produced single-family houses were constructed at affordable prices. A second automobile often became a necessity. The huge move to the suburbs led to the construction of shopping centers, roads, water supply systems, and sewage systems.

The cities changed. While young families left for the suburbs, minority groups and elderly people on **fixed incomes** stayed behind. Poor, unskilled workers from rural areas moved into the cities. They took lower paying jobs in city factories. Immigrants from war-torn Europe did the same.

As a result, the people that were earning money at good jobs were leaving the cities. They paid property taxes that funded development of the suburbs. The lower income groups that stayed in the cities paid less in taxes. City revenues declined and so did city services. The overall decline in city dwellers' income levels led businesses to leave the cities, too. Some businesses followed the skilled middle class workers into the suburbs. As businesses left the cities, unemployment rose. Cities went into decay. The media began calling the older cities in the Northeast and Mid-West "The Rust Belt." Some cities went into bankruptcy by the 1960s.

CITY POPULATION CHANGE 1950 AND 1970 (Source: U.S. Bureau of the Census)		
City	**1950**	**1970**
Baltimore, MD	949,708	905,787
Boston, MA	801,444	641,701
Buffalo, NY	580,132	462,768
Cincinnati, OH	503,998	453,514
Cleveland, OH	914,808	750,879
Detroit, MI	1,849,568	1,514,063
Philadelphia, PA	2,071,605	1,949,996
Pittsburgh, PA	676,806	520,089
Washington, DC	802,178	756,668

NEW EXPECTATIONS FOR MINORITIES

American society changed in many ways after World War II. The economy boomed, but some groups did not share in the expansion and improvement of life. African Americans had long faced legalized race discrimination in the South. In the North, they were denied job opportunities, decent housing, and educational opportunities. Groups such as the **NAACP** and the **Urban League** had battled in the courts to over-turn legal segregation laws. They made little progress, especially in the turmoil of the Great Depression.

World War II saw African Americans fighting overseas and working in defense plants at home. Many sacrificed their lives for a country that denied them basic rights. They returned home to race discrimination. After fighting for the freedom, equality, and dignity of others half a world away, they spoke out in stronger voices for the freedoms they were denied. President Truman ordered the armed forces desegregated in 1948. Congress defeated Truman's civil rights proposals. However, in the 1950s, the NAACP challenged school segregation in Topeka, Kansas. The case went on appeal to the U.S. Supreme Court.

In ***Brown v. the Board of Education of Topeka, Kansas*** (1954), the Court overturned *Plessy v. Ferguson* (1896) and said that separate public schools for the races were unconstitutional. The *Brown* decision was a landmark. It was the beginning of the end for the South's Jim Crow laws – legalized segregation.

Brown said that such separation on the basis of race violated the Fourteenth Amendment's guarantee of "equal protection of the law" for all citizens. The court ordered all segregation of schools to end. Southern states defied the Court's order. They claimed education was a state government matter and the federal government had no right to tell a state what it could do.

While states defied the *Brown* decision, it brought the whole question of racial discrimination into the open. The public put pressure on the federal government. Congress began debating civil rights laws to ban discrimination. Southern Senators and Representatives blocked the legislation.

NON-VIOLENT, DIRECT ACTION

As Congressional debate dragged on in Washington, the focus of action for equality broadened. From the campaign to desegregate schools, reformers sought to end segregation in all aspects of life.

The campaign took a different turn in 1955 and 1956. It went from the courtrooms to the streets. In Montgomery, Alabama, a tired African American working woman refused to give up her seat to a white male passenger on a city bus. **Rosa Parks** was arrested. African Americans were outraged. A young Baptist minister named **Martin Luther King, Jr.** organized a year-long boycott of city buses. (A **boycott** is when a group refrains from using a service or buying a product as an expression of protest.)

Rosa Parks breaks a Jim Crow Law in 1955
by sitting in the front of a bus.   UPI

The news media kept the Montgomery Bus Boycott story before the public. Ordinary people were using **non-violent protest** to call attention to injustice. The public became aroused. The bus company lost a great deal of money. The boycott ended in an agreement by the city to desegregate the transportation facilities.

In Arkansas, Governor Faubus defied federal court orders. In 1957, the Governor would not allow Little Rock's Central High School to admit African American students. At one point, the Governor ordered out the Arkansas National Guard to keep a handful of students out of the school. National television coverage aroused a public outcry. President Eisenhower said this was defiance of federal power. As Commander-in-Chief, he ordered the Arkansas National Guard demobilized and sent regular U.S. Army troops to escort the students into the school.

Civil rights leaders began an intense campaign of **civil disobedience** to overcome segregation in all public facilities. Civil disobedience means intentionally violating a law believed to be unjust. Civil rights groups used **non-violent**, **direct action**. In 1960, they peacefully began **sit-ins** at segregated lunch counters throughout the South. The **Freedom Riders** rode buses and tried to desegregate the bus terminals. In front of national television cameras, protesters were arrested and put in jail. When local officials used brutal tactics with these protesters, public interest and empathy grew.

In 1957, public pressure finally overcame Southern Senators' blocking tactics. Congress passed the first *Civil Rights Act* since Reconstruction. The 1957 law created a Civil Rights Commission to prose-

cute racial injustice. Another civil rights act in 1960 banned some of restrictions on African Americans' voting rights used by Southern states.

POLITICAL CHANGES

The 1950s ended with Cold War worries and civil rights tensions bothering Americans. In 1960, voters chose a young, action-oriented President – **John F. Kennedy**. The energetic JFK promised to lead the next generation to a "New Frontier." He offered proposals for a space program, civil rights, welfare, and a stronger foreign policy.

President John F. kennedy, 1961-1963
White House Historical Association, Washington, D.C.

Kennedy got Congress to lower tariffs, increase the minimum wage, and create the **Peace Corps** for humanitarian service overseas. Southerners in Congress still blocked civil rights reforms. Many of Kennedy's reforms in education, aid for the poor, and tax cuts were blocked, too. Kennedy sent federal marshals to the University of Mississippi when the Governor blocked African American students from enrolling.

In 1963, the nation was shocked when President Kennedy was murdered in Dallas. JFK had not been in office three years, and Congress had not yet acted on his "New Frontier" reforms.

Vice President **Lyndon B. Johnson** became President. LBJ was an experienced congressional leader. Johnson pushed many of JFK's social programs through Congress. Then he began his own social reform program. The heart of LBJ's "Great

Actions	Results
24th Amendment (1964)	Banned the use of poll taxes (voting fees) in federal elections.
Civil Rights Acts (1964, 1968)	The 1964 Act outlawed discrimination in employment and in public accommodations connected with interstate commerce; the 1968 Act banned discrimination in housing and real estate.
Project Head Start (1965)	Gave funds for developmental assistance to disabled children and children from low-income families.
Medicare (1965)	Extended Social Security benefits to provide health insurance for the elderly.
Elementary & Secondary Education Act (1965)	Funded libraries, textbooks, and supplementary education centers to help Native Americans, migrants, and low income families.
Voting Rights Act (1965)	Federal examiners registered African American voters; also suspended all literacy tests; (by the end of 1965 a quarter of a million new African American voters had been registered).
VISTA (1966)	This "domestic Peace Corps" used volunteers to run programs to help teach job skills in poverty areas.
Job Corps (1964)	Provides vocational training, health care, and personal counseling to disadvantaged youth in order to help them find work.
Medicaid (1966)	Provides medical payments for low income, blind, and disabled (funded jointly by U.S. federal and state agencies.
Department of Housing and Urban Development (1965)	Administers programs for mortgage insurance for home-buyers, low-income rental assistance, and programs for urban revitalization.
Department of Transportation (1966)	Administers environmental safety and an efficient national transportation system.

Society" program was a "war on poverty." In 1964, thirty-five million Americans lived below the poverty level. Most of the poor lived in rural regions such as Appalachia, on Indian reservations, and in poor urban neighborhoods.

By 1968, Great Society programs assisted millions of poor people. However, there were problems. The programs were costly and expanded the power of the federal government too much. Taxes rose to cover the costs. What really hurt the Great Society was the escalation of the Vietnam War in the late 1960s. The bitter struggle over the War tore the country apart, but it also undermined much support for social reform programs.

AN AGE OF LIMITATIONS (1965 – 1990)
ECONOMIC CHANGE AND UPHEAVAL

A great prosperity had carried the United States from the end of World War II into the 1960s. In the middle of the 1960s, the economy began to decline. There were a number of reasons for this. One reason had to do with the industrial countries that were ruined in World War II. With the Marshall Plan and other foreign aid, the United States had helped to rebuild many of them. By the 1960s, they were recovered enough to start competing again in

LBJ leads Congress, like a maestro conducts a symphonic orchestra.

world trade. In one sense, their factory production was better than that of older, less efficient American factories. The factories in the recovering countries were built for newer technology. With state of the art machinery, they produced more goods at cheaper prices. Also, the governments of countries such as Germany and Japan helped economic development. They did not tax corporations very much, and they kept minimum wages low. This meant their businesses could produce lower-priced goods and sell them to compete with American goods.

The improved quality and lower prices of foreign competitors put pressure on older industries in the United States. Manufacturers of electric appliances, tires, and steel felt the bite of foreign competition most. Mining was another industry affected by foreign competition. In addition, the coal industry was hurt by changing technology. Cheaply produced foreign oil replaced coal as an industrial and home heating fuel in the 1950s.

Not only were American businesses losing sales to foreign countries, but the great buying splurge of Americans slowed down in the 1960s. The market was saturated with goods. When consumer spending slows, so does the economy. Spending for food and clothing is usually stable. However, when spending falls for "big ticket items" (autos, large appliances, houses, vacations) the economy slows down noticeably. In the 1960s, the economy went into **recessions** (economic slowdowns). American corporations cut production and unemployment rose.

Another problem was **inflation**. When the general supply of goods and services is stable, but demand climbs, it is like an auction, and prices go up. Increased government demand was part of the problem. The government needed goods and services for Vietnam and the Great Society. It was as if the government was like a very rich person bidding against everyone else for goods, so prices rose even more. Average consumers could not buy as much because of these higher prices and taxes. As consumers demanded less, companies cut production and laid off workers. Unemployment rose. The economy slowed down into a recession.

In late 1960s and early 1970s, the country experienced limits on its military capability. The country was disturbed over its failure to achieve victory in Vietnam. Americans also came face to face with economic limitations (scarcity). In the years after World War II, the United States became very dependent on cheap foreign petroleum. Oil was the essential fuel for factory power, for transportation, and for home heating. However, more than half the petroleum used came from sources outside the United States.

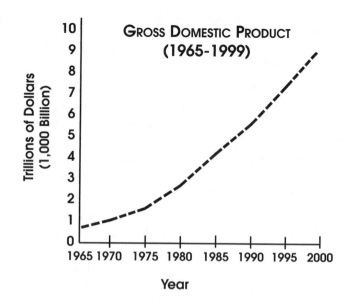

GROSS DOMESTIC PRODUCT (1965-1999)

In the early 1970s, an alliance of oil-producing countries called **OPEC** (Organization of Petroleum Exporting Countries) limited global production. OPEC cut production on purpose to limit the global supply. Limiting supply while demand remained the same drove up the price of oil. OPEC nations such as Saudi Arabia became very rich. However, there was more than economic gain behind this move. Some of the Middle East producers in OPEC wanted to punish the U.S. and some European industrial countries. The Western industrial countries had helped their enemy, Israel, defend itself in wars in 1968 and 1973.

OPEC's actions caused problems for Americans. The short supplies of oil drove up fuel prices and triggered inflation. Gas stations limited the amount of fuel motorists could buy. Deliveries of goods were delayed. Airlines cut the number of flights available. Americans were outraged at what OPEC did. However, they were also troubled and frustrated that, with all of their power, they could be at the mercy of other countries. The land of plenty had confronted the age-old economic problem of scarcity.

In more recent years, global competition created an "unfavorable balance of trade" for the United States. Actually, it was not a "balance" at all. Foreign countries poured goods into the U.S., and Americans were buying them because of their lower prices. However, the reverse was not true. American goods were not selling as well overseas. Countries such as Japan placed quotas on how much could be imported from the United States. Other countries put high tariffs (import taxes) on U.S. goods. Economists call this negative situation (imports exceeding exports) a **trade deficit**. Every year since 1980, the United States has had a trade deficit.

Administration	Actions
Richard M. Nixon 1969-1974	Esclated, then ended Vietnam War Détente with Red China and former Soviet Union (U.S.S.R.) Watergate scandal let to first Presidential resignation.
Gerald R. Ford 1974-1977	Pardon of Richard Nixon for any possible crimes committed during Presidency Greater control over CIA and FBI activities and violations of individual rights Economic campaign to cut government spending Began attempt to control inflation caused the 1973 oil crisis
James Earl "Jimmy" Carter 1977-1981	Oil shortages and energy crisis of 1979 Panama Canal Treaty to gradually return the Canal Zone to Panama Camp David Agreements brought peace between Israel and Egypt Fifty Americans held hostage in Iran U.S. boycott of Olympics, protesting Soviet invasion of Afghanistan
Ronald W. Regan 1981-1989	"Supply-side" budget and tax reductions Modernized military and built strong defense Anti-communist invasions of Grenada, Costa Rica, and Nicaragua Deregulation of U.S. banks Anti-terrorist actions Troop and arms reduction treaties with U.S.S.R. Iran-Contra aid and struggle with Congress
George W. Bush 1989-1993	Supported Soviet democratic and economic reforms Persian Gulf War against Saddam Hussein, freed Kuwait Invaded Panama in war against drugs Presided over the end of the Cold War
William Jefferson Clinton 1993-2001	Began reduction of federal budget deficit Used U.S. troops to restore civilian government in Haiti Impeached by the House of Representatives, acquitted by the Senate

ENVIRONMENTAL MOVEMENT

Just when Americans had run into limits on the economic front, they ran into limits in another place – the environment. Since the Industrial Era, America's industries had extracted natural resources at a rapid pace. There were very few regulations on industries. They dumped caustic chemical wastes into rivers and landfills. Factory smokestacks and automobiles spewed noxious waste products into the air. This went on for decades, and no one seemed to listen to people who protested.

> ### "We have acquired the fateful power to alter nature."
> - Rachel Carson, *Silent Spring*, 1963

In 1963, Rachel Carson's book, ***Silent Spring***, awakened the country to the effects of chemical pesticides on America's farmlands. She criticized the use of chemical pesticides, fertilizers, and weed killers. She showed that damage had already been done. The chemical industry fought back, but Carson's book triggered a strong public response. Environmental movements gained momentum, especially on college campuses. Environmentalists were concerned with the protection of natural surroundings from overuse and degradation by humans.

Congress responded to the public debate on the environment. Beginning in the 1960s, it passed many laws to preserve and restore the environment (see chart). There were trade-offs; however, businesses had to install expensive anti-pollution devices. This made almost every product more expensive. Americans had to work a little harder at recycling their waste.

In the 1980s, concern arose over serious global environmental problems. These included the acid rain controversy, the Chernobyl (Ukraine) nuclear catastrophe, the *Exxon Valdez* oil spill, tropical deforestation, and the concern over global warming. Dealing with international issues is always difficult. The United Nations sponsored two **Earth Summits** in the 1990s. These international conferences did much to publicize global environmental problems, but little to solve them. The remedies called for by the conferences involve great sacrifices and conflict with the goals of other nations.

Certain groups have been more seriously affected by environmental issues than the general public. For example, logging, mining and quarrying, fishing, and energy interests have threatened the lands and beliefs of Native Americans. The rural poor and minority groups fight efforts to locate landfills and nuclear waste facilities near the areas where they live.

CHANGES IN IMMIGRATION

In 1965, Congress repealed the prejudicial National Origins system. It passed the ***Immigration Act of 1965***, which created an enlarged annual ceiling for immigrants from the Eastern Hemisphere with an equal limit of 20,000 for every country. The Act gave preference to immigrants with close family ties in the U.S. or special skills. It placed a ceiling on immigrants from the Western Hemisphere of 120,000 with country limitations set at 20,000.

The countries of origin for immigrants changed after World War II. Before the War, immigrants were overwhelmingly European. By the end of the 1980s, no European country was a leading sender of immigrants. Almost half of all immigrants to the United States were coming from Asian countries. At least 25% of the remainder were coming from Spanish-speaking nations.

NATIONAL ENVIRONMENTAL ACTIONS	
Major Action	**Purpose**
Environmental Protection Agency (EPA, 1970)	Administers all federal environmental legislation.
Clean Water Act of 1972*	Tries to eliminate the discharge of pollutants into aquatic environments.
Environmental Pesticide Control Act (1972)	Sponsors control and education on use of chemicals to protect crops.
National Forest Management Act (1976)	Seeks to prevent neglect, exploitation, and destruction; provides for watershed protection, wildlife and fish habitats, and recreation.
National Acid Precipitation Act (1980)	Authorizes the study of acid deposition.
Superfund legislation of 1980	Creates a trust fund collected from producers or distributors of hazardous materials for the Environmental Protection Agency to cleanup abandoned hazardous waste sites.

*Note: In the late 1990s, Congress provided compensation for property owners who may not be permitted to develop their "wetlands" under provisions of the *Clean Water Act*.

HOW AMERICAN OCCUPATIONS CHANGED DURING THE 20TH CENTURY

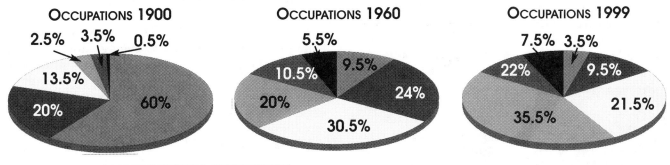

OCCUPATIONS 1900
2.5% 3.5% 0.5%
13.5%
20%
60%

OCCUPATIONS 1960
5.5% 9.5%
10.5%
20%
24%
30.5%

OCCUPATIONS 1999
7.5% 3.5%
22%
9.5%
21.5%
35.5%

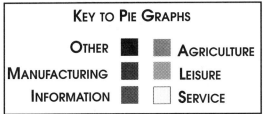

KEY TO PIE GRAPHS
OTHER ▪ ▪ AGRICULTURE
MANUFACTURING ▪ ▪ LEISURE
INFORMATION ▪ ☐ SERVICE

To help victims of political upheaval, Congress passed the *Refugee Act of 1980*. It also addressed the issue of illegal aliens. In 1986, Congress passed the ***Immigration Reform and Control Act***. It penalized employers who knowingly and willfully hired illegal aliens. The *Reform Act* set up programs for special agricultural workers to make them eligible for permanent resident alien status and eventual citizenship.

CHANGES IN THE WORK FORCE

The 20th century saw great changes in the way people made their living. Technology was behind the major changes in employment. Mechanization of farming allowed fewer workers to farm more acres more efficiently. "Smokestack industries" became the backbone of America's economy. Assembly lines led to the growth of factories and drew more workers into manufacturing. As the country became more urbanized, there was greater demand for services and entertainment.

After World War II, the expansion of cities and suburbs, international trade, and global military involvement increased the need for service industries. Jobs expanded rapidly in banking, transportation, health care, communications, education, public utilities, wholesale and retail trade, insurance, real estate, government, entertainment, and food services. Service industries replaced "smokestack industries" as the backbone of the economy. The arrival of computer technology caused another shift. By the end of the century, jobs in information/high tech industries replaced service industries as the backbone of the economy.

Throughout the 20th century, improvements in efficiency and productivity led to higher incomes and more time off from work. Improvements in medicine, diet, and health care meant Americans were living longer, too. (In 1900, only 4.1% of Americans were living beyond 65. In 2000, nearly 16% of the population was over 65.) As a result, there was steady growth in employment in **leisure activities** such as tourism, entertainment, and food services.

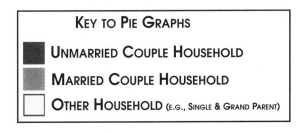

KEY TO PIE GRAPHS
▪ UNMARRIED COUPLE HOUSEHOLD
▪ MARRIED COUPLE HOUSEHOLD
☐ OTHER HOUSEHOLD (E.G., SINGLE & GRAND PARENT)

HOW AMERICAN HOUSEHOLDS CHANGED DURING THE 20TH CENTURY

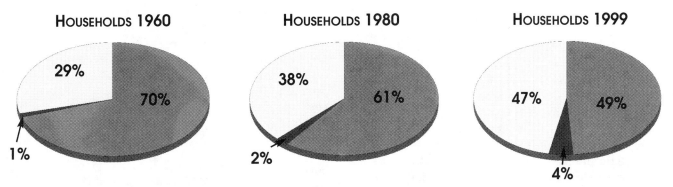

HOUSEHOLDS 1960
29%
70%
1%

HOUSEHOLDS 1980
38%
61%
2%

HOUSEHOLDS 1999
47%
49%
4%

NEW FAMILY PATTERNS

Family units changed considerably in the 20th century. In the early 20th century when agriculture was a major occupation, families were larger. There were more children; they were needed to help with the work. Farm families were **extended families**; there were

often three generations living in a household because older parents were supported by their children. Still, there were fewer elderly. In 1900, the average life expectancy was only 47 years.

By the middle of the 20th century rapid urbanization and the decline of the family farm changed the family unit. In cities and industrial towns, workers toiled on fixed salaries to support their families. Typically, there were **nuclear families** – married couple and their children

living in a household. Supporting large numbers of children in small city living quarters was difficult. The average number of children per family declined from earlier generations.

The family changed in other ways. The marriage rate dipped during the Great Depression, but rebounded after World War II. For the second half of the 20th century, it has averaged 11 per 1000 persons. The average divorce rate rose in the 20th century, from below 2 per 1000 persons to 4.2 per 1000 persons. It peaked at 5.3 per 1000 persons in 1981. Another change was that older parents no longer lived with their adult children as they had earlier. The elderly had to fend for themselves on employee pensions and later, on Social Security. There

were larger numbers of elderly; in 1960, the average life expectancy was 69 years.

By the end of the 20th century, rising costs and changing social needs led to even smaller families. However, in many families both parents were wage earners. Sometimes this was by choice as women sought to have careers of their own. Sometimes, it was of necessity as a single wage earner could not supply a family with all its needs. Nearly two-thirds of mothers with preschool-age children worked outside the home.

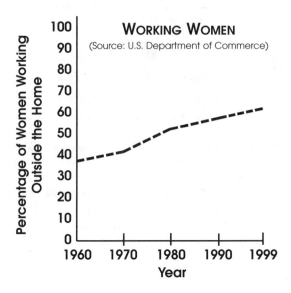

As the 20th century ended, traditional nuclear family structures changed. Family structures became more diversified. There were more single parent families. In 1998, twenty-eight percent of children under eighteen lived with just one parent, while sixty-eight percent lived with both parents.

As the 20th century ended, the elderly were playing a more prominent role in American families. There were many more elderly – in 1999 the average

life expectancy was 76 years. They often had good retirement income and usually lived on their own. In some cases, grandparents were playing a different role in families. In larger numbers, grandparents took responsibilities for rearing children when the single parent or both parents had

to work. From 1970 to 2000, the number of grandchildren under 18 living in their grandparents' households increased by 56%. Three-fourths of those children living with their grandparents had only one parent living in that same household.

While there were more older Americans because more people were living longer, the culture was becoming more youth oriented. In 1998, almost one third of the population was under nineteen years old. Television did more youth oriented programming – the prominence of MTV was evidence of this. Clothing manufacturers and retailers catered to youthful styles. The recording industry and media retailers were youth oriented.

> "Statistics show that in 1998, kids age 10 to 19 spent over $105 billion on such items as candy, fast food, clothing, and entertainment."
> – Rand Youth Poll, April 2000

By the end of the 20th century, government also was playing a greater role in family life. In 1998, over $20.5 billion in financial assistance went to more than 2.6 million needy families. Over 22.8% of those families had an employed wage earner. (In 1998, the U.S. government poverty level for a family of four was an annual income below $16,689.)

POPULATION BY AGE – YEAR 1999
(Source: Bureau of the Census, U.S. Department of Commerce)

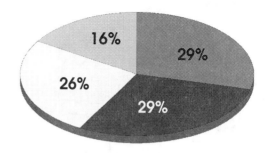

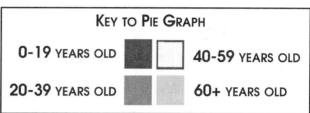

KEY TO PIE GRAPH

| 0-19 YEARS OLD | | 40-59 YEARS OLD |
| 20-39 YEARS OLD | | 60+ YEARS OLD |

As America moved into the 21st century, changing technology and the ability to move long distances affected how people lived and earned their living. Technology alters the pace of everyday life. It helps us live longer, more productive, and more exciting lives. During the 20th century, the basic way people made a living changed dramatically. It went from agriculture, to service, to high tech in very rapid succession. In the 21st century, the pace of change will continue to accelerate in every aspect of life.

REMINDER: For help in handling questions, see ADVICE CHART on page 184.

UNIT 11
MULTIPLE CHOICE

1 Which of the following was the result of the other three?
   1 pent-up savings
   2 G.I. Bill of Rights
   3 Marshall Plan
   4 postwar economic boom

2 Which statement about the American job market in the last half of the 20th century is most accurate?
   1 "Blue collar" jobs recorded their greatest increase in history.
   2 Few manufacturing jobs moved to foreign countries.
   3 Job security increased as few people changed their employers.
   4 Employment opportunities expanded in the service industries.

Directions: Base your answer to question 3 on the graph below.

3 Based on this graph, which is an accurate conclusion?
   1 In the postwar period, the GDP increased some years and decreased in other years.
   2 The GDP trend in the postwar period was one of consistent increase.
   3 In 1946, the GDP reached its highest point.
   4 The greatest increase in GDP occurred between 1955 and 1960.

Directions: Base your answer to question 4 on the cartoon below and on your knowledge of social studies.

WANTED

| Cleaning Woman $5 per hour | Sanitary Engineer $10 per hour |

4 The main point of the cartoon is the
  1 inequality of pay that women faced in the workplace
  2 hard work required of both men and women
  3 high hourly salaries paid to workers
  4 lack of technical advances in some job areas

5 A result of changing community patterns after World War II was
  1 a return of people to farming areas
  2 an increased suburban population
  3 improvement in the urban quality of life
  4 a revival of the cities of the northeast

Directions: Base your answer to question 6 on the quotation below and on your knowledge of social studies.

"Separate educational facilities are inherently unequal. (Separating children) solely because of their race generates a feeling of inferiority as to their status in the community that may affect their hearts and minds in a way unlikely to be undone."

– Brown v. Board of Education of Topeka Kansas, 1954

6 In this ruling, the Supreme Court overturned the
  1 right of religious groups to establish schools
  2 provision for the G.I. Bill of Rights
  3 decision for "separate but equal" education for African Americans
  4 decision to allow community based schools in northern states

7 Which environmental issue(s) have particularly affected Native Americans' lands?
  1 ozone depletion
  2 logging, mining, overfishing
  3 auto emissions
  4 acid rain

8 Both John F. Kennedy and Lyndon B. Johnson were strong supporters of
  1 providing programs to decrease poverty
  2 lowering the tax burden on the wealthy
  3 ending the U.S. space program
  4 eliminating foreign aid programs

Directions: Base your answer to question 9 on the graph below and on your knowledge of social studies.

PIE GRAPH

MAJOR OIL RESERVES (1991)

Western Europe 3.4%
Africa 3.5%
North America 5.5%
Asia 5.8%
Russia & E. Europe 9.8%
Latin America 11.7%
Middle East 60.3%

9 This graph helps to explain why
  1 gasoline prices are higher in Asia than in Western Europe
  2 U.S. foreign policy is often influenced by events in the Middle East
  3 environmentalists oppose oil exploration in Alaska
  4 the Exxon *Valdez* oil spill destroyed so much Alaska habitat

10 By the middle of the 20th century, changes were occurring in family structure which led to
  1 an increase in the number of farm families
  2 a decline in two earner families
  3 households containing several generations
  4 development of more nuclear families

Directions: Base your answer to question 11 on the quotation below and on your knowledge of social studies.

"It's not the big, dramatic things so much that get us down, but just being Indian (Native American), trying to hang on to our way of life, language, and values while being surrounded by an alien, more powerful culture."

– Mary Crow Dog and Richard Erdos, *Lakota Woman*, 1990

11 In this quotation, Mary Crow Dog is expressing her concern about the ability of Native Americans to
1 leave the reservations and enter the mainstream of American life
2 adopt the ways of the White communities that surround the reservations
3 continue the Native American way of life in the face of pressures to change
4 make the small changes required by modern education

CONSTRUCTED RESPONSE

SET 1

Directions: Base your answers to questions 1 through 3 on the quotations at the right and on your knowledge of social studies.

"I have a dream that one day the state of Alabama … will be transformed into a situation where little black boys and black girls will be able to join hands with little white boys and girls and walk together as sisters and brothers. …"

– Martin Luther King, Jr., 1963

"And the social philosophy of black nationalism means that we have to become socially mature to the point where we will realize the responsibility is upon us to elevate the condition, the standard of our community, to a higher level, so that our people will be satisfied to live in our own social circles. … instead of trying to force our way into the social circles of those who don't want us."

– Malcolm X, 1965

1 Which speaker states that "blacks" (African Americans) must take responsibility for their own future? _____

2 Which speaker states that African Americans and whites will join together in the future?

_____

3 What do these two speakers tell you about the views of African American leaders on the future of African Americans in the United States?

_____

_____

_____

SET 2

Directions: Base your answers to questions 4 through 6 on the illustration at the right and on your knowledge of social studies.

4 Identify TWO (2) forms of pollution evident in this sketch.

_____

_____

5   What is ONE (1) effect of pollution evident in the sketch? _____

_____

_____

_____

6   What is ONE (1) other problem that might result from the pollution shown in the sketch?

_____

_____

_____

PRACTICE SKILLS FOR DBQ

Directions: The following task is based on the accompanying documents. The documents may have been edited for the purposes of this exercise. The task is designed to test your ability to work with historical documents. As you analyze the documents, take into account both the source of the document and the author's point of view where relevant.

Historical Context: From the end of World War II to the end of the 20th century, the role that American women played in society and the economy underwent many changes. In some measure, the changes were the result of the civil rights movement that tried to ensure equality of opportunity. In some measure they were the result of the feminist movement which made women more aware of their potential. In some measure the changes came about as the economy offered chances for their involvement.

Part A - Short Answer

Document 1

> "They (suburban American women) baked their own bread, sewed their own and their children's clothes, kept their new washing machines and dryers running all day. ...They had no thought for the unfeminine problems of the world outside the home. ..."
>
> – Adapted from Betty Friedan, *The Feminine Mystique*, 1963

1a   According to Betty Friedan, what were TWO (2) things American women did in the early 1960s?

_____

_____

_____

1b   According to Friedan, what was NOT a concern of American women in the 1960s?

_____

_____

_____

_____

Document 2

2 Describe the trend in the percentage of women working outside the home in the U.S. between 1960 and 2000.

_____

_____

_____

_____

_____

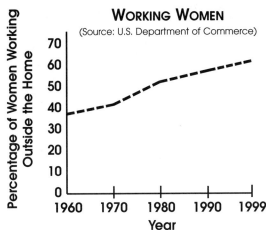

Document 3

Use the following data table, "Women As Percentage Of Total Employed," to answer questions 3a through 3c.

WOMEN AS PERCENT OF TOTAL EMPLOYED (Source: U.S. Department of Labor, Bureau of Labor Statistics)			
Occupation	**1975**	**1985**	**1996**
Waiter/Waitress	91.1	84.0	77.9
Data Entry Keyer	92.8	90.7	84.5
Lawyer, Judge	7.1	18.2	29.0
Physician	13.0	17.2	26.4

3a In what TWO (2) occupations did the percent of women employed increase between 1975 and 1996?

_____

3b In what TWO (2) occupations did the percent of women employed decrease between 1975 and 1996?

_____

3c What do the answers to the two questions above tell you about the type of jobs women are entering in increasing numbers?

_____

_____

Part B - Essay Response

Task: Discuss how the role of women changed from the end of World War II to the end of the 20th century. (State your thesis in the introduction.)

ADDITIONAL SUGGESTED TASK

From your knowledge of social studies, make a list of additional ways in which the role of women changed from the end of world War II to the end of the 20th century.

Unit 12

CITIZENSHIP IN TODAY'S WORLD

GO TO THE POLLS and VOTE "IT IS YOUR DUTY!"

We The People

> "**We the People** of the United States, in Order to form a more perfect Union, establish Justice, insure domestic Tranquility, provide for the common defense, promote the general Welfare, and secure the Blessings of Liberty to ourselves and our Posterity, do ordain and establish this Constitution for the United States of America."
>
> – Preamble to the *Constitution of the United States*

CITIZENSHIP IN THE UNITED STATES

The Preamble to the *Constitution of the United States of America* starts with the words: "We the People..." The words are simple, but their meaning is profound. The Constitution outlines a democracy and the people are the source of all power. The United States of America is a country where the citizens themselves run the government. To remain free, to have dignity, and to achieve happiness, a citizen must work to keep democracy alive and well.

Citizens have certain rights and privileges, but there are duties, too. Simply put, democracy dies without citizen participation. Free citizens must know their government. They must be clear on the principles that form its foundation. Those principles form a system that makes democracy work and opportunity grow so that the people remain free.

UNDERLYING PRINCIPLES OF THE U.S. CONSTITUTION

The *Constitution of the United States* is based on several important ideas. These include limited government, representative government, federalism, separation of power, protection of individual rights, and provision for change (amendments).

- **Limited Government** is the basic principle that places in writing what the national and state governments can and cannot do. This procedure means government activities are clearly stated in written constitutions. This makes it hard for government to go beyond what is stated.

- **Representative Government** is another basic principle. It guarantees that the people have direct and indirect processes to choose their leaders and deal with issues.

- **Federalism** is a core principle of American government. It sets up a system of government that divides power between a central authority and smaller political units. Clearly dividing power is a way of limiting any group.

A federal union sets up a dual system of government. In the federal union of the United States, the

---

U.S. CONSTITUTION LIMITS POWER BY DIVIDING IT BETWEEN THE NATIONAL AND STATE GOVERNMENTS.

FEDERALISM

Delegated Powers
(national government only)

interstate & foreign commerce
foreign relations
declares war
coins money
immigration
postal service

Implied Powers
Congress can stretch
the delegated powers.

Concurrent Powers
(both governments)
taxation
borrowing
court systems
penal systems
law enforcement agencies
general welfare of citizens
charter banks and
corporations

Reserved Powers
(state governments only)

intrastate commerce
local governments
public health
voter qualification
supervise elections
supervise education
license occupations

AMERICANS ARE CITIZENS UNDER TWO GOVERNMENTS:
NATIONAL (U.S. FEDERAL) GOVERNMENT AND THE STATE IN WHICH THEY RESIDE.

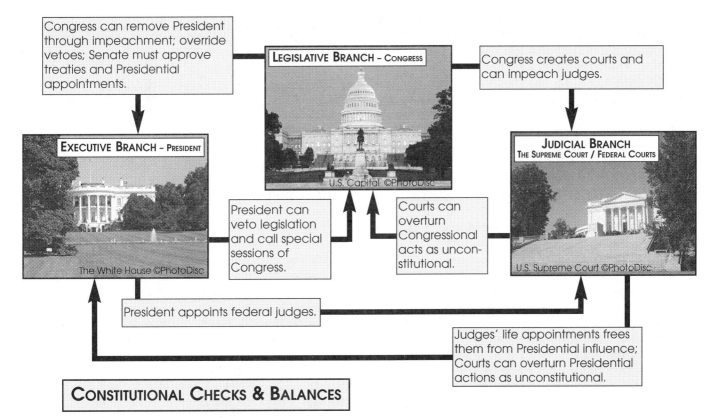

Congress can remove President through impeachment; override vetoes; Senate must approve treaties and Presidential appointments.

LEGISLATIVE BRANCH - CONGRESS

U.S. Capital ©PhotoDisc

Congress creates courts and can impeach judges.

EXECUTIVE BRANCH - PRESIDENT

The White House ©PhotoDisc

JUDICIAL BRANCH
THE SUPREME COURT / FEDERAL COURTS

U.S. Supreme Court ©PhotoDisc

President can veto legislation and call special sessions of Congress.

Courts can overturn Congressional acts as unconstitutional.

President appoints federal judges.

Judges' life appointments frees them from Presidential influence; Courts can overturn Presidential actions as unconstitutional.

CONSTITUTIONAL CHECKS & BALANCES

states accept the overall rule of the national government. However, the states keep power in local matters. (On the other hand, many nations have "unitary systems" in which all power rests with the central government. A unitary system is like a military chain of command – each level of government takes orders from the one directly above it.)

In a federal system, the levels have different functions and are mostly independent of each other. The Constitution says what the national government can and cannot do. The Constitution also says that remaining powers are left for the states. However, there is some power overlap, and the levels do interact. As new situations develop, sometimes the levels cooperate and sometimes they clash. Most of the time, the Supreme Court sorts out the problems.

In the 18th and 19th centuries, most countries were ruled by monarchs with absolute power. Division of power was a new idea. As soon as the new U.S. government began to function, there were arguments over how strong the national government was to be.

In the period before the Civil War (1861-1865), states claimed authority on certain issues. There were great debates over whether the national government could be taxed by the states; whether the states could refuse to collect federal taxes and tariffs; whether the states or the national government could make rules on slavery; and, whether the national government could control banks.

During the Civil War, the federal union nearly disintegrated over how much power the states had over issues such as slavery. After the Civil War, the federal government showed it had power in many issues, but questions about state power remained. Issues such as the death penalty, religion in the schools, and even a national speed limit still raise questions of state v. national power. Most of the time, the Supreme Court sorts out the issues in its decisions.

- **Separation of Power** is a basic principle that subdivides power within the the national government. The Constitution specifically assigns different functions and powers to the executive, legislative, and judicial branches. Each has specific tasks so that no one branch has too much power.

- **Checks and Balances** is a basic principle that keeps the branches separate. It limits the power of each branch of the national government. The Constitution gives each branch special controls to block the other branches from illegally expanding their powers.

All of this separating and checking flows from colonial experience. Royal governors overturned laws passed by colonial legislatures. In the new government, the framers of the Constitution allowed Presidents the veto power to block Congress, but they also gave Congress a way of overturning the veto. Similarly, each branch is given ways to prevent the other two branches from overstepping their bounds (see Checks and Balances diagram above).

A classic example of checks and balances is the Supreme Court's *Marbury v. Madison* decision (1803). In *Marbury*, the Supreme Court checked the power of Congress. The Court overturned a congressional law for the first time. In the *Judiciary Act of 1789*, Congress gave the Supreme Court the power to give orders to the President. Chief Justice John Marshall said Congress could not do this, for it violated the constitutional principle of separation of power. In *Marbury*, the Court declared that a portion of the *Judiciary Act of 1789* was unconstitutional. Marshall said that the judicial branch could not order the executive branch to do something. (In this case, Secretary of State Madison could not be ordered to give William Marbury an appointment as a federal judge.)

However, in another checks and balances situation, the Supreme Court said Congress could order the President to provide information for an investigation. In 1974, a special prosecutor appointed by Congress needed the President's tape recordings to investigate a burglary. President Nixon claimed "executive privilege." He said he did not have to give the tapes to Congress because they involved national security.

In the *United States v. Richard M. Nixon*, the Supreme Court ruled in favor of Congress. Chief Justice Burger said the separation of power did not outweigh the "fundamental demands of due process of law in the fair administration of criminal justice." The Court said that President Nixon could not hide behind separation of power – the Court ordered him to turn over the tapes.

> "...the doctrine of separation of powers... can (not) sustain an absolute, unqualified Presidential privilege of immunity from judicial process under all circumstances."
> – Chief Justice Warren Burger, *United States v. Richard M. Nixon, 1974*

- **Protection of Individual Rights** is a basic constitutional principle to insure individual liberty. Because the English people had long struggled for personal freedom, it was part of the American colonists' heritage. During and after the American Revolution (1775-1783), state governments guaranteed individual rights. The *Constitution of the United States* guarantees personal freedom – especially in its amendments.

Individual rights were important from colonial days. The trial of **John Peter Zenger** in 1733, in New York is an example. It shows that the colonists continued the English people's struggle for individual freedom. Zenger's paper, the *New York Weekly Journal*, criticized the colonial government. The government put Zenger in prison for nine months. Finally, it charged him with **libel** (false publication that viciously damages a person's reputation). His lawyer challenged the jury to decide whether what Zenger had printed was true. Zenger was acquitted. This was the first victory for the right of the press to print the truth.

MAJOR PROVISIONS OF THE *BILL OF RIGHTS*

I. Congress *shall not* pass laws infringing on freedoms of speech, press, peaceful assembly; free exercise of religion and separation of church and state.

II. Congress *shall not* pass laws infringing on the right to bear arms so that a well regulated militia can be maintained.

III. Congress *shall not* pass laws quartering troops in private homes in peacetime.

IV. Congress *shall not* pass laws authorizing unreasonable searches, seizures; warrants only on probable cause.

V. Congress *shall not* pass laws abusing legal proceedings. This amendment requires:
1. indictment by grand jury in felony cases
2. no double jeopardy (being tried a second time after acquittal)
3. self-incrimination cannot be forced
4. due process must be used (proper and equal legal procedures)
5. property cannot be taken without just compensation

VI. Congress *shall not* pass laws abusing accused citizens. This amendment requires:

1. speedy and public trial
2. impartial jury of peers
3. informing of charges
4. confrontation by accusers
5. calling of supportive witnesses
6. guarantee of counsel

VII. Congress *shall not* pass laws denying jury trials in certain civil (non-criminal) cases.

VIII. Congress *shall not* pass laws requiring excessive bail; cruel, or unusual punishment.

IX. Congress *shall not* pass laws denying other rights not listed in the Constitution.

X. Congress *shall not* pass laws denying to the states other powers not listed in the Constitution. (As part of the theory of federalism, powers not specifically assigned to the central government are reserved for the states.)

DUE PROCESS OF LAW

CONSTITUTIONAL RIGHTS OF THE ACCUSED

RIGHT TO REMAIN SILENT

INFORM OF RIGHT TO LAWYER

NO EXCESSIVE BAIL

NO UNREASONABLE SEARCH (NEED ARREST WARRANT)

NO EXCESSIVE PUNISHMENT

NO FORCED CONFESSION

SPEEDY & PUBLIC TRIAL BY JURY

Slavery is the opposite of personal liberty. The Thirteenth Amendment abolished slavery in 1865, at the end of the Civil War. Before the War, the Supreme Court tried to settle the slavery issue. In 1857, a question arose over whether a slave who had been brought to free territory was free. In *Dred Scott v. Sandford* (1857), the Supreme Court declared that slaves had no citizenship or rights as citizens. The Decision did not settle the issue. It worsened the situation and helped bring on the great tragedy of the Civil War.

The issue of personal freedom was at the core of **Plessy v. Ferguson** (1896). Could states make **de jure** (legalized) segregation laws that required separation of the races in public facilities? Critics said segregation violated the Fourteenth Amendment which guaranteed "equal protection of the law" for all citizens. In *Plessy*, the Supreme Court declared that African Americans could be legally separated as long as states made sure that facilities provided for each race were equal.

The inequality upheld in *Plessy* lasted another sixty years. In 1954, the fairness of separate facilities for races was challenged again. Could states make laws that required separate schools for the races? This time the Court looked beyond the facilities.

In **Brown v. the Board of Education of Topeka, Kansas** (1954), the Court looked at the idea of equality itself. It said that separate public schools for the races violated the personal freedom guaranteed by the Fourteenth Amendment. In *Brown*, the Court said that no matter how equal the facilities, legal separation based on race was unequal. The Court ordered all segregation of schools to end. As the Civil Rights Movement grew in the 1950s and 1960s, the Court condemned all de jure segregation of the races.

Another area of personal freedom is the rights of people accused of crimes. Because government can take freedom away, fair laws and fair treatment of accused persons are important. Scholars call fair treatment of the accused due process of law. Over more than two centuries, the courts of the U.S. have ruled on fair treatment. The question is always difficult because the courts must weigh the state's police power to keep society safe against individual liberty.

In 1966, the Supreme Court issued a landmark decision on rights of the accused – **Miranda v. Arizona**. In this case, the Court found a mentally handicapped man convicted of kidnapping and rape had not been told of his rights by the authorities. The Court overturned his conviction, but more important, it changed how police treated accused persons. The **Miranda Rule** requires that, before questioning suspects, police must tell an accused person that:

- they may remain silent
- anything they say may be used against them in court
- they have a right to have an attorney present
- if they cannot afford an attorney, one will be provided
- they may end police questioning at any time

Another example of the courts protecting individual freedom came in the 1969 case of **Tinker v. Des Moines School District**. In 1965, some Iowa high school students demonstrated their opposition to the Vietnam War by wearing black arm bands. They were suspended by school officials for violating the school dress code. The Supreme Court upheld the students' personal right to wear the arm bands as an extension of freedom of speech.

- **Provision for Change (Amendments)** is an important principle of government because change is so rapid in life. New technology and new ideas change people's behavior. Government must be able to make changes when the times call for them. Small changes can be made by using new procedures, but basic changes in the Constitution must be done by formal amendment.

CONSTITUTION OF THE UNITED STATES

PREAMBLE

We the people of the United States, in order to form a more perfect union, establish justice, insure domestic tranquility, provide for the common defense, promote the general welfare, and secure the blessings of liberty for ourselves and our posterity, do ordain and establish this Constitution of the United States of America.

ORIGINAL CONSTITUTION

Article I: Establishes Congress as a bicameral legislative branch (House of Rep. & Senate); how members are chosen and terms; lists 17 specific powers plus the "elastic clause;" Presidential veto and override; actions prohibited

Article II: Establishes executive branch with President and Vice President; duties of office; how elected; appointment power; checks on power, including impeachment procedure

Article III: Establishes judicial branch, with Supreme Court and its jurisdiction; how Congress sets up lower Federal courts; defines treason

Article IV: Declares equality among the states, extradition, admission of new states, Congress' authority over territories; requires republican form of government in all states

Article V: Establishes procedure for amending the Constitution

Article VI: Declares Constitution the Supreme law of the land

Article VII: Establishes procedure for the 13 states to ratify the new Constitution

CONSTITUTIONAL AMENDMENTS

Bill of Rights (1791)

1st Amendment - freedom of speech, press, assembly, free exercise of religion

2nd Amendment - right to bear arms

3rd Amendment - forbids government from quartering of troops in peacetime

4th Amendment - protects against unwarranted search

5th Amendment - protects rights of accused to due process; eminent domain

6th Amendment - protects rights to fair trial & counsel

7th Amendment - right of jury trial in civil cases

8th Amendment - protects against cruel punishment & excessive bail

9th Amendment - rights not specifically mentioned still exist

10th Amendment - powers not specified in Constitution left to states and people

---

SUBSEQUENT AMENDMENTS

11th Amendment (1795) - suits by citizens of one state against a particular state must be heard in the latter's courts not in Federal ones

12th Amendment (1804) - electors must use separate ballots for President and Vice President

13th Amendment (1865) - abolishes slavery

14th Amendment (1868) - defines citizenship, application of due process, and equal protection

15th Amendment (1870) - defines citizens' right to vote

16th Amendment (1913) - allows Federal income tax

17th Amendment (1913) - direct popular election of United States Senators

18th Amendment (1919) - manufacture, sale, importation, & transportation of alcoholic beverages forbidden in U.S. (repealed by 21st Amend.)

19th Amendment (1920) - right of women to vote

20th Amendment (1933) - redefines term of President & sessions of Congress

21st Amendment (1933) - repeal of prohibition amendment (18th)

22nd Amendment (1951) - limits Presidential term

23rd Amendment (1961) - provides Presidential electors for District of Columbia

24th Amendment (1964) - abolishes poll taxes: Federalelections

25th Amendment (1967) - defines succession to presidency & disability of President

26th Amendment (1971) - eighteen year-old citizens may vote in Federal elections

27th Amendment (1992) - sitting Congress may not raise own salary

One example was the direct election of Senators through the **Seventeenth Amendment** (1913). In the original Constitution, Senators were chosen by state leaders, not the people. The framers felt that average people in the 18th century were not well educated or travelled enough to pick statewide leaders. The process was riddled with corruption in the late 19th century. Reformers of the late 19th and early 20th centuries claimed the general public was better informed and educated to choose their Senators.

It took nearly two decades before the Seventeenth Amendment became part of the Constitution. There was opposition from Senators at first and from state officials who felt they were losing power. However, newspapers and writers worked along side reformers to finally get Congress to endorse the Amendment. Slowly public opinion pressured the needed three-fourths of the states to ratify the Amendment.

Alice Paul, 1920, a leader of radical tactics of the women's suffrage movement, later drafted the first *Equal Rights Amendment*.
(Library of Congress)

Women's suffrage is another example of how long it can take to change the Constitution. Serious demand for voting rights for women came from the Seneca Falls Convention in 1848. The campaign increased after former slaves were given the vote after the Civil War (Fifteenth Amendment, 1870). **Susan B. Anthony** and **Elizabeth Cady Stanton** formed the National Woman Suffrage Association to work for suffrage on the national level. The women's suffrage amendment was proposed in Congress in 1878. In 1890, Wyoming became the first state with general women's suffrage. In the same year, leaders formed the **National American Woman Suffrage Association** (NAWSA).

Carrie Chapman Catt and **Alice Paul** took over NAWSA leadership in the early 1900s. They used public rallies to call attention to their cause. In 1915, Alice Paul organized the **National Woman's Party**. It campaigned with mass marches and hunger strikes. Persistence on the part of both organizations led to victory. After nearly forty-one years, the 19th Amendment granted the ballot to American women in August of 1920.

LEGAL BASES FOR CITIZENSHIP

A **citizen** is a person who owes loyalty to state or nation and is entitled by birth or naturalization to its protection. A citizen possesses certain rights and privileges and accepts corresponding duties.

- **Citizenship by law and soil**
  The United States, most English-speaking countries, and most Latin American countries grant citizenship to those born on their soil. This rule is called **jus soli** (right of soil or place of birth).

- **Citizenship by birth**
  Most countries, including the United States, recognize **jus sanguinis** (right of blood or descent). This allows citizenship to be transmitted from a father, or sometimes a mother, to a child regardless of where the child is born.

For a child born outside of the United States or its possessions to be a citizen, either both parents must have been citizens or one must have resided in the United States for at least five years before the birth of the child.

- **Citizenship through naturalization**
  A person may also become a U.S. citizen by naturalization. The U.S. Constitution (Article I, Section 8) empowers Congress to pass uniform laws for naturalization. Congress did so for the first time in 1790. Most immigrants to the United States became citizens this way.

REQUIREMENTS FOR NATURALIZATION
• lawful entry for permanent residence
• five years residence (or, for spouses of U.S. citizens, three years)
• good moral character, as displayed during the period of residence
• support of the Constitution
• understanding of English, including an ability to read, write, and speak it except where physical disability prevents
• knowledge and understanding of the fundamentals of U.S. history and government
• residence for six months in the district of the naturalization court

RIGHTS AND RESPONSIBILITIES OF CITIZENSHIP ACROSS TIME AND SPACE
Citizens possess certain rights and privileges and have to perform certain duties.

Citizen **Rights**	Citizen **Responsibilities**
• Enjoy the country's protection and its laws • Hold and transfer all types of property • Vote • Seek elective office • Hold governmental positions • Receive welfare and social benefits • Be treated fairly in a legal system • Enjoy the protection of the Constitution and the laws	• Pay taxes • Obey the laws of the nation • Defend their nation • Serve jury duty

CIVIC KNOWLEDGE (POLITICAL AWARENESS)

Citizens in a democracy have to vote on many issues at many levels of government. They also have to choose officials at every level who will represent them. To vote responsibly, citizens have to keep up with issues in their community, county, state, and nation. They can be informed by going to local meetings, reading newspapers, and by listening to public affairs programs on radio and television. A democracy can only remain healthy if citizens take this responsibility seriously. When the work of staying informed is left to others, only the voices of the few are heard. When only a few people have power, democracy begins to crumble.

CITIZENSHIP IN STATE AND
LOCAL GOVERNMENT – NEW YORK STATE

The present state government is organized under the state constitution adopted in 1894, with subsequent amendments. Changing the New York state constitution is a two step process. An amendment must be approved by a majority at two sessions of the state legislature. Then a majority of voters must approve it in a general election.

The executive branch of New York state government consists of the Governor, elected to a 4-year term, assisted by three other elected officials—the Lieutenant Governor, the comptroller, and the attorney general. Under the Governor, there are twenty administrative departments. With Senate approval, the Governor appoints the heads of most of these departments. Examples include the Departments of Education, Conservation, Commerce, Health, and Social Assistance. The Governor is the central figure in state politics.

The New York state legislature has two houses, the Senate and Assembly. There are 61 senators and 150 assemblymen. They are elected to two-year terms. There are regular annual sessions of each house of the legislature, although the Governor may call special sessions.

New York has an extensive state court system. There are twelve judicial districts. Voters in each district elect justices to 14-year terms. The highest state court is the Court of Appeals. It consists of a chief judge and six associates selected for 14-year terms.

The Governor of New York is often a well-known figure in national politics. Three New York Governors have served as Presidents of the United States – Grover Cleveland, Theodore Roosevelt, and Franklin D. Roosevelt. Throughout U.S. history, other New York state Governors have been chosen by their parties to be candidates for the presidency. These include George Clinton, DeWitt Clinton, Horatio Seymour, Samuel J. Tilden, Charles Evans Hughes, Alfred E. Smith, and Thomas E. Dewey.

LOCAL GOVERNMENT

Besides the national and state governments, Americans are also citizens of many levels of local government.

County – A county is a territorial division and unit of local government. In 1990, the United States had 3,006 counties; Texas had the most (254) and Delaware the fewest (3). New York State has sixty-two counties. Counties usually have a full-time single elected executive or a part-time group of supervisors to administer the daily government activities. Most counties have a part-time elected legislative body representing geographic areas inside the county. County legislatures usually meet several times each month.

Town – A town is a population center, often incorporated, larger than a village and usually smaller than a city. A small group of elected representatives serve on a lawmaking council or board that meets weekly. There are usually an elected town supervisor and a town clerk who administer the daily government activities such as billing and collecting local property taxes, maintaining local roads and recreation facilities, and supervising town employees.

City – A city is a town of significant size and importance. It is usually a center of population, commerce, and culture. A city has boundaries and legal powers granted in a charter by the state. City governments vary greatly. Most cities have an elected mayor or city manager as the executive. In addition, a group of elected council representatives draws up local laws and budgets.

More than 88% of New York State's population lives in or near its ten largest cities (New York City, Buffalo, Rochester, Syracuse, Albany, Niagara Falls, Utica, Schenectady, Binghamton, and Troy). Nearly 60% of the population is concentrated in New York City and the counties around NYC.

Village – A village is a small group of dwellings in a rural area, usually ranking in size between a hamlet and a town. Many villages are just locations within towns, but some have organized governments. Village governments vary, but they are usually similar in structure to a town. The village executive is the mayor and the rules and problems are addressed by elected members of the village board.

School District – A school district is geographic area, the public schools of which are administered together. School districts are run by an elected group of citizens meeting at least once per month. The Board of Education sets tax rates, maintains buildings, formulates budgets, hires the Superintendent (the chief executive officer) and other administrators, and sets up elections.

EFFECT OF LOCAL GOVERNMENT ON THE CITIZEN

Local governments provide many services. However, not all the services are funded by local taxes.

SERVICES OF LOCAL GOVERNMENTS

EDUCATION
UTILITIES
LAWS
ROADS
SOCIAL SERVICES
TRAFFIC AND SMALL CLAIMS COURTS
ZONING
POLICE AND FIRE PROTECTION
RECREATION/CULTURE

NATIONAL

STATE

GOVERNMENTS

COUNTY

MIDDLETOWN

TOWN/CITY

Local governments receive funding assistance for administering certain programs required by the state and federal governments. In such cases, there are overlapping rules and regulations that are attached to using the funds provided by these other government units.

Education in New York State is an example of such government overlap. A locally elected school board makes certain independent decisions. It taxes local property owners for school expenses. However, most rules and regulations – and nearly half the district's funding – comes through the State Education Department (SED). For example, the SED orders the tests for which you are preparing by using this book.

The federal government also pays for some of the education programs run by the state. An example is school lunches for needy children. The federal government requires that state officials inspect local school districts' lunch programs to see that federal rules are being followed.

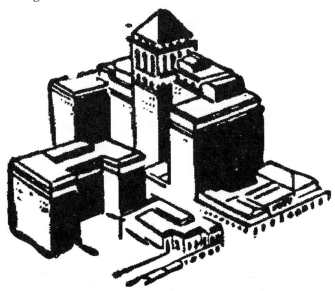

REMINDER: For help in handling questions, see ADVICE CHART on page 184.

UNIT 12
MULTIPLE CHOICE

1 Under the U.S. system of federalism, the power rests with the
   1 President and the judges
   2 national and state governments
   3 military and legislature
   4 chief executive and legislature

2 Disputes over power between the state and national governments are most often settled by (the)
   1 Congress
   2 wars
   3 Supreme Court
   4 system of checks and balances

3 In the case of *Marbury v. Madison*, the Supreme Court ruling protected the principle of
   1 federalism
   2 representative government
   3 individual rights
   4 separation of power

Directions: Base your answer to question 4 on the chart below and on your knowledge of social studies.

4 Based on the chart, it is possible to conclude that
   1 neither the President nor the Governor of New York plays a role in lawmaking
   2 the President and the Governor have very similar roles in their respective governments
   3 only the President is charged with the responsibility of enforcing laws
   4 both the President and the Governor conduct diplomatic relations with other nations

Directions: Base your answer to question 5 on the chart below and on your knowledge of social studies.

REQUIREMENTS FOR NATURALIZATION
• lawful entry for permanent residence
• five years residence (or, for spouses of U.S. citizens, three years)
• good moral character, as displayed during the period of residence
• support the Constitution
• understanding of English, including an ability to read, write, and speak it except where physical disability prevents
• knowledge and understanding of the fundamentals of U.S. history and government
• residence for six months in the district of the naturalization court.

5 According to this chart, naturalization requires that the person involved
   1 be born in the United States
   2 have served in the armed forces
   3 know the fundamentals of U.S. history and government
   4 be able to support him/herself

6 The trial of John Peter Zenger, the 13th Amendment, and *Brown v. Board of Education of Topeka, Kansas* have in common their
   1 protection of personal freedoms
   2 support for freedom of the press
   3 support for equal opportunity
   4 protection of trial by jury

7 When the police follow the Miranda Rule, they are
   1 making arrangements for bail
   2 advising an arrested person of his/her rights
   3 conducting an illegal search
   4 testifying in a jury trial

ROLES OF THE U.S. PRESIDENT AND N.Y.S. GOVERNOR COMPARED

Duties of the President of the United States	Roles of the Governor of New York State
• Chief Executive Runs Government Programs • Chief of State Ceremonial Head • Chief Diplomat Conducts Foreign Relations • Chief Legislator Proposes Laws • Chief Jurist Enforces Court Decisions • Commander in Chief Heads Military • Leader of Political Party in Nation	• Heads Executive Branch (enforces state laws; appoints department heads and commissioners) • Represents the state at National Meetings and Conferences • Influencer of Legislation (sends ideas to state legislature; signs all laws; can veto laws full or in part) • Judicial Influence (appoints high level judges; pardon criminals; commute sentences) • Leader of Political Party in State

8 Which group of people gained the right to vote in 1920 after the end of World War I?
   1 African Americans in Southern states
   2 everyone over the age of 18
   3 males over the age of 21
   4 women over the age of 21

9 Payment of taxes, obedience to the laws of the nation, service in the armed forces, and service on juries are all examples of the
   1 responsibilities of citizens
   2 requirements for naturalization
   3 rights of citizens
   4 delegated powers

10 Local governments are very important in the U.S. because they
   1 have primary responsibility for defense
   2 are the only government unit to impose taxes
   3 provide many services to citizens
   4 conduct foreign relations

CONSTRUCTED RESPONSE

SET 1

Directions: Base your answers to questions 1 through 3 on the quotations at the right and on your knowledge of social studies.

"The Supreme Court does not accept Homer Plessy's argument that segregation, or enforced separation of the races, stamps the colored race with a badge of inferiority. This argument also assumes that prejudices may be overcome by laws and that equal rights cannot be secured for the Negro except by an enforced mixing of the two races. The Supreme Court does not accept this assumption. The Court upholds Louisiana's 'equal but separate' law."

– Adaptation of decision in the case of *Plessy v. Ferguson*, 1896

"Separate education facilities are inherently unequal. (Separating children) solely because of their race generates a feeling of inferiority as to their status in the community that may affect their hearts and minds in a way unlikely to be undone."

– *Brown v. Board of Education of Topeka, Kansas*, 1954

1 In *Plessy v. Ferguson*, what is the attitude of the Supreme Court on separation of races?

_____

_____

_____

2 What view of separation of the races for education does the Supreme Court take in *Brown v. Board of Education*?

_____

_____

_____

3 What change occurred in the thinking of the Supreme Court between *Plessy v. Ferguson* in 1896 and *Brown v. Board of Education* in 1954?

_____

_____

_____

Directions: Base your answers to questions 4 and 5 on the diagram below and on your knowledge of social studies.

DUE PROCESS OF LAW

CONSTITUTIONAL RIGHTS OF THE ACCUSED

RIGHT TO REMAIN SILENT

INFORM OF RIGHT TO LAWYER

NO EXCESSIVE BAIL

NO UNREASONABLE SEARCH (NEED ARREST WARRANT)

NO EXCESSIVE PUNISHMENT

NO FORCED CONFESSION

SPEEDY & PUBLIC TRIAL BY JURY

4 List TWO (2) rights of the accused guaranteed by the *Constitution of the United States*.

_____

_____

5 For EACH right listed in answer 4, explain how it ensured due process of law for the accused.

_____

_____

_____

_____

PRACTICE SKILLS FOR DBQ

Directions: The following task is based on the accompanying documents. The documents may have been edited for the purposes of this exercise. The task is designed to test your ability to work with historical documents. As you analyze the documents, take into account both the source of the document and the author's point of view where relevant.

Historical Context: When our founding fathers wrote the *Constitution of the United States*, they included many ideas designed to protect democracy in the new country. Some of these ideas were included because of experiences under royal Governors and the control of the British government; others were the result of the ideas of writers during the period of the Enlightenment.

Part A - Short Answer

Document 1

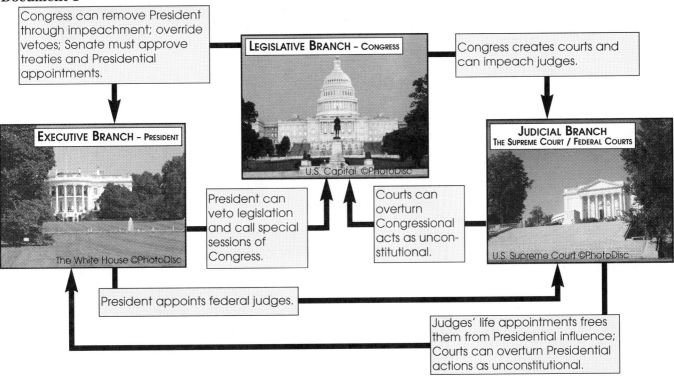

Congress can remove President through impeachment; override vetoes; Senate must approve treaties and Presidential appointments.

LEGISLATIVE BRANCH – CONGRESS

U.S. Capital ©PhotoDisc

Congress creates courts and can impeach judges.

EXECUTIVE BRANCH – PRESIDENT

The White House ©PhotoDisc

JUDICIAL BRANCH
THE SUPREME COURT / FEDERAL COURTS

U.S. Supreme Court ©PhotoDisc

President can veto legislation and call special sessions of Congress.

Courts can overturn Congressional acts as unconstitutional.

President appoints federal judges.

Judges' life appointments frees them from Presidential influence; Courts can overturn Presidential actions as unconstitutional.

1a Identify ONE (1) way that the executive branch can check the legislative branch and ONE (1) way it can check the judicial branch.

_____

_____

_____

1b Identify ONE (1) way that the legislative branch can check the executive branch and ONE (1) way it can check the judicial branch.

_____

_____

_____

1c Identify ONE (1) way that the judicial branch can check the executive branch and ONE (1) way it can check the legislative branch.

_____

_____

_____

Document 2

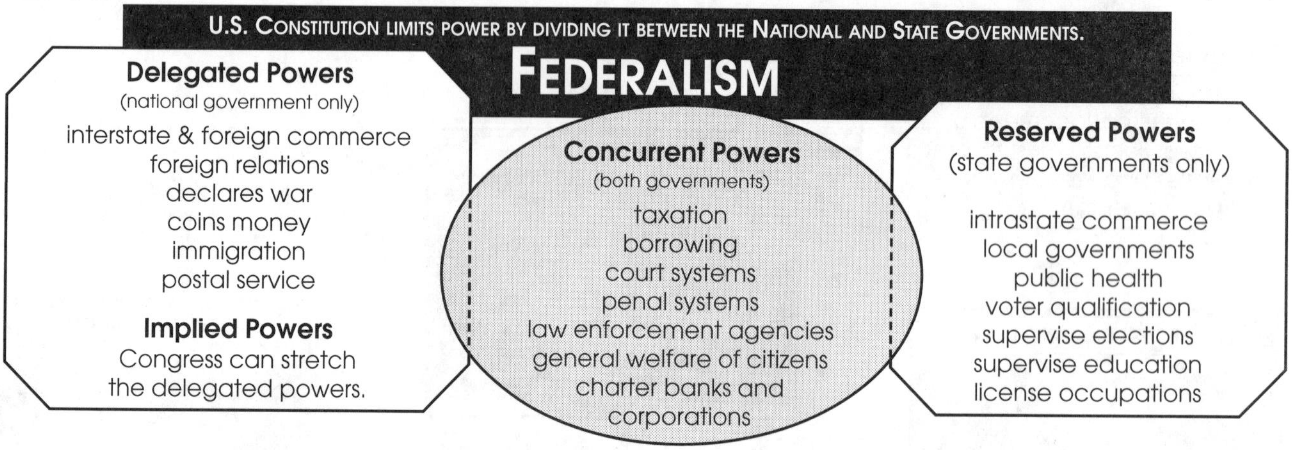

FEDERALISM

U.S. CONSTITUTION LIMITS POWER BY DIVIDING IT BETWEEN THE NATIONAL AND STATE GOVERNMENTS.

Delegated Powers
(national government only)

interstate & foreign commerce
foreign relations
declares war
coins money
immigration
postal service

Implied Powers
Congress can stretch
the delegated powers.

Concurrent Powers
(both governments)

taxation
borrowing
court systems
penal systems
law enforcement agencies
general welfare of citizens
charter banks and
corporations

Reserved Powers
(state governments only)

intrastate commerce
local governments
public health
voter qualification
supervise elections
supervise education
license occupations

AMERICANS ARE CITIZENS UNDER TWO GOVERNMENTS:
NATIONAL (U.S. FEDERAL) GOVERNMENT AND THE STATE IN WHICH THEY RESIDE.

2a Identify ONE (1) delegated power, ONE (1) concurrent power, and ONE (1) reserved power. For EACH power identified indicate which government(s) has the power.

_____

_____

_____

2b How does federalism help protect democracy?

_____

_____

_____

Part B - Essay Response

Task: Discuss at least TWO (2) ways in which the *Constitution of the United States* provided for the protection of democracy. (State your thesis in the introduction.)

ADDITIONAL SUGGESTED TASK

From your knowledge of social studies, make a list of other ways in which the *Constitution of the United States* provided for the protection of democracy.

UNIT 13

APPENDICES

TABLE OF CONTENTS

EXAM QUESTION STRATEGIES
MULTIPLE CHOICE & DOCUMENT BASED

GUIDE FOR MULTIPLE CHOICE QUESTIONS

Question Type	Strategies
Concept Question *see #1 on page 59* *see #2 on page 16*	• One of the answers illustrates a term or idea presented in the introduction of the question. • Try to define the term in the stem before looking at the answers. If you know the term, the illustration among the answers should pop out at you.
Reading Passage Question *see #6 on page 26* *see quest. 1-2 on pg. 109*	• Before you look at the question(s), read the passage. • Ask yourself what the passage is about. • Is there a title? • What (who) is the source? (Most times, it is clearly stated at the end of the quotation.) • From what time period is it? • What was happening in that time period?
Speaker A-B-C Question *see #5 on page 42* *see #12 on page 190*	• Before you look at the question(s), read the statements. • Identify the common theme. • List what you know about the topic. • Determine each person's position on the topic.
Series (events list or headlines) Questions *see #4 on page 59* *see #5 on page 16*	• Before you look at the question(s), look at the items. • See if you can detect a common thread among them – perhaps they are all about causes of wars, or they are all about civil rights.
Multi clue Question *see #14 on page 98* *see #18 on page 191* *see #34 on page 193*	• In these questions, there are several items in the introduction. You are looking for a common thread. • Focus on one item you really know. Look at the answers to see which one of them applies accurately to the event you know. Check to see if it applies to the other events in the stem, too.

Question Type	Strategies
Visual Stimulation Questions <u>Approximately 20% of exam</u>	*VSQs should be treated differently than other question types. Before reading the question or looking at the detractors (possible answers), cover them and just look at the visual. Then, use the strategies that follow to analyze and then choose the appropriate, correct answer.*

Map Questions
    see #7 on page 26
    see #9 on page 97
	• What is the title?
	• What is the area shown?
	• What time period is depicted?
	• Is there a legend (key) to show what different shades or lines stand for?

Graph Questions
    see #5 on page 60
    see #4 on page 96
	• What is the title?
	• What are the axes labeled?
	• Is there more than one graph? If so, what are the differences between or among them? (Example: do they show two different time periods?)
	• Is there a legend that says what the lines, bars, or shades stand for?
	• What item takes up the greatest portion of the graph(s)?
	• What item takes up the smallest portion of the graph(s)?

Cartoon Questions
    see #3 on page 33
    see #10 on page 97
	• What is the title?
	• In what time period is the action taking place?
	• Identify the persons or symbols shown.
	• How would you describe the action taking place? Where is the action taking place?
	• Is the cartoon poking fun at or condemning one of the figures?
	• What is the source?

Chart Questions
    see #9 on page 16
    see #10 on page 43
	• What is the title?
	• What is the source? Are dates used?
	• What do the columns stand for?
	• Are there differences among the columns?
	• What is the most striking difference among the items shown? (Which is largest? Which is smallest?)

Time Line Questions *see #1 on page 25*	• What events were happening during the range of years covered in the time line (i.e., Civil War, New Deal, Great Society)? • Is there a title? (It can hint at the connection of the time line items.) • What is the range of dates covered? • Are there similarities among the items on the time line (i.e., battles, similar laws, reforms, or amendments)?

DBQs

The Document Based Question (DBQ) is designed to prepare students for real life situations and to encourage those thinking skills necessary for responsible citizenship in the 21st century. **On the examinations, all parts of the Document-Based Question have to be answered.** DBQs usually consist of no more than eight documents, at least two of which are visuals as opposed to narrative quotations.

PART A

Each document (with source identified) is followed by a short-answer question. This is identified as "Part A." Think of this as prewriting designed to help you identify those aspects of the documents that might prove useful in building the Part B essay. Note that credit is awarded for correct answers to these short response Part A questions as well as for the Part B essay itself. **Note also that you must answer all of the Part A responses.**

PART B

The Part B essay should be answered by taking the information from the Part A document responses. However, you must also use additional relevant information that you learned in the course. You must use most of the Part A documents in writing the essay answer. The DBQ essay requires a specific format:

(1)   the **introduction** (including thesis),
(2)   the **body** (factual evidence), and
(3)   the **conclusion** (restate proven thesis and summarize supporting evidence).

PRACTICING DBQs

To best prepare for the Document Based Questions, you should do the following:

• Focus on the sample writing questions and responses in the Units and the Practice Exam.

• In the "Practice Skills for DBQs" at the end of each Unit, brainstorm possible answers to the practice questions.

• Analyze – relate the material to the thesis; do not simply paraphrase the documents.

• Take note of the author's nationality, religion, race, date when given.

• Assess the validity of a document – even when you do not know the author or source of the document. Contradictions within a document or with other documents may provide clues as to validity.

GRAPHIC ORGANIZER

• Use a "Graphic Organizer" (on the following pages) to see the pattern of your Part A answers. Placing answers in this compact format will assist you in seeing the overall structure needed for an effective presentation in the Part B essay. (Relying on the actual fill-ins on the test form is difficult because the answers are too spread out.)

• Experience is the best guide in how you use "Practice Skills for DBQ" exercises. Although they are designed to focus your attention on two critical skills – thesis formation and incorporating documents into essays, they offer fine opportunities for writing **conclusions** and **incorporating additional information**.

GRAPHIC ORGANIZER FOR THE DBQ ESSAY

The Graphic Organizer that follows will help you organize your DBQ essay [Part B]. There are 4 parts to this organizer: Steps 1, 2, and 3 focus on the theme of the essay; Step 4 helps organize the supporting evidence for the thesis; Step 5 focuses on the conclusion; and, Step 6 is the writing of the essay, itself. After you practice using this DBQ Graphic Organizer, you may want to modify this organizer to a shorter, customized one.

PART 1 – FORMULATING YOUR THESIS

Step 1   Review the Task [stated in Part B] and rewrite this task:

_____

_____

_____

_____

_____

PART 1 – FORMULATING YOUR THESIS CONTINUED

Step 2   Look back at each of your responses to the Document Questions [Part A]. Make a list (below) of key ideas, concepts, or facts from your responses that will help you write a defendable thesis statement [paragraph 1 of your final essay]:

_____

_____

_____

_____

_____

Step 3   Now, based on the task, state your [thesis] position to be "defended" in the main body of your DBQ Essay:

_____

_____

_____

_____

_____

PART 2 – ORGANIZING YOUR EVIDENCE

Step 4   Referring back to each Document [and Question Answer], fill in the columns below with the information needed to "defend" your above stated [thesis] position:

In this column, *identify each* document by (1) number, (2) subject [theme], and (3) source:	In this column, list *for each* document the support for your essay and the evidence from that document (i.e., facts, "quotes," statistics, examples, details):	In this column, list your related and relevant *outside* Information for inclusion in your essay (i.e., facts, "quotes," statistics, examples, details):

PART 3 – SHAPING YOUR CONCLUSION

Step 5   Review your column 2 and 3 supported facts. Circle the two or three strongest statements to be repeated in your conclusion paragraph. Rewrite them here:

_____

_____

_____

_____

_____

_____

PART 4 – WRITING THE ESSAY

Step 6   Now, write your DBQ Essay. Remember that your essay requires three distinctive parts [Introduction, Body, and Conclusion]:
- In the first paragraph [Introduction], state your thesis including reference to the Task.
- In the middle paragraphs [Body], state your supporting evidence for your thesis.
- In the last paragraph [Conclusion], restate your thesis together with the two or three strongest evidences supporting your thesis.

_____

_____

_____

_____

_____

_____

_____

_____

_____

_____

_____

_____

_____

_____

_____

_____

_____

_____

_____

_____

PRACTICE EXAM #1
SOCIAL STUDIES INTERMEDIATE LEVEL

PART I

MULTIPLE CHOICE

1   An examination of the process by which a bill becomes a law would most likely be studied by a (an)
    1   economist
    3   sociologist
    2   geographer
    4   political scientist

Directions: Base your answer to question 2 on the map below and on your knowledge of social studies

NORTH AMERICAN CULTURES (C 1500)

2   Based on this map, which is a correct conclusion about North American cultures?
    1   Eskimos primarily inhabited warm climates.
    2   Few North American cultures existed along the east coast of the U.S.
    3   There were more North American cultures in what became the U.S. than in what became Canada.
    4   The Mayan culture was the only one located in Mexico.

3   The Columbian Exchange led to
    1   disease and death for many Native Americans
    2   decreased trade between the Old and New Worlds
    3   a decline in the European standard of living
    4   isolation of Europe from North America

4   The alliance of the Algonquians with the French was the result of a
    1   desire to control the fur trade in eastern North America
    2   need for defense help against the Anasazi or Pueblo People
    3   the need for better farmlands
    4   concern about possible invasion from Spain

Directions: Base your answer to question 5 on the statements below and on your knowledge of social studies.

- People of the Great Plains spent their summers in portable tipis (teepees).

- The Anasazi built houses of stone and adobe masonry.

- The Eastern Woodland People lived in wooden longhouses.

5   These statements indicate that Native Americans
    1   rarely employed local materials to build their dwellings
    2   lived in very similar dwellings
    3   built dwellings suited to their environment
    4   inhabited permanent dwellings all year

6   Which event was the result of the other three?
    1   Marco Polo's account of his trip to China
    2   beginning of the Age of Exploration and Discovery
    3   improvements in methods of navigation
    4   increasing trade among towns and cities of Europe

7   Which statement about the early colonization of North America is most accurate?
    1   Sons and daughters of European nobles avoided the colonies.
    2   Few colonists were interested in economic gain.
    3   Religious freedom was a major goal for many colonists.
    4   Most early colonists came from southern Europe.

Directions: Base your answer to question 8 on the map below and on your knowledge of social studies.

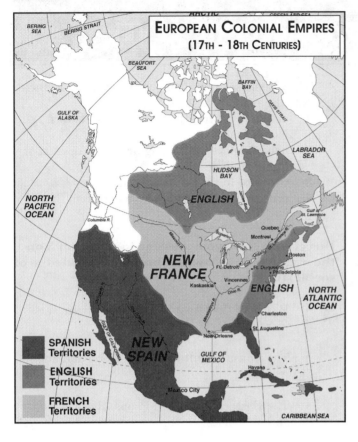

EUROPEAN COLONIAL EMPIRES
(17TH - 18TH CENTURIES)

8 Based on this map, which statement is correct?
1 Spanish territories were north of areas controlled by France.
2 French and Spanish territories blocked expansion of English coastal colonies.
3 France did not control any important waterways.
4 No part of the west coast was claimed by a European nation.

Directions: Base your answer to question 9 on the statements below and on your knowledge of social studies.

- Sell finished products to colonies

- Buy raw materials from colonies

- Increase gold and silver of mother country

9 The three goals listed are the objectives of
1 Protestant Reformers
2 American Patriots
3 Mercantilists
4 Federalists

10 British attempts to force their new tax policies on the colonists resulted in
1 acceptance by the colonists
2 protests and violence
3 emigration to Britain
4 colonial alliance with Spain

11 The American victory over the English at Saratoga, NY in 1777, was an important turning point in the American Revolution because it
1 led the French to form an alliance with the Americans
2 protected the South from attack by the sea
3 forced the British to withdraw from Canada
4 opened the St. Lawrence River Valley to the Americans

Directions: Base your answer to question 12 on the statements below and on your knowledge of social studies.

Speaker A: It is right and proper for Parliament to tax the American colonies to help pay for their defense.

Speaker B: Any taxation when the people taxed are not represented in Parliament is tyranny.

12 *Speaker A* is probably a (an)
1 American Patriot supporting colonial independence
2 believer in the ideas of Thomas Jefferson
3 supporter of the ideas of John Locke
4 Loyalist (Tory) living in the colonies

13 *The Articles of Confederation* proved to be a weak form of government because they gave
1 the right to interpret laws only to national courts
2 insufficient power to the national government
3 mercantilists control of the economy
4 no power to the state governments

Directions: Base your answer to question 14 on the time line below and on your knowledge of social studies.

```
     1800    1805    1810    1815    1820
__A__/__B__/_C__/__D__/__E___/__F_
```

14 In which time period does the Louisiana Purchase belong?
1 A
2 B
3 D
4 F

ARTICLES V. CONSTITUTION

ARTICLES OF CONFEDERATION	CONSTITUTION
• Unicameral legislature; each state had equal vote no matter size of population	• Bicameral legislature; representation proportional in House, states equal in Senate
• Two-thirds majority needed to pass laws	• Simple majority could pass laws
• No control of interstate or foreign trade	• Congress regulates interstate and foreign commerce
• Congress could levy but could not collect taxes	• Congress could levy and collect taxes
• No executive department to enforce laws	• Executive department headed by the President

Directions: Base your answer to question 15 on the chart above and on your knowledge of social studies.

15 Which is a correct conclusion about the *Articles of Confederation* and the *Constitution*?
1   Each provided the states with equal representation in the legislature.
2   It was easier to pass laws under the *Articles of Confederation*.
3   Only the Constitution provided for an executive.
4   Neither one allowed Congress to levy and collect taxes.

16 The *Federalist Papers* were important because they
1   helped to secure the ratification of the Constitution
2   presented the colonial reasons for independence from Britain
3   persuaded the French to come to the aid of the colonies
4   supported the election of George Washington as President

17 The issue involved in the Whiskey Rebellion was
1   neutrality
2   land speculation
3   territorial expansion
4   taxation

18 Elizabeth Cady Stanton, Henry Barnard, and Dorothea Dix have in common their desire to
1   establish new religions
2   improve the profits of industrialists
3   move Native Americans to reservations
4   make reforms in the American way of life

19 One immediate result of the territorial expansion associated with Manifest Destiny was a (an)
1   increased importance of the slavery issue
2   economic improvement for Native Americans
3   war with Britain over Oregon
4   Mexican annexation of Texas

Directions: Base your answer to question 20 on the map below and on your knowledge of social studies.

20 Which conclusion about the Northern battles of the War of 1812 is correct?
1   most battles occurred in Canada
2   the British won no battles
3   control of waterways was an objective
4   no battles occurred outside New York

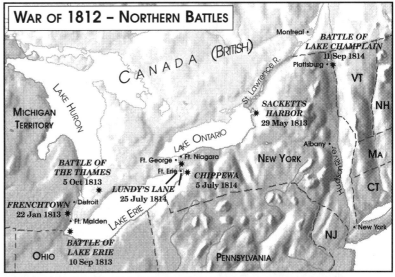

"A Southerner soon as a Northerner...
At home on the hills of Vermont or in the woods of Maine, or the Texan ranch
Comrade of Californians, comrade of free North-Westerners...
Of every hue and caste am I, of every rank and religion
A farmer, mechanic, artist, gentlemen, sailor, Quaker,
Prisoner, fancy-man, rowdy, lawyer, physician, priest."

– Walt Whitman, *Leaves of Grass*, 1855

21 Based on the views expressed in this poem, Whitman would most likely
1 support discrimination based on race and religion
2 prefer to live on a southern plantation
3 support strong class differences
4 take pride in the differences among Americans

22 In the early stages of the Civil War, the North lost a series of battles because it
1 lacked aggressive military leadership
2 failed to blockade Southern ports
3 refused to allow African Americans to serve in the army
4 had very low industrial production

Directions: Base your answer to question 23 on the list below and on your knowledge of social studies.

- Poll Taxes
- Literacy Tests
- Jim Crow Laws

23 All of the above were used in the South after the Civil War to
1 end the plantation system
2 deny African Americans their rights
3 stop the influence of Progressives
4 improve roads and build railroads

24 The Credit Mobilier Scandal and the Teapot Dome Scandal are associated with the administrations of
1 Abraham Lincoln and William McKinley
2 Andrew Jackson and James Polk
3 Ulysses S. Grant and Warren Harding
4 Theodore Roosevelt and Woodrow Wilson

Directions: Base your answer to question 25 on the list below and on your knowledge of social studies.

- Increased availability of capital
- Transferable ownership
- Losses limited to investment

25 These advantages are best associated with
1 unions
2 corporations
3 partnerships
4 proprietorships

Directions: Base your answer to question 26 on the cartoon below and on your knowledge of social studies.

26 This cartoon shows what some thought was the relationship between the Senate and the trusts in the late 19th century. Which statement best represents the main idea of the cartoon?
1 The trusts and the Senate had an equal partnership.
2 The trusts feared the Senate's lawmaking power.
3 The Senate was threatened by the trusts.
4 The trusts opposed wildlife conservation.

CHANGING PATTERNS OF IMMIGRATION: 1880-1909

1880-1889		1900-1909	
Asia	.1.3%	Asia	.3.2%
Northwestern Europe	.72.3%	Northwestern Europe	.17.5%
Eastern Europe	.3.6%	Eastern Europe	.18.7%
Central Europe	.6.8%	Central Europe	.18.6%
Southern Europe	.5.2%	Southern Europe	.24.6%
Americas	.9.9%	Americas	.16.9%

Directions: Base your answer to questions 27 and 28 on the chart above and on your knowledge of social studies.

27 Which area showed the greatest percentage increase of immigrants between 1880 and 1909?
 1 Northwestern Europe
 2 Americas
 3 Central Europe
 4 Southern Europe

28 One outgrowth in America of the rise in immigration from Eastern, Central, and Southern Europe between 1890 and 1909 was the formation of the
 1 Immigration Restriction League
 2 United Nations
 3 Republican Party
 4 the League of Nations

Directions: Base your answer to question 29 on the outline below and on your knowledge of social studies.

I. _____
   A. Reasons
      1. desire to increase trade
      2. need for coaling stations for steam ships
      3. desire to spread Christianity and Western ideas
   B. Results
      1. acquisition of less developed areas
      2. involvement in foreign wars

29 Which would be the best heading for this outline?
 1 Communism   3 Imperialism
 2 Nationalism   4 Capitalism

30 The Open Door Policy was designed to ensure that
 1 all nations had equal opportunity to trade in China
 2 American interests in the Philippines would be protected
 3 the Chinese Boxer Rebellion would be put down
 4 European nations limit their China trade

Directions: Base your answer to question 31 on the cartoon at the right and on your knowledge of social studies.

31 The best title for this cartoon would be
 1 "Roosevelt Prepares to Defeat Germany"
 2 "Roosevelt Brings U.S. into World War I"
 3 "Roosevelt Protects Latin America from Europe"
 4 "Roosevelt Wins Battle of San Juan Hill"

32 President Woodrow Wilson's primary goal at the Paris Peace Conference after World War I was to
 1 end European imperialism in Africa
 2 force Germany to pay large reparations
 3 protect the freedom of the seas
 4 establish the League of Nations

33 The administrations of Ulysses S. Grant and Warren Harding are similar in that both
 1 faced major scandals involving government officials
 2 led the nation into European wars
 3 oversaw the beginning of industrialization
 4 battled serious economic depressions

Directions: Base your answer to question 34 on the headlines below and on your knowledge of social studies.

Buy Now, Pay Later
Noble Experiment Fails
Jazz Hits New Popularity Highs
Babe Ruth Hits 60 Home Runs

34 In which decade would these newspaper headlines be found?
 1 the 1910s   3 the 1930s
 2 the 1920s   4 the 1940s

Directions: Base your answer to question 35 on the chart below and on your knowledge of social studies.

LABOR FORCE AND UNEMPLOYMENT: 1929-1941 (NUMBERS IN MILLIONS)		
YEAR	LABOR FORCE	NUMBER UNEMPLOYED
1929	49.2	1.6
1930	49.8	4.3
1931	50.4	8.0
1932	51.0	12.1
1933	51.6	12.8
1934	52.2	11.3
1935	52.9	10.6
1936	53.4	9.0
1937	54.0	7.7
1938	54.6	10.4
1939	55.2	9.5
1940	55.6	8.1
1941	55.9	5.6

35 Which statement about the labor force and unemployment (1929-1941) is accurate?
1 After Hoover assumed the Presidency, unemployment steadily fell.
2 From 1929 to 1941, the labor force decreased.
3 The worst year for unemployment was 1938.
4 After World War II began in 1939, U.S. unemployment fell.

36 A major difference between Hoover's and FDR's approach to dealing with the Great Depression was FDR's
1 aggressive approach to restore public confidence
2 willingness to allow the economy to heal itself
3 decision to concentrate on helping big business
4 refusal to allow a government role in a recovery program

37 Internationally, the Great Depression played a role in the
1 communist seizure of power in Russia
2 rise of totalitarian governments
3 refusal of the U.S. to join the League of Nations
4 outbreak of World War I

38 Faced with a two-front war at the beginning of World War II, FDR and his advisors decided to
1 launch an immediate invasion of Japan
2 deny military aid to communist Russia
3 use little air power against enemy nations
4 concentrate on winning the War in Europe first

Directions: Base your answer to question 39 on the speech below and on your knowledge of social studies.

"In the future days, which we seek to make secure, we look forward to a world founded upon four essential human freedoms.
The first is freedom of speech and expression, everywhere in the world.
The second is freedom of every person to worship God in his own way - everywhere in the world.
The third is freedom from want – everywhere in the world.
The fourth is freedom from fear – anywhere in the world."
    – Franklin D. Roosevelt, address to Congress, 6 January 1941

39 In this speech, President Roosevelt was
1 outlining his goals for peace after World War II
2 stating his concerns about the treatment of African Americans
3 expressing his hope that the U.S. would join the League of Nations
4 asking Congress to declare war on Japan

40 The *Truman Doctrine*, the Marshall Plan, and the North Atlantic Treaty Organization were designed to
1 protect the Philippines
2 contain the spread of communism
3 aid developing nations of Africa
4 ensure the supply of foreign oil

Directions: Base your answer to question 41 on the cartoon at the right and on your knowledge of social studies.

41 What allowed President Truman to take the action shown in the cartoon?
1 Congress can veto all the President's actions.
2 The Supreme Court was on his side.
3 A majority of the states were against public opinion.
4 The Constitution makes the President Commander in Chief

Directions: Base your answer to question 42 on the events below and on your knowledge of social studies.

- Berlin Airlift
- Korean War
- Cuban Missile Crisis

42 All of these events were a part of the
1 lead up to World War II
2 domino effect
3 Cold War
4 end of the Soviet Union

43 When the Freedom Riders rode buses and tried to desegregate bus terminals, they were employing
1 boycotts
2 strikes
3 civil disobedience
4 violent confrontation

44 President Lyndon B. Johnson's "Great Society" Program was aimed at helping
1 Americans below the poverty line
2 people in developing nations
3 women gain the right to vote
4 European fight communism

45 Environmental concerns have led to national debates because
1 protection of the environment has a cost
2 it is a Cold War issue
3 Congress has passed no environmental protection laws
4 global warming is no longer a concern

PART II
CONSTRUCTED RESPONSE

Directions: Base your answers to questions 1 through 3 on the quotation at the right.

"When in the course of human events, it becomes necessary for one people to dissolve the political bonds which have connected them with another, and to assume, among the powers of the earth, the separate and equal station to which the laws of nature and nature's God entitle them, a decent respect to the opinions of mankind requires that they should declare the causes which impel them to the separation. ... We hold these truths to be self-evident, that all men are created equal; that they are endowed by their Creator with certain unalienable rights; that among these are life, liberty, and the pursuit of happiness. ... That, to secure these rights, governments are instituted among men, deriving their just powers from the consent of the governed;... That, whenever any form of government becomes destructive to these ends, it is the right of the people to alter or to abolish it, and to institute a new government, laying its foundation on such principles, and organizing its powers in such form, as to them shall seem most likely to effect their safety and happiness..."

– Thomas Jefferson, *Declaration of Independence*, 1776

1 According to Jefferson, why was it necessary to declare the causes which led the colonists to separate from Britain?

_____

_____

_____

2 What are the THREE (3) "unalienable rights" mentioned in the *Declaration of Independence*?

_____

_____

3 How does Jefferson justify declaring independence from Britain?

_____

_____

Directions: Base your answers to questions 4 through 5 on the map at the right and on your knowledge of social studies.

4 What is ONE (1) mountain range that many pioneers had to cross?

_____

_____

_____

_____

5 What are TWO (2) additional problems that many pioneer wagon trains faced in the movement West?

_____

_____

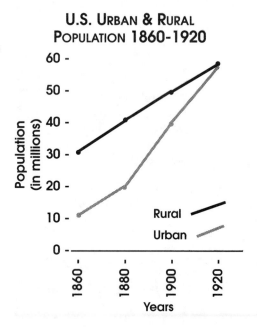

_____

_____

Directions: Base your answers to questions 6 through 8 on the chart at the right and on your knowledge of social studies.

U.S. URBAN & RURAL POPULATION 1860-1920

6 What was the overall trend in total U.S. population between 1860 and 1920?

_____

_____

_____

7 In approximately what year did urban and rural populations become equal?

_____

8 What is ONE (1) reason for the sharp increase in urban population between 1880 and 1920?

_____

_____

Directions: Base your answers to questions 9 and 10
on the illustration below and your knowledge
of social studies.

9   Use the illustration above to identify TWO (2) events and/or people from the time period between 1900 and
    1920 which had an impact on the time period or later history.

    _____

    _____

    _____

10 For ONE (1) of the events and/or people identified above, explain how the person or event affected the time
    period or later history.

    _____

    _____

    _____

    _____

    _____

    _____

PART III

DOCUMENT BASED QUESTION

This question is based on the accompanying documents (1-7). Some documents have been edited for the purpose of this question. The question is designed to test your ability to work with historical documents. As you analyze the documents, take into account both the context of each document and any point of view that many be presented in the document.

Historical Context: From the coming of the *Mayflower* in 1620 and on into the 21st century, the U.S. has experienced the arrival of waves of immigrants. Some of these immigrants have come to American shores because of problems in their native lands; others have come because they viewed this country as a land of opportunity; and still others have come for a combination of reasons.

Task: Using information from the documents and your knowledge of social studies, answer the questions that follow each document in Part A. Your answers to the questions will help you write the Part B essay in which you will be asked to:

- Identify and discuss at least TWO (2) problems that immigrants experienced in their native lands that led them to come to the United States.

- Identify and discuss at least TWO (2) reasons why immigrants saw the U.S. as a land of opportunity.

Part A: Short Answer

Directions:

Analyze the documents and answer the questions that follow each document in the space provided. Your answers to questions will help you write the essay.

Document 1

1 In the documents at the right, what are TWO (2) indications that the early colonists came here to have a more democratic society?

> *Mayflower Compact*, 1620
>   Colonists agree to meet and decide upon just and equal laws for the common good, and to obey such laws.
>
> *Fundamental Orders of Connecticut*, 1639
>   Each year there will be two general assemblies to organize government and elect officials. The governor will not be allowed to serve two years in a row.
>
> *Maryland Act of Toleration*, 1649
>   There will be religious freedom for Protestants and Catholics. (Discrimination against Jews and atheists remained.)

_____

_____

_____

_____

Document 2

Sawyer

Potter

Blacksmith

Wheelwright

Cooper

Miller

2a   Identify and explain THREE (3) occupations available in the colonies.

_____

_____

_____

2b   Why might the availability of these occupations encourage immigration?

_____

_____

_____

_____

_____

_____

Document 3

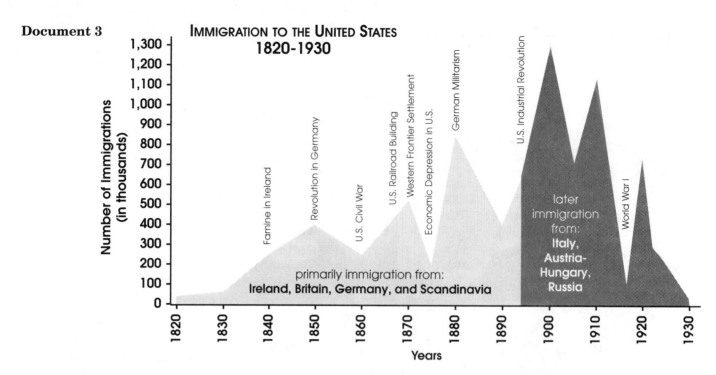

IMMIGRATION TO THE UNITED STATES
1820-1930

Number of Immigrations (in thousands)

1,300
1,200
1,100
1,000
900
800
700
600
500
400
300
200
100
0

Famine in Ireland
Revolution in Germany
U.S. Civil War
U.S. Railroad Building
Western Frontier Settlement
Economic Depression in U.S.
German Militarism
U.S. Industrial Revolution
World War I

primarily immigration from:
Ireland, Britain, Germany, and Scandinavia

later immigration from:
Italy, Austria-Hungary, Russia

1820 1830 1840 1850 1860 1870 1880 1890 1900 1910 1920 1930

Years

3a Identify TWO (2) events in Europe that led to large numbers of immigrants coming to the U.S.

_____

_____

3b For ONE (1) of the two events cited above, explain why many people left Europe because of it.

_____

_____

Document 4
The advertisement at the right appeared in Europe in the 1860s.

4 Why would this poster attract immigrants to the U.S.?

_____

_____

_____

_____

_____

THE FINEST FARMING LANDS
EQUAL TO ANY IN THE WORLD
MAY BE PROCURED
AT FROM $8 TO $12 PER ACRE
Near Markets, Schools, Churches, and all the blessings of Civilization
1,200,000 Acres in Farms of 40, 80, 120, 160 Acres and upwards in ILLINOIS, the Garden State of America.

The Illinois Central Railroad Company offers, on long credit, the beautiful and fertile Prairie Lands lying along the whole line of their railroad, 700 miles in length, upon the most favorable terms, for enabling farmers, manufacturers, mechanics, and workingmen to make for themselves and their families a competency, and a home they can call their own.

Document 5

> "The public school has done its best for us foreigners, and for the country, when it made us into good Americans. ... Education was free. That subject my father had written about repeatedly, as comprising his chief hope for us children, the essence of American opportunity, the treasure that no thief could touch, not even misfortune or poverty... No application made, no questions asked, no rulings or exclusions, no plotting, no fees. The doors stood open for every one of us..."
>
> – Mary Antin, *The Promised Land*, 1885

5a What was the main reason Mary Antin's father brought his family to the U.S.?

_____

_____

5b How was the American education system different from that of Russia, the Antin's native land?

_____

_____

Document 6

"Working" class Immigrants

"Wealthy" class Immigrants

6a What are TWO (2) differences between the immigrants pictured in the cartoon?"

_____

_____

6b Compared to the "wealthy" immigrant, how did coming to America improve the quality of life for the "working" class immigrant?

_____

_____

_____

Document 7

7 Why were people anxious to leave South Vietnam?

_____

_____

_____

_____

_____

"The *Midway* (an aircraft carrier off the coast of Vietnam) was our base of operations. We were real close to shore at the time, right off Saigon. We heard that we were taking on a whole bunch of civilians. They were coming out in boats, half-sinking boats. There were people who had their own airplanes who were flying out.

"It was total chaos. The Purple Heart Trail, the road that came into Saigon from the paddies west of the city, was so jammed, from the air I could see columns of people that were at least twenty miles long. ... Some had clothes they picked off dead bodies. Most were barefoot. ...The army of North Vietnam was lobbing these rockets all over the place, they were wiping out civilians.

"On April 30 Saigon fell. South Vietnam had fallen to Communist North Vietnam."

– Stephen Klinkhammer as told to Al Santoli, *Everything We Had*, 1981

_____

_____

Document 8

8 What are TWO (2) reasons given for why some believed that Elian Gonzalez should have been allowed to remain in the United States?

"The boy will have far greater opportunities here than in Cuba."
– Lazaro Gonzalez, uncle of Elian Gonzalez (child survivor of a shipwreck while attempting to enter the U.S. from Communist Cuba) as quoted in *Newsweek*, 12/20/99

"The child should be able to live in freedom and not in slavery."
– U.S. Senator John McCain, as quoted in *Newsweek*, 12/20/99

_____

_____

Part B: Essay

Directions:
- Write a well-organized essay that includes an introduction, several paragraphs, and a conclusion.
- Use evidence from the documents to support your response.
- Include specific, related outside information.

Historical Context: From the coming of the *Mayflower* in 1620 and into the 21st century, the U.S. has experienced the arrival of waves of immigrants. Some of these immigrants have come to American shores because of problems in their native lands; others have come because they viewed this country as a land of opportunity; and still others have come for a combination of reasons.

Task: Using information from the questions that follow each document in Part A write the Part B essay in which you:

- Identify and discuss at least TWO (2) problems that immigrants experienced in their native lands that led them to come to the U.S.

- Identify and discuss at least TWO (2) reasons why immigrants saw the U.S. as a land of opportunity.

Be sure to include specific historical details. You must also include additional information from your knowledge of social studies.

Anthropology (study of the origin, the behavior, and the physical, social, and cultural development of human beings), 12, 13

Appalachian Mountains (mountain system of eastern North America extending about 1,600 miles), 9, 10, 13, 15, 16, 17, 47

Appeasement (European countries concede to Hitler's aggressive acts, c. 1938-40), 132

Aristrocrats (noble or well to do class), 24

Armstrong, Louis (1900-1971; musician; greatly influenced the development of jazz), 118

Articles of Confederation (first U.S. national gov't structure, 1778-1789), 38

Assembly line (workers, machines, and equipment in which the product being assembled passes consecutively from operation to operation until completed), 90, 118

Assimilation (to absorb immigrants into the prevailing culture), 90

Astair, Fred (1899-1987; Hollywood entertainer; 1930s musicals), 125

Austin, Stephen (1793-1836; colonizer and political leader; helped Texas settlers gain their independence), 66

Axis Alliance (1936 informal cooperation between Italy and Germany, formalized in 1939, Japan joined in 1940), 133, 134 [+map], 138

Aztec (people of central Mexico whose civilization was at its height at the time of the Spanish conquest in the early 16th century), 14

B

Backlash (negative reaction usually to civil rights campaigns), 75

Balboa (Spanish explorer), 21, 22 [charts]

Bank of the United States (Jackson's controversial veto), 46, 52, 56

Bara, Theda (1890?-1955; American actress of the silent film era.), 119

Barnard, Henry (1811-1900; educator-reformer; sought higher standards in public schools; the first U.S. Comm. of Ed., 1867-1870), 58

Baseball (professional sport emerged in the 19th c. industrial era), 91, 92 [illustration], 119

Battle of Bunker Hill (Boston, MA; 1st major Revolutionary War battle on nearby Breed's Hill on 17 June 1775), 31

Bay of Pigs in Cuba (CIA attempt to overthrow Castro), 142

Beecher, Lyman (1775-1863; fiery Calvinist theologian; militant abolitionist, temperance crusader), 58

Bell, Alexander Graham (1847-1922; inventor of the telephone in 1876), 84 [chart]

Benign neglect (lax enforcement of mercantilist trade restrictions by 17th and 18th century British officials to encourage economic growth in the American colonies), 31

Benny, Jack (mid 20th c. vaudeville, radio, TV, cinema comedian), 125

Berlin Blockade and Airlift (1948-1949; Soviet blockade of city relieved by Allies air supplies), 140

Bessemer Process (see Kelly-Bessemer Process)

Bethune, Mary McLeod (1875-1955; educator sought improved racial relations and educational opportunities for African Americans; advisor to FDR; delegate to first U.N. meeting, 1945), 125

Bicameral legislature (lawmaking body divided into 2-houses), 25 [chart], 38, 39 [chart], 41

"Big Bull Market" (1920s optimism in the stock market that led to prolific buying in anticipation of a rise in prices), 123

"Big Stick, The" (T. Roosevelt's aggressive foreign policy in Latin America), 105

Bill of Rights, English (1689 – declared that suspending of laws or the execution of laws by regal authority without consent of the Parliament is illegal), 31

Bill of Rights, American (791 – U.S. Constitutional amendments 1-10 stating fundamental personal rights of citizens), 41 [chart], 41 [chart], 46, 172 [chart]

Black codes (laws set up in southern states after the Civil War to regulate social, economic, and political life of freed slaves; racial separation laws, see also Jim Crow laws), 74

Black Death (bubonic plague that wiped out nearly 1/3rd of Europe's population in the late Middle Ages), 20

Black Friday (financial panic of 1869), 84

Blacklist (employers in an industry circulate lists of unwanted union workers), 88

Blitzkrieg (swift, sudden military offensive, usually by combined air and mobile land forces; Nazis - WW II attack on Poland), 133, 135

Blue collar jobs (industrial workers; ["white collar" usually means clerical/managerial jobs]), 154

Bolsheviks (communist group that led late 1917 revolution in Russia), 117

Bonaparte, Napoleon (Emperor of the French, 1804-1814), 49

Bond rallies (raised money; WW II home front), 137

Bootlegger (one who produces, distributes, or sells something without permission or illegally), 118

Boss (professional politician who controls a party or a political machine), 91

Boston Massacre (1770; squad of British troops fired into an unruly crowd killing three men outright and mortally wounding two others), 31

Boston Tea Party (1773; colonial protest against Parliament's *Tea Act*), 31

Bow, Clara (1905-1965; American actress whose roles in silent films, such as *Mantrap*,1926, and *It*, 1927, made her a symbol of the Roaring Twenties), 119

Boxer Rebellion, The (anti-imperialist movement in China, 1900), 104

Boycott (organized abstaining from doing business with someone to force them to accept a condition), 88, 155

Bragg, Braxton (1817-1876; Confederate general in the Civil War; defeated in the Chattanooga Campaign, 1863), 73 [chart]

Brown, John (1800-1859; abolitionist; aborted raid on U.S. arsenal at Harper's Ferry (VA) to liberate Southern slaves), 69

Brown v. Board of Ed. of Topeka (1954 - school desegregation), 155, 173

Buchanan, James (1791-1868; 15th President, 1857-1861; could not prevent the South from seceding), 70

Budget deficit (amount by which gov't. revenue falls short of meeting expenses; a shortage of income), 124

Bunche, Ralph (1904-1971; 1940s civil rights leader; U.N. activist; Nobel Peace Prize, 1950), 125

Burger, Warren E. (1907-1995; Chief Justice, 1969-1986; advocate of judicial restraint), 172

Burr, Aaron, (1756-1836; Vice President of the U.S. [1801-1805] under Jefferson; mortally wounded rival Alexander Hamilton in a duel in 1804), 48

Busch, Adolphus (19th century American manufacturer, inventor,), 84 [chart]

Business cycle (see cycle of demand)

C

Cabinet (collective heads of the various executive agencies functioning as an advisory group to the President), 46

Cabot, John (1450-1498; Italian-born explorer [Giovanni Caboto]; commanded English expedition that discovered the North American mainland in 1497), 22 [chart]

Calhoun, John C. (1782-1850; Senator, Vice President, Southern rights spokesman), 51, 55-56

Cahokia (southwest Illinois group of approximately 85 prehistoric Native American earthworks), 13

Call of the Wild, The (Jack London story - realism of industrial era writers), 92

Canada, 7, 51

Capital (as a factor of production in an economic sense, the financial resources as well as the tools, machinery, and equipment used to produce goods and services), 82-83

Capitalism (system in which the means of economic production and distribution are privately owned;

development is balanced by accumulation and reinvestment of profits), 85 [feature box]

Capone, Alphonse (Italian-born American gangster who ruthlessly ruled the Chicago underworld in the Prohibition Era and was imprisoned for tax evasion), 118

Carnegie, Andrew (1835-1919; industrialist and philanthropist who amassed a fortune in the steel industry), 82, 88, 103

Carpetbagger (Northerner who went to the South after the Civil War for political or financial advantage), 75

Cartier, Jacques (1491-1557; French explorer who navigated the St. Lawrence River in 1535 and laid claim to the region for France), 22 [chart]

Castro, Fidel (1936- ; Cuban rebel leader; created communist state, 1959), 142

Catt, Carrie Chapman (1859-1947; major role in the ratification of the *19th Amendment* giving women the vote; founded the League of Women Voters), 93

Central Intelligence Agency (CIA; U.S. espionage agency created in 1947; coordinates other agencies in the intelligence community), 142

Central Pacific Railroad Company (transcontinental railroad built eastward from San Francisco; joined Union Pacific in 1869), 84 [chart]

Central Powers (Austria, Germany, Turkey WW I alliance), 106

Champlain, Samuel de (1567-1635; French explorer ; founded Nova Scotia and Quebec), 22 [chart]

Chaplin, Charles Spencer "Charlie" (1889-1977; British-born actor, director, and producer who gained fame for his role as a tramp in baggy trousers and a bowler hat; productions include *The Kid*, 1921, *The Gold Rush*, 1925, and *City Lights*, 1931), 119

Charter (document issued by a sovereign, legislature, or other authority, creating a public or private corporation; colonies were often chartered as private enterprises), 25 [chart], 139

Charter colony (colonies operated as private enterprises by permission of sovereign, a share of the revenues went to the monarch or national gov't.; operated as self-governing), 25 [chart]

China, 140-141

Checks and Balances (system that grants power to various branches to keep the other branches within specific bounds), 39, 171

Cherokee Nation (Native American people formerly inhabiting the western Carolinas, eastern TN, and northern GA; gov't. removed them to Indian Territory in the 1830s), 55

Chicasaw (Native American people inhabiting northeast Mississippi and northwest Alabama, with present-day populations in central Oklahoma), 55

Chinese Nationalists (also Guomindang; party of Jiang Jieshi; ruling power group in China 1924-1947), 140-141

Chiang Kai-shek (see Jiang Jieshi)

Choctaw (Native American people inhabiting central and southern Mississippi and southwest Alabama, with present-day populations in Mississippi and southeast Oklahoma), 55

Churchill, Winston (1874-1965; British prime minister, 1940-1945 and 1951-1955; led Great Britain through WW II), 133, 139 [photo], 147 [quotation]

CIA (see Central Intelligence Agency)

Cities (center of population, commerce, and culture; a town of significant size and importance; urban areas of the U.S.), 155, 177

Citizenship (duties, rights, and privileges of a person entitled by birth or naturalization to the protection of a state or nation), 175-177

Civil disobedience (intentional public breaking of laws deemed unjust), 156

Civil Rights Acts (1866, 1964, 1968; laws guaranteeing and elaborating rights belonging to an individual by virtue of citizenship, especially the freedoms and privileges guaranteed by the *13th* and *14th Amendments*; include due process, equal protection of the laws, and freedom from discrimination), 75, 154, 156

Civil Rights Commission (1957; evaluates federal laws and policies on equal rights and the effectiveness of equal opportunity programs; makes recommendations to the President and Congress), 156

Civil Rights Movement (1957-1965 intense public pressure and massive demonstrations that produced Congressional legislation to overcome local and state obstruction to the exercise of citizenship rights by African Americans), 156, 173

Civil service (distribute gov't. jobs through fair competitive examinations; see *Pendleton Act*), 85

Civil War ([general: a war between factions or regions of the same country] in U.S., the 1861-1865 war between the Union and the Confederacy; also called The War Between the States;), 68-75, 171, 173

Civil War Amendments (see 13th, 14th, & 15th Amendments), 74, 75

Civilian Conservation Corps (CCC; 1933-1942; unemployed, unmarried young men enlisted to work on conservation and resource-development projects), 123

Clay, Henry (1777-1852; U.S. Representative, KY; Speaker of the House; Senator; Sec'y of State; Presidential candidate, 1824, 1832, 1844), 51, 52, 53, 55, 56

Clayton Anti-Trust Act (1914; made up deficiencies in the *Sherman Anti-Trust Act* of 1890 in combatting monopolistic practices), 95

Clean Water Act (1972; curbed aquatic pollution), 160 [chart]

"Clear and present danger rule" (gov't. can suspend civil liberties in time of national stress), 107, 138

Clemenceau, Georges (1841-1929; French news correspondent and politician; WW I leader), 141 [quote], 108

Cleveland, [Stephen] Grover (1837-1908; 22nd and 24th President, 1885-1889 and 1893-1897), 88, 102, 176

Climate (U.S. regions), 8

Clinton, DeWitt (1769-1828; Governor of New York, 1817-1823 and 1825-1828; principal supporter of the Erie Canal [completed 1825].), 176

Clinton, George (1739-1812; Vice Pres. [Jefferson & Madison]; NY Gov., 1777-1795), 40, 176

Collective bargaining (labor-management negotiation on wages and working conditions), 87, 123

Collective security (mutual defense agreement among several nations pledged to come to the aid of any member attacked; e.g., NATO), 140

Cold war (political tension and military rivalry between nations that stops short of full-scale war), 139-144

Columbian Exchange (early contacts between Native Americans and Europeans), 20-21 [chart]

Columbus, Christopher (1451-1506; Italian explorer in the service of Spain; attempted to reach Asia by sailing west from Europe, encountered America in 1492; made three other voyages to the Caribbean), 20, 21, 22 [chart]

Commander in Chief (official role of the President as head of the U.S. military forces), 133, 156

Command economy (arrangement for exchange of goods and services following decisions by gov't. agencies), 106-107

Communism (a system in which state plans and controls the economy, or a social order in which all goods are equally shared by the people; the Marxist-Leninist version advocates the overthrow of capitalism by the revolution of the working class), 117, 142, 143, 144

Compromise of 1850 (an omnibus bill of five laws enacted by Congress aimed at ending sectional disputes that threatened the Union), 68

Concurrent power (power shared by several divisions of gov't.), 39 [chart]

Confederate States of America (name adopted by the states that seceded from the U.S. in 1860-61 to form an independent nation, also "The Confederacy"), 69-71

Congregational churches (self-governing Protestant churches descending from those established by the New England Puritans), 24, 102

Confederation (union of sovereign states retaining power locally), 38

Congress, The (federal legislative body of U.S.), 40 [chart], 41 [chart], 46, 47, 48, 49, 50, 51, 52, 55, 67, 69, 70, 71, 74, 75, 85, 86, 88, 90, 103, 106, 116, 122, 123, 124, 126, 133, 137, 140, 143, 154, 155, 156, 160, 161, 172

Connections (the basic transportation and communication facilities, services, and installations needed for economic functioning of a society), 83-84

Conservation (attempts to preserve the natural environment)

Constitution (fundamental law), 39

Constitution of the United States (1789- present; system of fundamental laws and principles that outlines the functions and limits of the U.S. gov't.), 39-40, 41 [summary chart], 48-49, 74, 75, 118-119, 170-171, 174, 175

Constitutional Convention (1787, Philadelphia gathering to reform the national government, produced the *Constitution of the United States*), 39, 74

Containment policy (post WW II foreign policy to restrain growth of communism on global scale), 140-145

Continental Congress (delegates from the 13 original American colonies /states; U. S. gov't., 1774-1789; declared independence, fought Am. Revolution, managed country under the *Art. of Confederation*), 31

Contraction (economic decline; see depression, recession)

Coolidge, President (1872-1933; 30th President, 1923-29), 116, 120

Cooper, James Fenimore (1789-1851; novels of frontier life – *The Last of the Mohicans*), 59 [chart]

Cooper, Peter (19th century American manufacturer, inventor,), 84 [chart]

Cooperatives (late 19th C. farmers' organizations to combat high railroad shipping charges), 90

Cordoba (Spanish explorer), 21 [chart]

Cornwallis, Charles (1738-1805; British commander in NC during the Am. Rev.; surrendered at Yorktown in 1781), 32

Cortés (Spanish conquistador), 21, 22 [charts]

Corporations (business organization drawing capital from large group of share holding owners), 85 [+chart]

Cotton (shrubby plants of the genus Gossypium, grown for the soft, white, downy fibers surrounding oil-rich seeds; used in making textiles and other products.), 8, 39,

Coughlin, Charles E. (1891-1979; isolationist, anti-Semitic, and pro-fascist "radio priest" of the 1930s-40s; broadcasts critical of New Deal), 124

County (territorial division of a state or colony exercising administrative, judicial, and political functions), 176, 177 [map]

Court Packing Plan (FDR's 1936 attempt to influence Supreme Court decisions), 124

Coureurs de bois (15th-16th C. fur trappers of New France / Canada), 22

Craft unions (labor organizations set up for skilled trades), 87

Crane, Stephen (1871-1900; realist author of industrial era), 92

Credit Mobilier Scandal (Grant era RR scandal), 85 [chart]

Creek (confederacy of Native American people formerly inhabiting eastern Alabama, southwest Georgia, and northwest Florida), 55

Criollos (also creoles; American born children of Iberian nobles in the colonial era), 21 [chart]

Critical Period (1781 to 1789 - near collapse under Articles of Confederation), 38

Crosby, Bing (20th C. singer-actor, radio, cinema, TV), 125

Crow (Native American people formerly inhabiting northern Great Plains between the Platte and Yellowstone Rivers), 13

Cuba (U.S. protectorate after Spanish American War; 1962 missile crisis), 103, 142

Cullen, Countee (1903-1946; Harlem Renaissance poet; collections: *Colors, Copper Sun*), 118

Cultural diffussion (cultural patterns spreading from one people to another), 20 [chart]

Cumberland Road (also National Road; authorized by Congress in 1806; built from Cumberland, MD., to Vandalia, IL, between 1811 and 1852), 53 [map]

Cycle of demand (ebb and flow of demand; causes the economy to expand and contract at intervals; also business cycle), 121

D

DaGama (Portuguese explorer), 22 [chart]

Davis, Jefferson (1808-1889; president of the Confederacy, 1861-1865), 69 [+ photo], 73 [monument]

Debs, Eugene V. (1855-1926; industrial era labor union and Socialist Party leader), 88, 107

DeCuellar (Spanish explorer), 21 [chart]

Deciduous (shedding or losing foliage at the end of the growing season), 8 [chart]

Declaration of Independence (summary of the reasons the colonies revolted against Britain in 1776; employs the natural-rights theories of John Locke), 32 [+chart], 58, 92

Declaration of Sentiments (Elizabeth Stanton's proclamation at the 1848 Seneca Falls women's rights convention), 58, 92

Deere, John (1804-1886; industrialist who pioneered the manufacture of plows especially suited to working prairie soil), 57

Deficit spending (spending of public funds obtained by borrowing rather than by taxation), 124

E

English Bill of Rights (1689; limited the power of English monarchs and increased power of Parliament), 30 [illus], 31

Enlightenment (18th C. European intellectual liberation movement), 31

Entrepreneur (a person who organizes, operates, and assumes the risk for a business venture), 82

Environmental concern (relating to the ecological impact of altering the environment), 160

Environmental Protection Agency (EPA; established in 1970, as an independent agency coordinated effective gov't. action on behalf of the environment), 160 [chart]

Equal protection of the law (see *14th Amendment*)

Era of Good Feeling (1820s - a time of political cooperation), 52-53

Erie Canal (1817 - 1825; artificial waterway extending about 360 miles across central NY from Albany to Buffalo), 53 [map], 57

Ethiopia (East African nation invaded and annexed by Italy as a colony in 1935), 132

Ethnic (sizable group of people sharing a common and distinct racial, national, religious, language, or cultural heritage), 91

European Recovery Act (see Marshall Plan)

Excise Tax (tax imposed on the production, sale, or consumption of a commodity or the use of a service within a country; tobacco, liquor, and long-distance telephone calls are examples), 46, 47

Executive (branch of gov't. charged with putting into effect a country's laws and the administering of its functions; in U.S. national gov't., the Presidency), 40 [chart], 171

Executive privilege (claim by Presidents refusing to share information with Congress or the courts that disclosure would compromise either national security or the principle of separation of powers; see *United States v. Nixon*), 172

Export (to sell or trade merchandise abroad), 39, 50, 74

Extradition (legal surrender of a fugitive to another state, country, or government for trial), 41

F

Fair Labor Standards Act (1937- federal minimum wage, other labor rights), 123 [chart]

Fascist (system of gov't. marked by centralization of authority under a dictator; suppression of opposition through terror and censorship), 126

FDIC (see Federal Deposit Insurance Corporation)

"Fed" (see Federal Reserve System)

Federal Deposit Insurance Corporation (1933; FDIC-New Deal agency protects depositors by insuring their bank accounts; absorbed FSLIC in 1989), 123 [chart]

Federal Emergency Relief Act (FERA- New Deal relief measures), 123

Federal Reserve Board (administers Federal Reserve Banking System), 95 [chart], 120

Federal Reserve System (1913; "The Fed"; central bank of the U.S.; holds deposits of the commercial banks and operates a nationwide check-clearing system; serves as the basic controller of credit in the economy), 95 [chart], 120, 122

Federal System (see federalism)

Federal Theater Project (New Deal aid for arts), 125

Federal Trade Commission (maintains free and fair competition in business; takes action against monopoly, restraints on trade, and unfair or deceptive trade practices), 95 [chart], 120

Federal union (see federalism)

Federalism (political union with a strong central gov't. with some power shared among smaller components), 39, 170-171

Federalist Papers, The (essays in defense of new U.S. Constitution by Hamilton, Jay, and Madison, 1788), 40

Federalists (supporters of the Constitution in ratification struggle, also early political party founded by Hamilton and John Adams), 40 [chart], 47 [chart],48, 51, 52

Field, Stephen Dudley (19th century American manufacturer, inventor,), 88 [chart]

Fifteenth Amendment (1870; states could not deny citizens suffrage because of race or previous slavery), 41 [chart], 74, 174

Finney, Charles Grandison (1792-1875; religious leader and educator; key figure in the Second Great Awakening), 58

"Fireside Chats" (FDR's radio messages), 123

First Continental Congress (see Continental Congress)

Fisk, Jim (1834-1872; industrial era speculator), 84

Fitzgerald, F. Scott (1896-1940; writer who epitomized the Jazz Age disillusion), 119

Fixed income (household revenue stagnant as with only income being a pension, Social Security, disability, or insurance), 155

Florida (peninsula of S.E. United States, acquired from Spain between 1810 and 1819), 49 [map], 66 [map + chart]

Ford, Henry (1863-1947; automobile manufacturer; mass-produced a gasoline-powered automobile in 1893; founded the Ford Motor Company in 1903), 118

Fort Orange (Dutch colonial name for the trading outpost that later became Albany, NY under the British), 23

Fort Sumter (Union installation in Charleston, SC surrendered 12 April 1861 in first action of the Civil War), 70

Fourteen Points, The (Wilson's plan for post-WW I world peace), 107 [chart], 108

G

H

Hamilton, Alexander (1755-1804; soldier and politician; first U.S. Secretary of the Treasury, 1789-1795; established the National Bank and public credit system), 40, 46, 47, 48

Hancock, John (1737-1793; Revolutionary War leader; president of the Continental Congress; first to sign the *Declaration of Independence*; served nine terms as governor of MA), 31

Harding, Warren G. (29th President, 1921-1923; corrupt administration), 116, 120

Harlem Renaissance (1920s and early 1930s composers, novelists and poets renewed racial pride; emphasis on African cultural heritage), 118

Harte, Bret (19th C. writer noted for his stories about California mining towns), 92

Haudenosaunee Union (see Iroquois League), 15

Hawaii, 7, 102

Hawthorne, Nathaniel (1804-1864; writer; moralistic and spiritual novels and short stories), 59

Hay, John, (1838-1905; public official / writer; Sec'y. of State, 1898-1905), 104

Haymarket Riot (1886; violent labor confrontation at Chicago's McCormick Reaper Co. strike), 87

Hayes, Rutherford B. (1822-1893; 19th President, 1877-1881), 75

Hayne, Robert Y. (1791-1839;U.S. Senator from SC, 1823-1832; states' rights advocate), 55

Hearst, William Randolph (1863-1951; newspaper and magazine publisher; built the world's largest publishing empire; see yellow journalism), 91, 103

Hemingway, Ernest (1899-1961; post WW I author; work: *The Sun Also Rises*), 119

Henry, Patrick (1736-1799; Revolutionary War leader and orator; member of the VA House of Burgesses and the Continental Congress; Gov. of Virginia, 1776-1790), 31

Hepburn Act (l906; continued earlier civil service reforms), 94

Hirohito (1901-1989; Emperor of Japan, 1926-1989; advocated unconditional surrender that ended WW II; renounced his divine status), 136

Hiroshima (city of southwest Honshu, Japan; site of U.S. nuclear bombing, 1945), 136

History and historians (overview chart), 12

Hitler, Adolf (1889-1945; leader of Nazi Germany), 126, 132, 133, 135

Ho Chi Minh (1890-1969; communist rebel leader; North Vietnamese leader), 143

Holocaust, The (genocide of European Jews and others by the Nazis during WW II), 135

Home front (civilian activities of a country at war), 137-138

Homestead Act (1862; offered free land to promote settlement of the West), 88

Homestead Strike (1892; bloody strike against Carnegie Steel Co. in PA), 88

Hoover, Herbert (1874-1964; 31st President, 1929-1933), 122-123

House of Burgesses (colonial VA legislature, c. 1619), 31

House of Representatives, U.S. (lower chamber of U.S. national legislature), 48, 52, 53, 55, 93

Houston, Sam (1793-1863; led the Texan struggle for independence; president of the Republic of Texas, 1836-1844; served as U.S. Senator and Governor), 67

Howe, Elias (19th century American manufacturer, inventor,), 84 [chart]

Huckleberry Finn (188; Mark Twain's novel of Mississippi boyhood), 92

Hudson, Henry (b? - d. 1611; English navigator and explorer who discovered the Hudson River on an expedition for the East India Company, 1609), 22 [chart]

Hughes, Charles Evans (1862-1948; Associate Justice U.S. Supreme Court, 1910-1916; ran for President, 1916; Secretary of State, 1921-1925; Chief Justice, 1930-1941), 176

Hughes, Langston (1902-1967; Harlem Renaissance writer; works include *Weary Blues*, *The Ways of White Folks*), 118

Hull House (1889; Jane Addams' Chicago settlement house), 93-94

Human rights (fundamental entitlements that all persons enjoy as protection against state conduct prohibited by international law or custom; mistreatments condemned include extrajudicial or summary execution, disappearance [in which people are taken into custody and never heard of again]; torture; arbitrary detention or exile; slavery or involuntary servitude; discrimination on racial, ethnic, religious, or sexual grounds; violation of free expression, free association)

"Hundred Days, The" (whirlwind New Deal legislation of first three months of FDR's administration in 1933), 123

Hydrogen bomb (nuclear weapon in which atomic nuclei of hydrogen are joined in an uncontrolled nuclear fusion reaction), 142

Hypothesis (tentative explanation that accounts for a set of facts and can be tested by further investigation; a theory)

I

Immigration (to enter and settle in a country or region to which one is not native), 90-91, 106, 117, 160-161

Immigration Act of 1965 (repealed 1920s National Origins system; created an enlarged annual ceiling for immigrants), 160

Immigration Reform and Control Act (1986; addressed the problem of illegal aliens), 161

J

Joint stock company (16th-19th C. private investment groups used by English to finance exploration routes and colonies), 21

Jones, Robert Tyre "Bobby" (1902-1971; golfer who won (1930) the Grand Slam of golf, the amateur and open championships in the United States and Great Britain), 119

Judicial Branch, The (federal court structure), 41, 49, 124, 172, 174

Judicial review (Supreme Court power to declare acts of Congress, President, Federal agencies or state laws and actions unconstitutional), 48-49, 172

Judiciary Act of 1789 (see *Marbury v. Madison*)

Jungle, The (1906; muckraking Sinclair novel led to *Meat Inspect. Act*), 93

Jurisdiction (extent of authority or control of a government or the territorial range of authority or control), 41

Jus sanguinis (to grant citizenship by virtue of parents citizenship), 175

Jus soli (to grant citizenship by virtue of being born in a country), 175

K

Kansas-Nebraska Act (1854; established the territories of KA and NE with slave status determined by popular sovereignty; repealed the Missouri Compromise of 1820), 68

Kellogg-Briand Pact (1928; attempt to outlaw aggression among nations), 117

Kelly, William (1811-1888; Pittsburgh iron manufacturer; patented a pneumatic process for making steel in 1857), 88 [chart]

Kelly-Bessemer Process (pneumatic process for making steel by blowing air through molten iron), 74, 88 [chart]

Kennedy, John F. (1913-1963; "JFK," 35th President, 1961-63; U.S. Sen., MA; assassinated), 142, 143, 156

Kent State (anti-Vietnam protest), 143

King, Jr., Martin Luther (1950s-'60s non-violent civil rights leader, assassinated, 1968), 155

Knights of Labor (early national labor union), 87

Knox, Henry (Revolutionary War commander; 1st Sec'y of War for Washington), 46

"Know-Nothings" (19th C. anti-immigrant party), 91

Korean Conflict (1950-53), 141

Korematsu v. U.S. (1944; suit against internment of Am. citizens of Japanese ancestry during WW II, see "clear & present danger" rule), 138

Khrushchev, Nikita S. (1894-1971; Soviet leader, 1956-64), 142

Ku Klux Klan (racist, nativist group), 75, 117

L

Labor (as a factor of production in an economic sense the human energy expended to do the work necessary in a society), 82, 86-88, 123

LaFollette, Robert (1855-1925; Progressive Era reformer served as a U.S. Senator from Wisconsin, 1906-1925; ran unsuccessfully for President on the Progressive Party ticket in 1924), 93

Laissez-faire (the philosophy that promotes minimal gov't. interference with the economy), 120, 122, 123, 124

Land (as a factor of production in an economic sense, not just solid earth, but what is on and under the earth, such as minerals, water, forests, factories, roads, etc.), 82

Landon, Alf (1887-1987; governor of KS, 1933-1937; 1936 Republican presidential candidate), 124

Landslide vote (overwhelming election victory), 123, 124

Lange, Dorothea (1895-1965; photographer; portraits of rural workers in Depression), 125

Latin America (region of W. Hemisphere influenced by Spanish/Portuguese), 51, 105, 144, 175

Law (body of rules and principles governing the affairs of a community and enforced by a political authority), 40, 41, 48-49, 86, 123, 176

LDCs (see Less Developed Countries)

League (association of states, organizations, or individuals for common action; an alliance), 15, 91, 108,116, 132 [chart]

League of Nations (post-WW I international peace organization - U.S. never joined), 108, 116, 132 [chart]

Lee, Ann (1736-1784; "Mother Ann"; British religious leader; founder of the Shakers in U.S., 1776), 58

Lee, Robert E. (1807-1870; Confederate commander in Civil War), 73

Lend-Lease Act (1941; U.S. aid to Britain v. Nazis; expanded to all WW II Allies), 133

Less Developed Countries (LDCs; low level of industrial development, high poverty level, vulnerability to international economic conditions, and poor quality of life), 141

Levittown (post WW II suburban growth), 155

Lewis, Meriwether and Clark, William (led the 1803-1806 Louisiana Territory expedition), 50

Lewis, Sinclair (1885-1951; novelist satirized middle-class America; *Main Street, Babbitt*), 119

Libel (a false publication that maliciously damages a person's reputation), 172

Liliuokalani (1838-1917; Lydia Kamekeha Paki - last Hawaiian ruler, 1891-1893), 102

Limited government (principle of restricting gov't. power), 39, 170

Lincoln, Abraham (1809-1865; 16th President, 1861-65; led the Union during the Civil War; emancipated slaves in the South), 69, 70-71, 74

Literacy tests (citizens must pass exam to vote, kept poor blacks from voting in the South), 75

Little Rock Crisis (1957; desegregating Southern schools), 156

Lloyd, Harold Clayton (1894-1971; American silent film actor whose most famous stunt was hanging from a clock face at the top of a building in *Safety Last*, 1923), 119

Lobbying (groups pooling resources and efforts to influence the thinking of legislators or other public officials for or against a specific cause), 92

Lockout (employer closes down to deny work to employees during a labor dispute), 88

Locke, John (1632-1704; English Enlightenment political philosopher), 31, 32

Lodge, Henry Cabot (1850-1924; Senate majority leader, 1918-1924, rejected Wilson's Versailles Treaty), 108

London, Jack (1876-1916; writer of rugged adventure novels), 92

Long, Huey (1893-1935; Gov. of LA, 1928-1932 and U.S. Sen., 1930-1935; opponent of FDR), 124

Longfellow, Henry Wadsworth (1807-1882; 19th century poet), 59

Loose construction (broad, flexible interpretation of the Constitution, allowing expansion of federal power), 47 [chart]

Lost Colony (Raleigh's 1588 attempt to establish a permanent english settlement in NC) , 21-22

Louisiana Purchase (1803; 1st major addition of territory; constitutionality questioned), 49-50, 66

Loyalists (see Tories)

M

MacArthur, Douglas (1880-1964; WW II Pacific commander; military governor of occupied Japan; Korean War commander fired by Truman), 139 [box], 141 [map]

Madison, James (1751-1836; 4th President, 1809-1817; member of the Continental Congress and Constitutional Convention, 1787), 40, 46, 48, 50, 51

Magellan (Spanish explorer), 21 [chart]

Magna Carta (charter of English political and civil liberties granted by King John in June 1215)

Mahan, Alfred (1840-1914; naval officer and historian; called for a worldwide buildup of naval strength prior to World War I), 102

Maine (Extreme Northeastern state; first claimed by MA, came into the union in 1820 with the MO Compromise, northern 1/2 gained by treaty with Britain in 1842), 42 [map], 66 [map + chart]

Manhattan Project (1942-1945; developed atomic bomb), 136

Manifest Destiny (emotional drive for territorial expansion), 66

Mann, Horace (1796-1859; educator who introduced reforms and regulations that greatly influenced public education), 58

Mao Zedong (communist Chinese revolutionary leader), 140

Marbury v. Madison (1803, decision that established Supreme Court's power of judicial review), 48-49, 172

Marco Polo (13th C. Italian traveller to the Orient), 20

Margin (buying stocks on credit arrangement; difference between the cost and the selling price of securities or commodities), 120

Market economy (exchange of goods and services following decisions made through the interaction of buyers and sellers), 85, 106-107, 120, 153

Marshall Plan (1948-1952; 16 participating countries received $13.15 billion in U.S. aid, post-WW II economic recovery), 140, 152

Marti, José (19th C. Cuban revolutionary), 102

Marshall, John (Chief Justice, U.S. Supreme Court, 1801-1835), 49, 172

Massachusetts Bay Colony (the Puritan-dominated Massachusetts Bay Company unified several earlier commercial settlements at Plymouth, Gloucester, and Salem and governed by charter from 1629-1684), 22

Maximilian Affair (French attempt to take over Mexico, 1860s), 105

Maya (also Mayan culture; Mesoamerican Indian people inhabiting southeast Mexico, Guatemala, and Belize, whose civilization reached its height around A.D. 300-900), 14 [chart]

Mayflower Compact (Plymouth settlers agreed to establish and to be bound by a "Civil Body Politic"– a temporary gov't. modeled after a Separatist church covenant), 22

McClellan, George B. (1826-1885; overcautious commander of the Union Army, 1861-1862), 73

McCormick, Cyrus (1809-1884; inventor and manufacturer who developed a mechanical harvester in 1831), 57

McClure's (19th and early 20th C. popular magazine, carried muckraker articles in Progressive Era), 93

McKay, Claude (1890-1948; poet of Harlem Renaissance), 118

McKinley, William (1843-1901; 25th President, 1897-1901; Spanish-American War, 1898), 102-103

Meade, George G. (1815-1872; Union general commanded at Gettysburg, 1863), 73 [chart]

Meat Inspection Act (1906; first major consumer legislation), 94

Medicaid (1960s Great Society welfare system providing medical treatment of poor), 157 [chart]

Medicare (1960s Great Society welfare system providing medical treatment of elderly), 157 [chart]

Melville, Herman (1819-1891; writer of allegorical masterpiece *Moby Dick,* 1851), 59

Mentally ill (reforms for), 58

Mercantilism (also mercantile system; closed trading system involving immense profit for mother country, while using colonies as market for goods), 20 [chart], 30

Merganthaler, Otto (19th century American manufacturer, inventor,), 84 [chart]

Mergers (strongest firm(s) in an industry absorbing competition to form a monopoly), 86

Mesoamerican (Native American civilizations in Mexico, Central America, and northern South America), 14 [chart], 20

Mexico, 7, 66-67

Mexican cession (1848; large land area ceded to the U.S. by the treaty ending the Mexican War), 42 [map], 66 [map + chart], 66-67

Mexican War (1846-1848 conflict incited by U.S. annexation of Texas), 67

Midway (central Pacific island territory of U.S.; WW II turning point battle), 135 [+map]

Military Reconstruction Plan (1867; Radical Republicans set up harsh post-Civil War occupation), 74

Minutemen (rebels pledged to be ready to fight on a minute's notice just before and during the Revolutionary War), 31

Miranda v. Arizona (1966; Supreme Court clarified rights of criminally accused persons), 173

Mississippi River (chief river of the U.S., rises in the lake region of northern MN and flows generally southward about 2,350 mi.; enters the Gulf of Mexico through a huge delta in S.E. Louisiana), 8, 9, 10, 13, 32, 50, 55, 66, 71

Mississippian People (ancient Native American civilizations in what is now the central U.S.), 13

Missouri Compromise (1820; an attempt to solve the sectional disputes between free and slave states), 53, 68 [map], 69

Mohawk (Native American people formerly inhabiting northeast NY along the Mohawk and upper Hudson Valley, north to the St. Lawrence River), 15

Monopoly (company or group having exclusive control over a commercial activity), 82, 86, 94, 95

Monroe Doctrine, The, (1823; declared U.S. opposition to European interference in the Americas), 52, 105

Monroe, James (1758-1831; 5th President, 1817-1825; acquisition of FL, 1819; Missouri Compromise, 1820; Monroe Doctrine, 1823), 51-52, 105

Montgomery Bus Boycott (1955-1956; bus desegregation led by Dr. King), 155-156

Montgomery Ward (early mail-order business, 19th C.), 90

Morgan, J.P. (John Pierpont Morgan, 1837-1913; Wall St. financier - philanthropist), 94

Mormonism (way of life practiced by members of the Church of Jesus Christ of Latter-day Saints, founded in the 1830s), 58

Moody, Helen Wills (1906- ; American tennis player who was the dominant woman player in the 1920's and 1930's), 119

Morrill Land Grant Act (1862; created agricultural colleges), 88

Morse, Samuel F.B. (1791-1872; artist and inventor; refined and patented the telegraph [1854]), 57, 84

Mott, Lucretia (1793-1880; feminist social reformer; active in the antislavery movement), 58

Mountain (natural elevation of the earth's surface having considerable mass, generally steep sides, and a height greater than that of a hill), 9

Muckrakers (journalists who expose corruption and scandal), 93 [+ chart]

Munich Conference (1938; Britain and France gave in to Hitler's demand for German occupation of the German-speaking Sudetenland in northwest Czechoslovakia), 132

Munn v. Illinois (1876; states could regulate railroads), 90

Mussolini, Benito (1883-1945; fascist dictator of Italy), 126, 132, 133

N

NAACP (see National Association for the Advancement of Colored People)

NAFTA (see North American Free Trade Agreement)

Nagasaki (city of western Kyushu, Japan; nuclear bombing by U.S., 1945), 136

Napoleon I (1769-1821; Napoleon Bonaparte, military commander, and consul, Emperor of the French [1804-1814]), 49, 50

Napoleonic Wars (1803-1815; European wars with France; U.S. tried to remain neutral), 50-51

National American Woman Suffrage Association (founded in 1890 to work for women's vote), 92, 175

National Association for the Advancement of Colored People (NAACP; major civil rights group, founded 1909), 95, 155

National nominating convention (formal meeting of members, representatives, or delegates of a political party as method of selecting presidential candidates; began c. 1830), 54

National Industrial Recovery Act (1933; NIRA - New Deal regulation/stimulation of industry; permitted businesses to draft "codes of fair competition" [subject to presidential approval] that regulated prices, wages, working conditions, plant construction, and credit terms; administered and better known by initials NRA [Nat. Recovery Admin.]), 123 [chart]

National Labor Relations Act (1935; *Wagner Act* - assured right of organization and collective bargaining for unions; set up National Labor Relations Board for oversight), 123 [chart]

National Origins Act (1924-1968; immigration system based on preference quotas for certain groups), 117, 160

National Organization for Women (1966; NOW; works to achieve "full equality for women in truly equal partnership with men"), 154

National Recovery Administration (NRA; see *National Industrial Recovery Act*)

National Road (see Cumberland Road)

National Woman's Party (founded in 1915 and took non-violent actions to press Congress for women's suffrage), 93, 175

Native Americans (member of any of the aboriginal peoples of the Western Hemisphere; see also American Indian or Amerindian), 13-15, 22, 55, 125

Nativist (organized opposition to immigrants), 91

NATO (see North Atlantic Treaty Organization)

Natural resources (material source of wealth, such as timber, fresh water, or a mineral deposit, that occurs in a natural state and has economic value), 10, 13

Naturalization (to grant full citizenship to one of foreign birth), 175

Naval stores (forest by-products used by shipwrights in the days of sail), 23

Navigation Acts (17th C. series of statutes by the English Parliament, formed the basis of the mercantilist trading system in the early British Empire), 24, 30 [chart]

Nazis (National Socialist German Workers' Party, founded in Germany in 1919 and brought to power in 1933 under Adolf Hitler), 126

Nelson, Donald (industrialist managed WW II military production), 137

Neutrality (belonging to neither side in a controversy, especially nonparticipation in war), 48, 50, 106, 133-134

Neutrality Acts (of 1935, 1936, 1937; pre-WW II isolationist sentiment; see chart for differences), 133-134

New Amsterdam (Dutch colonial name for what later became New York City under the British), 23

New Deal (FDR's reform programs to help in Great Depression), 123-125

New England, 7

New England Town Meeting (assembly of the qualified voters of a community to conduct public business), 38

New Freedom (President Wilson's domestic Progressive reform program), 95 [+chart]

New Frontier (JFK's legislative program), 156

Newlands Act (1902; national parks), 94

New Netherland (Dutch colonial name for what later became the eastern portion of New York State), 24

New York State, 40, 176, 176

Nimitz, Admiral Chester (1885-1966; WW II Pacific naval commander), 135

Nineteenth Amendment (1920; provides men and women with equal voting rights), 93

Nisei (person born in America of parents who emigrated from Japan), 138

Nixon, Richard M. (1913-1994; 37th President, 1969-74; Watergate scandal; only President to resign, pardoned by Pres. Ford), 143

Non-violent, direct action (protest tactics of the civil rights movement), 156

Normalcy (normality – state or fact of being typical; Warren Harding's 1920 campaign misnomer for wanting the country to return to normal, pre-Progressive and pre-war conditions), 116, 120

Norris, Frank (early 20th C. muckraking writer; works include: *The Octopus*, *The Pit*), 93 [chart]

North American Free Trade Agreement (NAFTA – 1994, U.S., Can., Mex. phased out trade barriers over 15 yr. period), 144

North Atlantic Treaty Organization (1949; NATO; 12 nation defense alliance; first permanent peacetime military alliance for the U.S, now 18 nations are members), 140

North Korea (Soviet satellite, attacked South Korea, 1950 to begin the Korean War), 141

North, Lord Frederick (1732-1792; British prime minister who lost most of the American colonies), 31, 32

Northern migration (movement of southern African Americans to northern industrial cities in the early 20th century), 117

Northern Securities Co. v. U.S. (1904, first federal prosecution and breakup of a monopoly), 94

Northwest Ordinance (1787; procedures for admission of states), 38

Nuclear family units (smaller family in industrial society households as opposed to larger extended families in rural areas), 24, 162

Nullification (individual states declaring a federal law is invalid and refusing to enforce it), 55

Nuremberg Trials (Allied trials of Axis war criminals, 1945-1946), 136

O

OAS (see Organization of American States)

Ocean (any principal division of the body of salt water that covers 70% of the Earth, including the Arctic, Atlantic, Pacific, and Indian Oceans), 9

Office of Economic Opportunity (OEO; major Great Society job retraining and anti-discrimination agency), 154

Office of Price Administration (OPA; administered WW II rationing), 137 [chart & cartoon]

Oil (1973, 1978, Arab and OPEC nations used economic embargo and supply manipulations against Western nations, 1973), 142, 158

OPA (see Office of Price Administration)

OPEC (see Organization of Petroleum Exporting Countries)

Open Door Policy (1900; U.S. call for equal trading rights in China be guaranteed to all foreign nationals), 104

Operation Overlord (code name for WW II - Allied invasion of Europe 6/6/44), 134

Oppression of Protestants (arbitrary, cruel exercise of power resulting in harassment and persecution), 22

Oregon (extreme North western territory of the U.S. acquired by treaty with Britain in 1846), 42 [map], 66 map + chart]

Organization of American States (OAS; Western Hemisphere peace & mediation organization; formerly the Pan American Union, 1910-1948), 144

Organization of Petroleum Exporting Countries; OPEC; cartel created by 5 oil producing countries in 1960 to counter oil price cuts of American and European oil companies; oil boycotts of the mid-1970s; now 12 members), 158

Orlando, Vittorio (Italian Premier at Versailles, 1918-19), 108

P

Paine, Thomas (1737-1809; revolutionary; wrote the pamphlets *Common Sense* and *The Crisis* in 1776; also involved in the French Revolution), 31

Palmer Raids (1919-20; federal raids against alleged radicals and subversives during the Red Scare period following WW I), 117

Panama Canal Zone (1903-1999; 648 sq.mi. U.S. corridor that ran through the middle of the Republic of Panama from the Atlantic to the Pacific Ocean), 105

Parks, Rosa (defiance of racially segregated bus seating triggered Montgomery Bus Boycott, 1955-56), 155

Parliament (Great Britain's national legislature), 30-31

Partnership (limited business contract arrangement entered into by two or more persons in which each agrees to furnish a part of the capital and labor for a business enterprise, and by which each shares a fixed proportion of profits and losses), 86 [box]

Patroon (under Dutch colonial rule: New Netherland granted proprietary and manorial rights to a large tract of land in exchange for bringing 50 settlers to the colony), 23, 24

Paul, Alice (1885-1977; suffragist; founded National Woman's Party in 1916; wrote the first equal rights amendment considered by Congress, 1923), 93, 175

Peace Corps (JFK's international volunteer program to aid people in underdeveloped nations), 156

Pearl Harbor (naval base in Hawaii; 1941 attack by Japan drew U.S. into WW II), 134

Pendleton Act (1883; initiated federal civil service examination system), 85

Peninsulares (15th-17th century Spanish and Portuguese nobles who became landholders in the colonial period), 21 [chart]

Perry, Oliver Hazard (1785-1819; U.S. naval commander in War of 1812), 51

Pershing, John (1860-1948; U.S. general; WW I commander), 107

Philippines (U.S. possession after Spanish-American War 1898-1946; fell to Japan in WW II; independent 1946), 103, 104, 134, 135

Philipse (Colonial Era, Dutch patroon family of the Hudson Valley), 24

Picketing (group of persons stationed outside a place of employment, usually during a strike, to express grievance or protest and discourage entry by non-striking employees or customers), 88

Pilgrims (English Separatists from the Anglican Church who founded the Plymouth colony in 1620), 22

Pizarro (Portuguese conquistador), 21, 22 [charts]

Plessy v. Ferguson (1896 - allowed de jure segregation, sets "separate but equal" rule), 173

Plymouth Plantation (initial English MA colonial settlement c. 1620 by the Pilgrims), 22

Pocahontas (1595?-1617; Powhatan princess who befriended the English colonists at Jamestown), 22

Poe, Edgar Allan (1809-1849; writer known especially for his macabre poems and short stories), 59

Political boss (professional politician who controls a party or a political machine), 91

Political parties (organizations of common political interest), 46, 54

Political science (study of principles & structures of gov't.), 12

Polk, James K. (1795-1849; 11th President, 1845-1849, establishment of the 49th parallel as the U.S. northern border; Commander in Chief during Mexican War), 67

Poll taxes (fees charged in order to vote, see *24th Amendment*), 41 [chart], 75

Pools (combination of firms for monopolistic ends), 86

Popular Sovereignty (1850s idea that the status of slavery should decided by each new state as it was admitted to the Union), 68

Populist Party (People's Party; c. 1892; western / midwestern agrarian reform group), 90

Powderly, Terence V. (1849-1924; idealist reform leader of Knights of Labor; mayor of Scranton, PA), 87

Powhatan (16th and 17th C. confederacy of Native American peoples of eastern VA), 22

Prairie (extensive area of flat or rolling, predominantly treeless, grassland, especially the large tract or plain of central North America), 88

Preamble (preface to *U.S. Constitution*), 41 [chart], 170, 174 [chart]

Precedents (initial actions in gov't. that become basic pattern for subsequent actions of similar nature), 22, 46, 48

Price controls (gov't. sets ceilings and floors for specific goods and services to stabilize economy), 152 [chart]

Primary source (document or artifact created at the same time as historical period being examined), 12

Primogeniture (all inheritance rights given to first-born son), 23

Privateer (captain of or ship privately owned and manned but authorized by a government during wartime to attack and capture enemy vessels), 48

Proclamation of 1763 (British stopped settlement beyond Appalachian Mts), 30

Proclamation of Neutrality (1793; Washington sought isolation from European wars), 48

Proclamation of Neutrality (1914,\; Wilson sought isolation from WW I in Europe), 106

Progressive Era (period from 1900 to WW I; age of reform; trust-busting, railroad legislation, pure food and drug acts), 92-95, 116

Prohibition (temperance movement [anti-alcohol movement]; 1920-1933 period when the *18th Amendment* forbade the manufacture and sale of alcoholic beverages), 58, 118-119

Project Head Start (1960s Great Society program for pre-school help for minority children), 157 [chart]

Proprietorships (single-owner businesses), 24, 86 [chart]

Proprietary colonies (set up as private enterprises by a business group who chose the governor), 25 [chart]

Propaganda (information reflecting the views and interests of people advocating a doctrine or cause), 68

Prosperity (period of the economic cycle when there is high employment, and productivity), 121

Protective tariffs (high import duties to insure competitive pricing for domestic producers; e.g., Tariff of Abominations, Fordney-McCumber Tariff, 1922), 55, 121

Protestant Reformation (16th C. movement in W. Europe aimed at reforming doctrines and practices of the Roman Catholic Church; resulted in the establishment of Protestant churches in America), 22

Psychology (deals with mental processes and behavior), 12

Pueblo (some 25 Native American peoples, including the Hopi, Zuñi, and Taos, living in established villages in northern and western NM and northeast AZ; descendants of the cliff-dwelling Anasazi peoples), 15

Puerto Rico (central Caribbean island taken as U.S. colony in Spanish-American War), 104

Pulitzer, Joseph (1847-1911; NY newspaper publisher; endowed the Pulitzer Prizes; yellow journalism), 91, 103

Pullman Boycott or Strike (1894; bloody national railroad strike), 88

Pump-priming theory (gov't. stimulation of economy through assistance to the poor to promote market demand; also demand-side economics), 123

Pure Food and Drug Act (1906; Progressive consumer reform), 94 [chart]

Puritans, Puritan Revolution (In England, a Calvinist reform faction in the Anglican Church in the 16th and 17th century; led a revolution and civil war against King Charles I; set up a commonwealth in 1650s; others populated Massachusetts Bay Colony beginning in 1630s), 22, 31

Q

Quartering Act (1765 act by Parliament forced colonists to provide housing for British troops), 30

Quotas (legally set limitation; ethnically biased immigration restrictions of 1920s), 117

R

Radical (one who advocates fundamental or revolutionary changes in current practices, conditions, or institutions), 117

Radical Republicans (extreme wing of Republican Party bent on punishment of the South; led Reconstruction Era), 74-75

Railroad Land Grants (large areas of land in the western territories given to railroad developers by Congress in the late 19th century), 83 [map], 84 [+ chart]

Raleigh, Sir Walter (1552-1618; English, navigator and colonizer of VA; introduced tobacco and the potato to Europe), 21

Randolph, A. Philip (1889-1979; labor and civil rights leader, 1920s-1960s; organized FDR's Fair Employment Practices Committee), 125

Randolph, Edmund (1753-1813; Revolutionary War leader; member of the Constitutional Convention, 1787; served as U.S. Attorney General and Secretary of State), 46

Rankin, Jeannette (1880-1973; leader in the women's suffrage movement; first woman U.S. representative, 1917-1919 and 1941-1943; pacifist), 93

Ratification (1787-88 battle to accept the *U.S. Constitution*), 72-73

Rationing program (WW II gov't. controlled consumer supplies of critical goods), 137

Recall (a public election to remove an official from office; reform sought by Populists & Progressives), 93 [chart]

Recession (economic slowdown characterized by declining production and rising unemployment for more than 9 straight months of falling GDP), 86, 121 [chart], 158

Reconstruction (1865-1877; Congressional program for reform of South after Civil War), 74-75

Recovery (short-term gov't. actions to stimulate economic activity), 121 [chart]

Red Scare (1918-1919; paranoiac response to socialist and anarchist activities after WW I; see Palmer Raids), 117

Referendum (deciding public issues in a general election; democratic reform sought by Populists and Progressives), 93 [chart]

Reform (actions to abolish abuse or malpractice; improve by alteration, correction of error, or removal of defects; put into a better condition), 58, 92-95, 123 [+chart]

Relief (gov't. actions to relieve economic misfortune), 123 [+chart]

Reparations (compensation required from a defeated nation as indemnity for damage or injury during a war; especially as a cause of economic difficulties in Europe after WW I), 108, 126

Representative government (agents of the people having decision-making power; see republic; republican forms), 39, 170

Republic (political order in which the supreme power lies in a body of citizens who are entitled to vote for officers and representatives responsible to them)

Republican Party (emerged in the 1850s from anti-slavery, free-soil wing of the Whig Party; the more conservative of the two major modern parties; support comes from the upper middle class, suburban and rural populations, and corporate, financial, and farming interests; generally favors laissez-faire, free enterprise, and fiscal responsibility and opposes the welfare state and expansion of state power), 69, 74-75, 93, 116, 124

Reserved powers (by virtue of the *10th Amendment*, powers not specifically assigned or delegated to the national gov't., are left to the states), 39 [chart]

Riis, Jacob (investigative journalist of the industrial-Progressive Era), 93 [chart]

River (large natural stream of water emptying into an ocean, a lake, or another body of water and usually fed along its course by converging tributaries), 9

Rockefeller, John D. (1839-1937; oil industry monopolist), 82

Rocky Mountains (western U.S. range), 9

Rogers, Ginger (1930s-'40s Hollywood film actress / dancer), 125

Roosevelt Corollary to the Monroe Doctrine (1903; U.S. to act as protector of the Western Hemisphere, adopts interventionist approach), 106

Roosevelt, Franklin D. (FDR; 1882-1945; 32nd President, 1933-1945; Governor of NY, 1929-1932), 123-124, 133, 137, 138, 152 [chart], 176

Roosevelt, Theodore (1858-1919; 26th President, 1901-1909; hero of the Spanish American War; Governor of NY, 1899-1900; U.S. Vice President, 1901), 94, 104-107, 176

"Rosie the Riveter" (fictional American heroine - symbolic of women's home front role in WW II), 137-138

Royal colony (large tract of land owned and operated by a sovereign, who appointed the governor; revenues went to the monarch or national gov't.), 25 [chart]

Ruth, George Herman "Babe" (1895-1948;. American baseball player of 1920s), 119

Russia (see also Soviet Union), 7, 106, 107, 117, 117, 139

"Rust Belt, The" (decaying industrial centers of Northeast and Mid-west in 1960s-80s), 155

S

Sacajawea (1787-1812; guide and interpreter for Lewis and Clark Expedition, 1805-1806), 50

St. Lawrence River (major river of S.E. Canada/ N.E. U.S., flowing N.E. from Lake Ontario to the Atlantic Ocean), 9, 22

"Salary Grab " (1873; Grant rra scandal), 85

Saratoga (1777; American Revolution battle; colonists defeat of invading British armies from Canada and the west convinced French to form an alliance with Patriot side), 32

"Scabs" (worker who refuses membership in a labor union; employee who works while others are on strike; a strikebreaker; person hired to replace a striking worker), 88

Schechter Poultry Corp. v. United States (1935; court struck down New Deal's NIRA), 124

Schenck v. United States (1919; civil rights in wartime; see clear and present danger rule), 107, 138

Socialism (social system in which the means of producing and distributing goods are owned collectively and political power is exercised by the whole community), 107, 124

Socialist Party (early 1900s coalition of worker interests weakened after WW I; regained strength during the Great Depression but abandoned presidential campaigns after 1948; Socialist Workers Party, more militantly allied with international communism, was founded in 1937), 107

Sociology (study of origins, organization, institutions, and development of human society), 12

South Carolina Exposition and Protest (Calhoun's 1830 statement on states rights), 55

Southeast Asia Treaty Organization (SEATO - U.S. backed regional collective security arrangement, 1953), 143 [cartoon caption]

Soviet Union (U.S.S.R.; Union of Soviet Socialist Republics; lands of the old Russian Empire governed by the Communist Party of the U.S.S.R., 1917-1991), 117, 133, 139, 140, 141, 142

Spanish American War (1898; marked emergence of the U.S. as a great power; advent of overseas imperialism), 102, 103-104

Speakeasy (place for the illegal sale and consumption of alcoholic drinks, as during Prohibition in the United States), 118

Spheres of Influence (area of exclusive control by one country in another), 104

Spoils System (political jobs and rewards being distributed among party faithful instead of on merit), 55

Square Deal (President Theodore Roosevelt's Progressive reform program), 94

Stalin, Josef (1879-1953; successor to Lenin, dictator / premier of the U.S.S.R. from 1926-1953), 126, 139

Stamp Act (1765-66; first direct tax imposed by Britain on its American colonies), 30

Stanton, Elizabeth Cady (1815-1902; feminist and social reformer), 58, 92, 175

Steffens, Lincoln (1866-1936; journalist; managing editor of *McClure's* Magazine, 1902-1906), 93 [chart]

Steinbeck, John (1902-1968; novelist; *The Grapes of Wrath* about the migrants forced out of the Dust Bowl in the 1930s), 128

Stephens, Uriah (early U.S. labor leader; Knights of Labor), 87

Stone, Lucy (1818-1893; social reformer; founder of the American Woman Suffrage Association, 1869), 92

Strict constructionists (believers in precise, verbatim interpretations of the Constitution and no expansions of its power), 47 [chart]

Strike (to cease working, in support of demands made upon an employer), 87-88 [+ chart], 107, 116, 137 [chart]

Strip mining (clearing a natural covering or growth for extracting minerals near the earth's surface, especially coal), 153

Strong, Rev. Josiah (1847-1916; social justice advocate and pro-imperialist of 1880s), 102

Submarine warfare (use of underwater attack boats; a cause of U.S. entry into WW I), 106

Subversive activities (actions intended to overthrow or undermine an established government), 117

Suburbs (residential region around a major city; growth after WW II), 154-155

Suffrage (the right to vote), 54, 92, 175

Suffragist (crusader for women's right to vote ["suffragette" was used in Britain, not in the U.S. movement]), 92

Summit meetings (personal diplomacy among world leaders), 139

Supply (economics: amount of a commodity available for meeting a demand or for purchase at a given price), 54, 85, 118, 120, 121

Supreme Court (highest court in the U.S. federal system; exerts a commanding influence on public and legal policies of the U.S.; currently consisting of nine justices), 46, 48-49, 55, 69, 86, 107, 120, 124, 155, 171, 172, 173, 174

Suzuki (Japanese premier, surrendered in WW II), 136

Sweatshops (factory with poor working conditions), 86

T

Taft, William Howard (1857-1930; 27th President, 1909-1913; Chief Justice of the Supreme Court, 1921-1930), 104

Tammany Hall (19th & early 20th C. NYC Democratic political club), 91

Tarbell, Ida (1857-1944; muckraker: *History of the Standard Oil Co.*, 1904), 93 [chart]

Tariff of Abominations (1828; exceptionally high duties became subject of Southern protests), 55-56

Tariffs (duties, taxes on imports), 39, 55, 158

Taylor, Zachary (1784-1850; 12th President, 1849-1850; commander in Black Hawk, 2nd Seminole, and Mexican Wars), 67

Tax revenue (see revenue)

Teapot Dome Affair (1920s Harding era scandal), 116

Temperance (restraint in the use of or abstinence from alcoholic liquors), 58

Tenement houses (run-down, low-rental apartment building whose facilities and maintenance barely meet minimum standards), 90

Texas (south-central territory of the United States; admitted as the 28th state, 1845; held by the Spanish from the 16th century, it was a province of Mexico until it won independence in 1836; independent republic until 1845), 42 [map], 66-67

U

United States Constitution (see *Constitution of the United States*)

United States v. Butler (1935; Supreme Court struck down New Deal's agricultural program), 124

United States v. Nixon (1974; Supreme Court ruled against "executive privilege"), 172

Universal Declaration of Human Rights (1947; backing for basic rights), 139

U.S.S.R. (see Soviet Union)

Unwritten constitution (precedents, judicial decisions, expansions of legal power and procedure not in the Constitution), 46, 47, 49

Urban League (civil rights group founded in 1910 to provide jobs for southern African Americans in industry and aid southern migrants moving into northern cities), 155

V

V-2 rockets (Germany's "vengeance weapon 2"; liquid-propellant rocket; more than 4,300 were launched against London, southeastern England, & Antwerp, 1944-1945), 135

Valentino, Rudolph (1895-1926; Italian-born American actor known for his romantic leading roles in silent films such as *The Sheik*, 1921, and *Blood and Sand*, 1922), 119

Van Rensselaer (Dutch patroon family; founded the only successful private colony in America in upstate New York c , 1635), 24

Versailles Peace Conference (ended WW I; also called the Paris Peace Conference), 108, 116, 126, 132

Veto (the power of a chief executive to reject a bill passed by the legislature and thus prevent or delay its enactment into law), 40, 56, 171

Viceroys (15th-19th century Spanish colonial governors), 21 [chart]

Viet Cong (communist insurgent forces in Vietnam War), 143

Vietnam War (U.S. involvement in containing communist expansion in southeast Asia, 1954-1974), 143-144

Vigilante groups (sought unofficial law and order in old west), 88

Village (small group of dwellings in a rural area, usually ranking in size between a hamlet and a town), 176

VISTA (Volunteers in Service to America, 1960s Great Society Program to help inner cities and rural poor), 157 [chart]

Voting Rights Acts (1965, 1970, 1975 insured proper procedures against racial discrimination), 157 [chart]

W

Wabash, St. Louis, and Pacific Railway v. Minn. (1886; states could regulate railroads), 90

Waddell, "Rube" (George E., 1876-1914; 19th & early 20th century Hall of Fame baseball pitcher with Pittsburgh *Pirates*, Philadelphia *A's*, and St. Louis *Browns*), 92

War of 1812 (fought between the U.S. and Great Britain from June 1812 to the spring of 1815), 50-51, 52, 54, 57, 66

War bond drives (WW II patriotic pressures to finance war effort), 107, 137

War Hawks (land-hungry pro-war Congressmen in 1812 era), 51

War Manpower Commission (WW II management of labor), 137 [chart]

War Production Board (WPB; WW II economic command structure for industry), 137 [chart]

Warsaw Pact (1950s Soviet alliance of Eastern European nations; gave Soviet commanders control over the satellite's armies; ended in 1991), 140

Washington Conference (1921-1922; diplomatic attempt to stop naval arms race after WW I), 117

Washington, Booker T. (1856-1915; post Civil War civil rights leader), 95 [chart]

Washington, George (1732-1799; Commander of American forces in the Revolutionary War, 1775-1783; presided over Constitutional Convention, 1787; first President of the U.S., 1789-1797), 31, 32, 40, 47, 48, 125

Weaver, Robert (1907-1997; served in FDR administration; later he was the first African American to hold a cabinet post under LBJ), 125

Webster, Daniel (1782-1852; U.S. Rep.and Sen., [MA]; Secretary of State twice; argued for preservation of the Union), 55

Webster-Ashburton Treaty (1842; negotiation settled disputes the U.S.-Canadian boundaries), 66 [chart/map]

West Point, U.S. Military Academy at (on the Hudson River in SE NYS, military post since 1778 and the seat of the U.S. Military Academy since 1802), 71

Whigs (The National Republicans, a short-lived party that split off the Democratic-Republicans in the 1830s, favored high tariffs and a loose interpretation of the Constitution), 54

Whiskey Rebellion, The (PA farmers' protest of Hamilton's excise tax, 1792), 47

Whiskey Ring (scandal in Grant era), 85

White House (official residence of the President since 1800; also journalistic phrase denoting executive branch of the U.S. gov't.), 40 [illus.], 122

Whitman, Walt (1819-1892; poet who used unconventional meter and rhyme), 59

Y

Z